JOHN WILLIS'

SCREEN WORLD

1978

Volume 29

CROWN PUBLISHERS, INC.

ONE PARK AVENUE

NEW YORK, N.Y. 10016

ISBN: 0 517 534517

TO

MILES KREUGER

*dedicated film historian, archivist, and author whose kindness
and generosity have made him an invaluable friend*

DIANE KEATON AND WOODY ALLEN
in "Annie Hall" *1977 Academy Awards for Best Picture, Best Actress (Diane Keaton), Best
Director (Woody Allen), and Best Original Screenplay (Woody Allen and Marshall Brickman)*

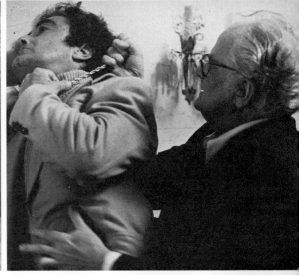

Art Carney, Bill Macy Above: Joanna Cassidy, Lily Tomlin Top: Howard Duff

Lily Tomlin, Eugene Roche Above: Art Carney, Tomlin Top: John Considine, Carney

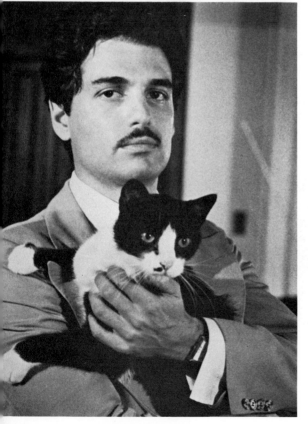

THE SENTINEL

(UNIVERSAL) Producers, Michael Winner, Jeffrey Konvitz; Director, Michael Winner; Screenplay, Jeffrey Konvitz from his novel; Photography, Dick Kratina; Designer, Philip Rosenberg; Music, Gil Melle; Editors, Bernard Gribble, Terence Rawlings; Assistant Directors, Charles Okun, Ralph Singleton, Larry Albucher; Costumes, Peggy Farrell; In Technicolor; 92 minutes; Rated R; February release.

CAST

Michael Lerman	Chris Sarandon
Alison Parker	Cristina Raines
Professor	Martin Balsam
Halliran	John Carradine
Robed Figure	Jose Ferrer
Miss Logan	Ava Gardner
Franchino	Arthur Kennedy
Chazen	Burgess Meredith
Gerde	Sylvia Miles
Jennifer	Deborah Raffin
Gatz	Eli Wallach
Rizzo	Christopher Walken
Film Director	Jerry Orbach
Sandra	Beverly D'Angelo
Brenner	Hank Garrett
Hart	Robert Gerringer
Girl at end	Nana Tucker
Man at end	Tom Berenger
Perry	William Hickey
Malcolm Stinnett	Gary Allen
Rebecca Stinnett	Tresa Hughes

and Kate Harrington (Mrs. Clark), Jane Hoffman (Lilian Clotkin), Elaine Shore (Emma Clotkin), Sam Gray (Dr. Aureton), Reid Shelton (Priest), Fred Stuthman (Alison's Father), Lucie Lancaster (Alison's mother), Anthony Holland (Party Host), Jeff Goldblum (Jack), Zane Lasky (Raymond), Mady Heflin (Professor's student), Diane Stilwell (Brenner's secretary), Ron McLarty (Real Estate Agent)

Chris Sarandon
Top: Cristina Raines

Top: John Carradine

Burgess Meredith
Top: Cristina Raines, Ava Gardner

Cristina Raines

11

TWILIGHT'S LAST GLEAMING

(ALLIED ARTISTS) Executive Producer, Helmit Jedele; Producer, Merv Adelson; Screenplay, Ronald M. Cohen, Edward Huebsch; Based on novel "Viper 3" by Walter Wager; Music, Jerry Goldsmith; Designer, Rolf Zehetbauer; Photography, Robert Hauser; Editor, Michael Luciano; Assistant Directors, Wolfgang Glattes, Peter Eitzert; A Geria Production; Presented by Lorimar-Bavaria; In Technicolor; Rated R; 146 minutes; February release.

CAST

Lawrence Dell	Burt Lancaster
Martin MacKenzie	Richard Widmark
David T. Stevens	Charles Durning
Zachariah Guthrie	Melvyn Douglas
Powell	Paul Winfield
Garvas	Burt Young
Arthur Renfrew	Joseph Cotten
James Forrest	Roscoe Lee Browne
Michael O'Rourke	Gerald S. O'Loughlin
Capt. Stanford Towne	Richard Jaeckel
Victoria Stevens	Vera Miles
William Klinger	William Marshall
Colonel Bernstein	Charles Aidman
Ralph Whittaker	Leif Erickson
Peter Crane	Charles McGraw
Phil Spencer	Simon Scott
1st Lt. Louis Cannellis	Morgan Paull
Hoxey	William Smith
Willard	Bill Walker

Charles McGraw, Gerald S. O'Loughlin, Charles Durning, Leif Erickson, Melvyn Douglas, Joseph Cotten, Simon Scott, William Marshall Top Left: Richard Widmark

Burt Lancaster, Paul Winfield, Charles
Durning Top: Burt Young, Paul Winfield,
Burt Lancaster

Burt Lancaster Top: Melvyn Douglas,
Charles Durning

FREAKY FRIDAY

(BUENA VISTA) Producer, Ron Miller; Director, Gary Nelson; Screenplay, Mary Rodgers; Photography, Charles F. Wheeler, Associate Producer, Tom Leetch; Music, Johnny Mandel; Words and Music, Al Kasha, Joel Hirschhorn; Art Directors, John B. Mansbridge, Jack Senter; Editor, Cotton Warburton; Assistant Directors, Ronald R. Grow, Cheryl Downey; A Walt Disney Production in Technicolor; Rated G; 95 minutes; February release.

CAST

Ellen Andrews	Barbara Harris
Annabel Andrews	Jodie Foster
Bill Andrews	John Astin
Mrs. Schmauss	Patsy Kelly
Virginia	Ricki Schreck
Harold Jennings	Dick Van Patten
Mr. Dilk	Sorrell Booke
Mr. Joffert	Alan Oppenheimer
Coach Betsy	Kaye Ballard
Opposing Coach	Ruth Buzzi
Boris Harris	Marc McClure
Mrs. Murphy	Marie Windsor
Ben Andrews	Sparky Marcus
Miss McGuirk	Ceil Cabot
Mrs. Gibbons	Brooke Mills
Mary Kay Gilbert	Karen Smith
Carpet Cleaner	Marvin Kaplan
Drapery Man	Al Molinaro
Bus Passenger	Iris Adrian
Mrs. Benson	Barbara Walden

and Shelly Juttner (Hilary), Charlene Tilton (Bambi), Lori Rutherford (Jo-Jo), Jack Sheldon (Lloyd), Laurie Main (Mills), Don Carter (Delivery Boy), Fuddle Bagley (Bus Driver), Fritz Feld (Jackman), Dermott Downs (Harvey Manager), Jimmy Van Patten (Cashier)

Barbara Harris, Sparky Marcus
14 Top: Barbara Harris, John Astin

Jodie Foster Top: Brooke Mills, Jodie Foster, John Astin

ISLANDS IN THE STREAM

(PARAMOUNT) Producers, Peter Bart, Max Palevsky; Director, Franklin J. Schaffner; Screenplay, Denne Bart Petitclerc; Based on novel by Ernest Hemingway; Photography, Fred Koenekamp; Editor, Robert Swink; Music, Jerry Goldsmith; Design, William J. Creber; Assistant Director, Kurt Neumann; In Metrocolor; Rated PG; 105 minutes; March release.

CAST

Thomas Hudson	George C. Scott
Eddy	David Hemmings
Captain Ralph	Gilbert Roland
Lil	Susan Tyrrell
Willy	Richard Evans
Audrey	Claire Bloom
Joseph	Julius Harris
Tom	Hart Bochner
Andrew	Brad Savage
David	Michael-James Wixted
Constable	Charles Lampkin
Helga Ziegner	Hildy Brooks
Andrea	Jessica Rains
Herr Ziegner	Walter Friedel

Right: George C. Scott, Claire Bloom

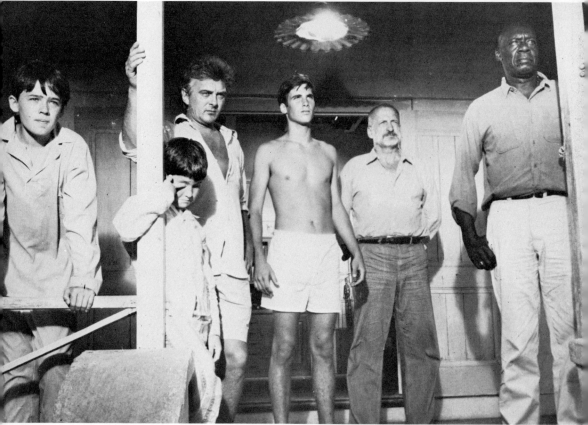

Michael-James Wixted, Brad Savage, David Hemmings, Hart Bochner, George C. Scott, Julius Harris

16

George C. Scott, Gilbert Roland Above: Jessica
Rains, Hildy Brooks, Scott, Richard Evans
Top: Scott, Claire Bloom

George C. Scott, David Hemmings
Top: Hart Bochner, Scott

17

SLAP SHOT

(UNIVERSAL) Producers, Robert J. Wunsch, Stephen Friedman; Associate Producer, Robert L. Crawford; Director, George Roy Hill; Screenplay, Nancy Dowd; Editor, Dede Allen; Photography, Victor Kemper; Art Director, Henry Bumstead; Assistant Directors, James Westman, Tom Joyner, Wayne Farlow, Peter Burrell; Costumes, Tom Bronson; In Panavision and Technicolor; 122 minutes; Rated R; March release.

CAST

Reggie Dunlop	Paul Newman
Ned Braden	Michael Ontkean
Lily Braden	Lindsay Crouse
Francine Dunlop	Jennifer Warren
Joe McGrath	Strother Martin
Dave "Killer" Carlson	Jerry Houser
Denis Le Mieux	Yvon Barrette
Steve Hansen	Steve Carlson
Jeff Hansen	Jeff Carlson
Jack Hansen	Dave Hanson
Jim Carr	Andrew Duncan
Dickie Dunn	Emmett Walsh
Jim Ahern	Stephen Mendillo
Johnny Upton	Allan Nicholls
Helen Upton	Swoosie Kurtz
Drouin	Yvan Ponton
Wanchuk	Brad Sullivan
Anita McCambridge	Kathryn Walker
Tim McCracken	Paul D'Amato
Charlebois	Guido Tenesi
Brophy	John Gorfton
LeBrun	Ronald L. Docken
Carlie	Mathew Cowles
Hyannisport Announcer	Paul Dooley
Peterboro Referee	Lawrence Block

Left: Paul Newman

Paul Newman (C)

Strother Martin, Jeff Carlson, Lindsay Crouse, Paul Newman

BLACK SUNDAY

(PARAMOUNT) Producer, Robert Evans; Executive Producer, Robert L. Rosen; Director, John Frankenheimer; Screenplay, Ernest Lehman, Kenneth Ross, Ivan Moffat; Based on novel by Thomas Harris; Photography, John A. Alonzo; Editor, Tom Rolf; Music, John Williams; Art Director, Walter Tyler; Costumes, Ray Summers; Assistant Director, Jerry Ziesmer; In Movielab Color; 143 minutes; Rated R; March release.

CAST

Kabakov	Robert Shaw
Lander	Bruce Dern
Dahlia	Marthe Keller
Corley	Fritz Weaver
Moshevsky	Steven Keats
Fasil	Bekim Fehmiu
Muzi	Michael V. Gazzo
Pugh	William Daniels
Col. Riaf	Walter Gotell
Nageeb	Victor Campos
Fowler	Walter Brooke
Watchman	James Jeter
Freighter Captain	Clyde Kusatsu
Farley	Tom McFadden
Vickers	Robert Patten
Israeli Ambassador	Than Wynn
Themselves	Pat Summerall, Joseph Robbie, Robert Wussler, Tom Brookshier

Left: Fritz Weaver, Robert Shaw

Bruce Dern, Marthe Keller

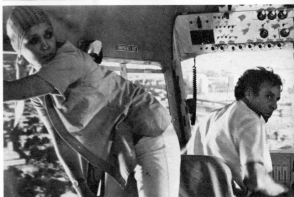

Bruce Dern, Marthe Keller
Above: Robert Shaw (also top)

Marthe Keller Above: Keller, Bruce Dern
Top: Steven Keats, Keller

AIRPORT '77

(UNIVERSAL) Executive Producer, Jennings Lang; Producer, William Frye; Director, Jerry Jameson; Screenplay, Michael Scheff, David Spector; Photography, Philip Lathrop; Design, George C. Webb; Editors, J. Terry Williams, Robert Watts; Music, John Cacavas; Sung by Tom Sullivan; Costumes, Edith Head; Assistant Directors, Wilbur Mosier, Bob Graner, Jim Nasella; In Panavision and Technicolor; 113 minutes; Rated PG; March release.

CAST

Don Gallagher	Jack Lemmon
Karen Wallace	Lee Grant
Eve Clayton	Brenda Vaccaro
Nicholas St. Downs III	Joseph Cotten
Emily Livingston	Olivia de Havilland
Stan Buchek	Darren McGavin
Martin Wallace	Christopher Lee
Chambers	Robert Foxworth
Eddie	Robert Hooks
Banker	Monte Markham
Julie	Kathleen Quinlan
Frank Powers	Gil Gerard
Ralph Crawford	James Booth
Anne	Monica Lewis
Dorothy	Maidie Norman
Lisa	Pamela Bellwood
Mrs. Jane Stern	Arlene Golonka
Philip Stevens	James Stewart
Steve	Tom Sullivan
Dr. Williams	M. Emmett Walsh
Walker	Michael Richardson
Wilson	Michael Pataki
Gerald Lucas	George Furth

and Richard Venture (Cmdr. Guay), Ross Bickell (Johnson), Peter Fox (Lt. Norris), Beverly Gill (Stewardess), Charles Macaulay (Adm. Corrigan), Tom Rosqui (Hunter), Arthur Adams (Cmdr. Reed), Anthony Battaglia (Benjy), Elizabeth Cheshire (Bonnie), Charlotte Lord (Stewardess), Paul Tuerpe (Deck Officer), Dar Robinson (Larry), Ted Chapman (Chef), Jim Arnett, Ron Burke, Chuck Hayward, Janet Brady, Johana De Winter, George Whiteman, Jean Coulter (Passengers), John Clavin (FAA Supervisor), John Kerry (Lt. Cmdr.), James Ray Weeks (Pilot), William Whitaker (Radioman), Mary Nancy Burnett (Radar Controller), Bill Jelliffe, Rick Sorenson (Controllers), Peter Greene, Asa Teeter (Frogmen), George Kennedy (Joe Patroni)

Jack Lemmon, Brenda Vaccaro

Top: Joseph Cotten, Olivia de Havilland

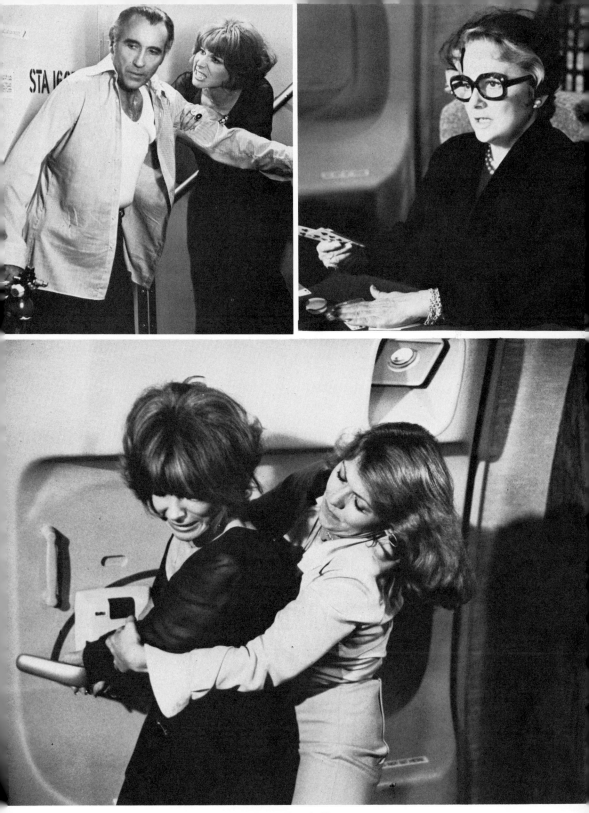

Lee Grant, Brenda Vaccaro
Top: Lee Grant, Christopher Lee; Olivia de Havilland

23

DEMON

(NEW WORLD PICTURES) Produced, Directed and Written by Larry Cohen; Photography, Paul Glickman; Sound, Jeffrey Hayes; Music, Frank Cordell; Song "Sweet Momma Sweetlove" by Janelle Webb and Robert O. Ragland; Performed by George Gentre Griffin; A Larco Production in Metrocolor; 90 minutes; Rated R; March release.

CAST

Peter Nicholas	Tony Lo Bianco
Casey Forster	Deborah Raffin
Martha Nicholas	Sandy Dennis
Miss Mullin	Sylvia Sidney
Everett Lukas	Sam Levene
David Morten	Robert Drivas
Deputy Commissioner	Mike Kellin
Vernard Phillips	Richard Lynch
Harold Gorman	Sammy Williams
Mrs. Gorman	Jo Flores Chase
Richards	William Roerick
Board Chairman	Lester Rawlins
Cookie	Harry Bellaver
Zero	George Patterson
Junkie	Walter Steele
Bramwell	John Heffernan
Bramwell as a youth	Alan Cauldwell
Fletcher	Robert Nichols
Police Assassin	Andy Kaufman

and Al Fann, James Dixon, Bobby Ramsen, Peter Hock, Alex Stevens, Harry Madsen, Randy Jurgensen (Detective Squad), Sherry Steiner (Mrs. Phillips as a girl), James Dukas (Doorman), Mason Adams (Obstetrician), William Bressant (Policeman), Armand Dahan (Vendor), Vida Taylor (Miss Mullin as a girl), Adrian James (Prostitute), Leila Martin (Nurse), Michael Pendry (Attendant), Harry Eno (Medical Examiner), Dan Resin, Alexander Clark, Marvin Silbisher (Wall St. Executives)

Sandy Dennis, Deborah Raffin
Top: Tony LoBianco, Deborah Raffin (and below)

LOOKING UP

(LEVITT-PICKMAN) Producer-Director, Linda Yellen; Co-Producer, Karen Rosenberg; Screenplay, Jonathan Platnick; Photography, Arpad Makay, Lloyd Friedas; Art Director, John Annus; Editor, John Carter; Music, Brad Fiedel; "Rose's Theme" sung by Robin Grean; In Movielab Color; Presented by First American Films; 94 minutes; Rated PG; April release.

CAST

Rose Lander	Marilyn Chris
Manny Lander	Dick Shawn
Libby Levine	Doris Belack
Sy Levine	Harry Goz
Becky	Jacqueline Brookes
Grandma	Naomi Riseman
Grandpa	Will Hussing
Myra	Neva Small
Stan	George Reinholt
Ann Reeny	Gillian Goll
Francine Levine	Ellen Sherman
Barbara Lander	Susan McKinley
Larry	Anthony Mannino
Michael Lander	Paul Lieber
David Lander	Paul Christopoulos
Judy	Lee Wilson
Irma	Estelle Harris
Gene	Izzy Singer
Harbey	Barry Burns
Sweedler	Michael Vale

Andrew Smith (Burger Crown Man), Jack Weissbluth (Lou), Barbara Andress (Natalie), Ruth Franklin (Bernice), Miguel Pinero, Dadi Pinero, Lefty (Muggers), Jaqueline Tuteur (Check-out Girl), June Berry (Phyllis), Sally DeMay (Gussie), Edith Weissbluth (Mrs. G), Jill Weissbluth (Genevieve), Sarah Phillips (Mrs. Combs), Ted Butler (Walter), Frederica Minte (Antique Customer), Joshua Freund (Jaymen), Ginger James (Cory), Gizella Mittleman (Lady in window)

Top: (L) Neva Small, George Reinholt, Gillian Goll (R) Harry Goz, Ellen Sherman Below: Naomi Riseman, Marilyn Chris (L) Chris, Doris Belack, Jacqueline Brookes

Marilyn Chris, Dick Shawn
Above: Shawn, Michael Vale

25

ANNIE HALL

(UNITED ARTISTS) Producer, Charles H. Joffe; Director, Woody Allen; Screenplay, Woody Allen, Marshall Brickman; Executive Producer, Robert Greenhut; Associate Producer, Fred T. Gallo; Photography, Gordon Willis; Editors, Ralph Rosenblum, Wendy Greene Bricmont; A Jack Rollins-Charles H. Joffe Production; In color; 93 minutes; Rated PG; April release.

CAST

Alvy Singer	Woody Allen
Annie Hall	Diane Keaton
Rob	Tony Roberts
Allison	Carol Kane
Tony Lacey	Paul Simon
Mom Hall	Colleen Dewhurst
Robin	Janet Margolin
Pam	Shelley Duvall
Duane Hall	Christopher Walken
Dad Hall	Donald Symington
Grammy Hall	Helen Ludlam
Alvy's Dad	Mordecai Lawner
Alvy's Mom	Joan Newman
Alvy at 9	Jonathan Munk
Alvy's Aunt	Ruth Volner
Alvy's Uncle	Martin Rosenblatt
Joey Nichols	Hy Ansel
Aunt Tessie	Rashel Novikoff

Woody Allen (also top left), Diane Keaton

Woody Allen, Tony Roberts, Diane Keaton
Top: Woody Allen, Jonathan Munk

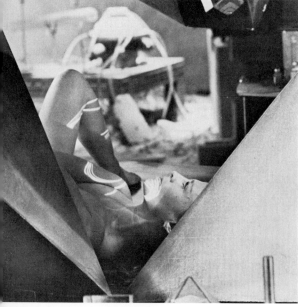

DEMON SEED

(UNITED ARTISTS) Producer, Herb Jaffe; Director, Donald Cammell; Screenplay, Robert Jaffe, Roger O. Hirson; Based on novel by Dean R. Koontz; Photography, Bill Butler; Editor, Francisco Mazzola; Music, Jerry Fielding; Design, Edward C. Carfagno; Assistant Director, Edward A. Teets; In Metrocolor; 94 minutes; Rated R; April release.

CAST

Susan Harris	Julie Christie
Alex Harris	Fritz Weaver
Walter Gabler	Gerrit Graham
Petrosian	Berry Kroeger
Soon Yen	Lisa Lu
Cameron	Larry J. Blake
Amy	Dana Laurita
Voice of Proteus IV	Robert Vaughn
Royce	John O'Leary
Mokri	Alfred Dennis
Warner	David Roberts
Babies	Tiffany Potter, Felix Silla

Julie Christie also top
with Fritz Weaver

Fritz Weaver, Julie Christie
Top: Gerrit Graham, Julie Christie

Julie Christie

29

AUDREY ROSE

(UNITED ARTISTS) Producers, Joe Wizan, Frank De Felitta; Director, Robert Wise; Screenplay, Frank De Felitta from his novel; Photography, Victor J. Kemper; Music, Michael Small; Editor, Carl Kress; Costumes, Dorothy Jeakins; Designer, Harry Horner; In Panavision and color; 113 minutes; Rated PG; April release.

CAST

Janice Templeton	Marsha Mason
Elliot Hoover	Anthony Hopkins
Bill Templeton	John Beck
Ivy Templeton	Susan Swift
Dr. Steven Lipscomb	Norman Lloyd
Scott Velie	John Hillerman
Brice Mack	Robert Walden
Judge Langley	Philip Sterling
Mary Lou Sides	Ivy Jones
Russ Rothman	Stephen Pearlman
Maharishi Gupta Pradesh	Aly Wassil
Mother Veronica	Mary Jackson
Policemen	Richard Lawson, David Wilson
Detective Fallon	Tony Brande
Carole Rothman	Elizabeth Farley
Customer in store	Ruth Manning
Cashier in store	Stanley Brock
Dominick	David Fresco
Dr. Webster	Pat Corley
Mrs. Carbone	Eunice Christopher
Maria (Waitress)	Karen Anders

Left: Susan Swift

Marsha Mason, Susan Swift, John Beck

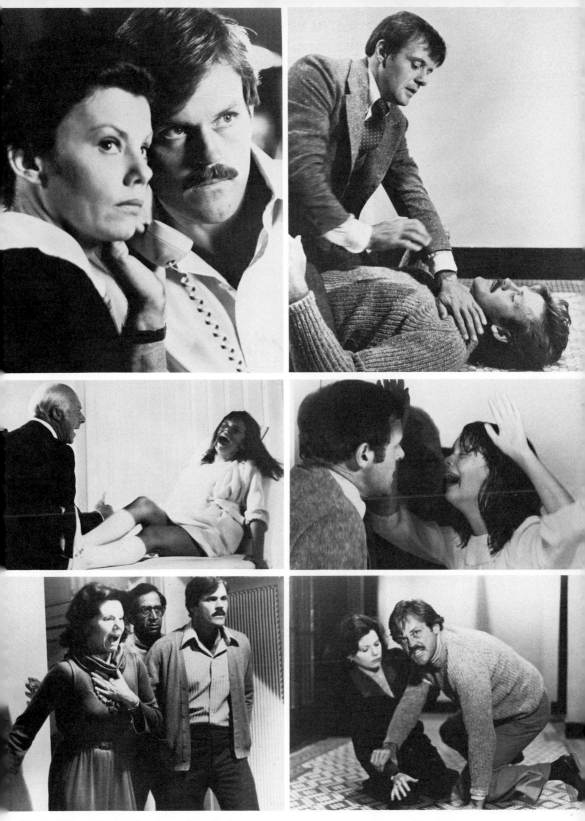

Marsha Mason, Stephen Pearlman, John Beck
Above: Norman Lloyd, Susan Swift
Top: Marsha Mason, John Beck

Marsh Mason, John Beck Above: Anthony
Hopkins, Susan Swift Top: Hopkins, Beck

BETWEEN THE LINES

(MIDWEST) Producer, Raphael D. Silver; Director, Joan Micklin Silver; Screenplay, Fred Barron; Story, Fred Barron, David M. Helpern, Jr.; Music, Michael Kamen; Photography, Kenneth Van Sickle; Design, Stuart Wurtzel; Editor, John Carter; Costumes, Patrizia Von Brandenstein; Assistant Directors, Mike Haley, Laurie Eichengreen; In Panavision and TVC color; Rated R; 101 minutes; April release.

CAST

Harry	John Heard
Abbie	Lindsay Crouse
Max	Jeff Goldblum
Lynn	Jill Eikenberry
David	Bruno Kirby
Laura	Gwen Welles
Michael	Stephen Collins
Stanley	Lewis J. Stadlen
Hawker	Michael J. Pollard
Roy	Lane Smith
Danielle	Marilu Henner
Sarah	Susan Haskins
Herbert Fisk	Ray Barry
Doug Henkel	Douglas Kenney
Frank	Jon Korkes
Ahmed	Joe Morton
Wheeler	Richard Cox
Jason	Gary Springer
Paul	Charles Levin
Austin	Guy Boyd

and Southside Johnny & The Asbury Jukes

John Heard, Lindsay Crouse
(also at top)

Stephen Collins, John Heard
Top: **Lindsay Crouse, Gwen Welles, Jill Eikenberry**

ROLLERCOASTER

(UNIVERSAL) Producer, Jennings Lang; Executive Producer, Howard G. Kazanjian; Director, James Goldstone; Screenplay, Richard Levinson, William Link; Story, Sanford Sheldon, Richard Levinson, William Link; Story, Tommy Cook; Photography, David M. Walsh; Design, Henry Bumstead; Editors, Edward A. Biery, Richard Sprague; Music, Lalo Schifrin; Associate Producer, Tommy Cook; Costumes, Burton Miller; Assistant Directors, L. Andrew Stone, David O. Sosna, Peter J. Burrell; In Panavision and Technicolor; 119 minutes; Rated PG; April release.

CAST

Harry Calder	George Segal
Hoyt	Richard Widmark
Young Man	Timothy Bottoms
Simon Davenport	Henry Fonda
Keefer	Harry Guardino
Fran	Susan Strasberg
Tracy Calder	Helen Hunt
Helen	Dorothy Tristan
Benny	Harry Davis
Lyons	Stephen Pearlman
Wayne Moore	Gerald Rowe
Christie	Wayne Tippit
Demerest	Michael Bell
Rock Concert M. C.	Charlie Tuna

Lonny Stevens, Tom Baker (Federal Agents), Ava Readdy, Craig Wasson (Hippies), William Prince (Quinlan), Dick McGarvin, Quinn Redeker, Harry Basch, Arthur Peterson (Owners), Richard Altman (Mandell), Gloria Calomee (Jackie), Robert Quarry (Mayor), Jean Rasey (Girl in line), Greg Elliot (Boy in line), Bruce Kimbell, Bruce French, Stephen Mendillo, Charles W. Bennett, Jr., Larry Holt, Gene Tyburn (Bomb Squad), Bill Sorrells (Selby), Monica Lewis (Tourist mother), Dick Wesson (Tourist father), Joe George (Guard), Gary Franklin (Radio Reporter), Dave Milton (Man in robe), David Byrd (Pet store owner), Henry Olek (Smoking Technician), Dennis Speigel (Pierce), Bill Saito, Takayo Doran (Orientals), Roger Steffens (Radio Technician), Dianne T. Murray (Pregnant Agent), Mark Hulcher (Delivery Boy), John F. Swanson (Lansing), Denice Harlow (Hertz girl), Mark Thomas (Agent), J. Michael Hunter (Shooting Gallery Attendent), Tara Buckman, Louis Weisberg (Coaster attendants)

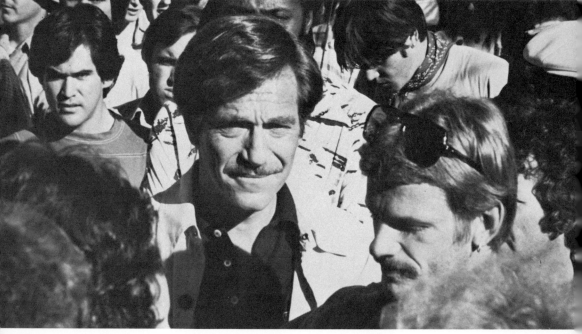

George Segal (C) Top Left: Timothy Bottoms

Top: Lonnie Stevens, Richard Widmark,
Tom Baker, Harry Guardino

Timothy Bottoms

FRATERNITY ROW

(PARAMOUNT) Formerly "Oh Brotherhood"; Produced and Written by Charles Gary Allison; Director, Thomas J. Tobin; Photography, Peter Gibbons; Editor, Eugene A. Fournier; Music, Don McLean, Michael Corner, John Phillips Hutton, Mathew Roe; Art Director, James Sbardellati; Costumes, Beverly Ihnen, Richard A. Davis; Assistant Directors, Richard N. Graves, James M. Davidson; Associate Producers, Thomas W. Joachim, Thomas W. Pope; In CFI Color; Rated PG; 101 minutes; April release.

CAST

Rodger Carter	Peter Fox
Zac Sterling	Gregory Harrison
Chunk Cherry	Scott Newman
Jennifer Harris	Nancy Morgan
Betty Ann Martin	Wendy Phillips
Brother Bob Abernathy	Robert Emhardt
Lloyd Pope	Robert Matthews
Professor	Bernard R. Kantor
Narrator	Cliff Robertson

Right: Scott Newman

Nancy Morgan, Gregory Harrison

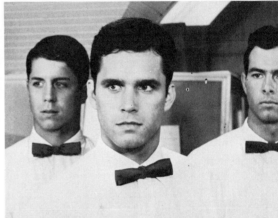

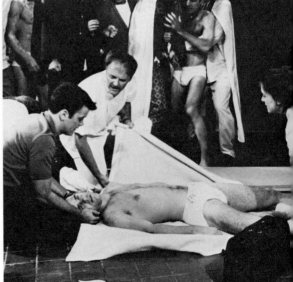

**Shelley Duvall, Sissy Spacek
(also top)**

THREE WOMEN

(20th CENTURY-FOX) Produced, Directed and Written by Robert Altman; Photography, Chuck Rosher; Editor, Dennis Hill; Music, Gerald Busby; Art Director, James D. Vance; Assistant Director; In DeLuxe Color; 122 minutes; Rated PG; April release.

CAST

Millie	Shelley Duvall
Pinky	Sissy Spacek
Willie	Janice Rule
Edgar	Robert Fortier
Pinky's Parents	Ruth Nelson, John Cromwell
Bunweill	Sierra Pecheur
Mr. Maas	Craig Richard Nelson
Hospital Attendants	Maysie Hoy, Belita Moreno
Hospital Twins	Leslie Ann Hudson, Patricia Ann Hudson
Deidre	Beverly Ross
Dr. Norton	John Davey

**Janice Rule
Top: Sissy Spacek**

Henry O'Brien Above: Ernie Orsatti, James
Brolin, Ronny Cox

Kathleen Lloyd Top: Kim Richards,
James Brolin, Kyle Richards

FUN WITH DICK AND JANE

(COLUMBIA) Producers, Peter Bart, Max Palevsky; Director, Ted Kotcheff; Screenplay, David Gilber, Jerry Belson, Mordecai Richler; Based on story by Gerald Gaiser; Photography, Fred Koenekamp; Editor, Danford B. Greene; Music, Ernest Gold, Lamont Dozier, Gene Page; Design, James G. Hulsey; Costumes, Donfeld, Lambert E. Marks, Margo Baxley; Assistant Director, Charles Okun; In Metrocolor; 95 minutes; Rated PG; May release.

CAST

Dick Harper	George Segal
Jane Harper	Jane Fonda
Charlie Blanchard	Ed McMahon
Doctor Will	Dick Gautier
Loan Company Manager	Allan Miller
Raoul Esteban	Hank Garcia
Jane's Father	John Dehner
Jane's Mother	Mary Jackson
Mr. Weeks	Walter Brooke
Billy Harper	Sean Frye
Immigration Officer	James Jeter
Blanchard's Secretary	Maxine Stuart
Bob	Fred Willard
Mr. Johnson	Thalmus Rasulala
Guard	Ji-Tu Cumbuka

Left: Sean Frye, George Segal, Jane Fonda

George Segal (L), Jane Fonda (R)

Jane Fonda, George Segal, Sean Frye Above: George Segal, Jane Fonda, Ed McMahon
Top: Jane Fonda, Thalmus Rasulala, George Segal

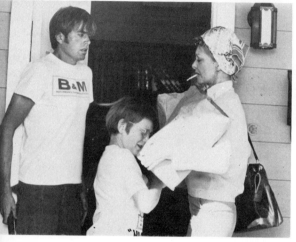

HANDLE WITH CARE

(PARAMOUNT) Formerly "Citizens Band"; Executive Producer, Shep Fields; Director, Jonathan Demme; Screenplay, Paul Brickman; Photography, Jordan Cronenweth; Editor, John F. Link II; Music, Bill Conti; Design, Bill Malley; Costumes, Jodie Lynn Tillen; Assistant Director, Charles Okun; In Movielab Color; 98 minutes; Rated PG; May release.

CAST

Spider (Blaine)	Paul LeMat
Electra (Pam)	Candy Clark
Joyce Rissley	Ann Wedgeworth
Blood (Dean)	Bruce McGill
Dallas Angel (Connie)	Marcia Rodd
Chrome Angel (Harold)	Charles Napier
Hot Coffee (Debbie)	Alix Elias
Papa Thermadyne (Father)	Roberts Blossom
Smilin' Jack (Garage Owner)	Richard Bright
Priest	Ed Begley, Jr.
Cochise	Michael Rothman
Hustler	Michael Mahler
Red Baron	Harry Northrup
Warlock	Will Seltzer

Top: Candy Clark Below: Paul LeMat, Michael Mahler, Micki Mann

Ed Begley, Jr. Above: Marcia Rodd, Alix Elias, Ann Wedgeworth Top: Paul LeMat

**Ann Wedgeworth, Marcia Rodd, Charles Napier
Above: Bruce McGill, Paul LeMat Top: LeMat,
Candy Clark, Roberts Blossom**

Candy Clark, Paul LeMat
(also above)

THE WHITE BUFFALO

(UNITED ARTISTS) Producer, Pancho Kohner; Director, J. Lee Thompson; Screenplay, Richard Sale from his novel; Music, John Barry; Photography, Paul Lohmann; Designer, Tambi Larsen; Editor, Michael F. Anderson; Presented by Dino DeLaurentiis; In color; 97 minutes; Rated PG; May release.

CAST

Bill Hickok/James Otis .... Charles Bronson
Charlie Zane .... Jack Warden
Crazy Horse/Worm .... Will Sampson
Poker Jenny Schermerhorn .... Kim Novak
Whistling Jack Kileen .... Clint Walker
Winifred Coxy.. Stuart Whitman
Abel Pinkney.. Slim Pickens
Amos Briggs .... John Carradine
Cassie Ollinger .... Cara Williams
Tim Brady... Shay Duffin
Amos Bixby ....Douglas V. Fowley
Pete Holt... Cliff Pellow
Capt. Tom Custer.................................. Ed Lauter
Jack McCall .... Martin Kove
Gyp Hook-Hand .... Scott Walker

Left: Charles Bronson

Jack Warden, Charles Bronson, Will Sampson

Will Sampson Above: Jack Warden, Charles
Bronson Top: Kim Novak, Charles Bronson

John Carradine

53

Jacqueline Bisset

THE DEEP

(COLUMBIA) Producer, Peter Guber; Director, Peter Yates; Screenplay, Peter Benchley, Tracy Keenan Wynn; From novel by Peter Benchley; Designer, Tony Masters; Photography, Christopher Challis; Music, John Barry; Associate Producer, George Justin; Art Director, Jack Maxsted; Editor, Robert Wolfe; Assistant Director, Derek Cracknell; Costumes, Ron Talsky; A Casablanca Filmworks Production in color; 123 minutes; Rated PG; June release.

CAST

Romer Treece	Robert Shaw
Gail Berke	Jacqueline Bisset
David Sanders	Nick Nolte
Cloche	Lou Gossett
Adam Coffin	Eli Wallach
Kevin	Robert Tessier
Slake	Dick Anthony Williams
Ronald	Earl Maynard
Wiley	Bob Minor
Mate	Peter Benchley
Young Adam Coffin	Peter Wallach
Young Romer Treece	Colin Shaw

**Top: Nick Nolte, Robert Shaw,
Jacqueline Bisset**

54

THE THREE SISTERS

(NTA) Executive Producer, Cheryl Crawford; Producer, Ely Landau; Screen Direction, Paul Bogart; Based on the theatre production of the Chekhov play staged by Lee Strasberg; English version by Randall Jarrel; Transferred to film from videotape; 166 minutes; Not rated; June release.

CAST

Andrei	Gerald Hiken
Natalya	Shelley Winters
Olga	Geraldine Page
Masha	Kim Stanley
Irina	Sandy Dennis
Kulygin	Albert Paulsen
Vershinin	Kevin McCarthy
Baron Tuzenbach	James Olson
Solyony	Robert Loggia
Chebutykin	Luther Adler
Fedotik	John Harkins
Roday	David Paulsen
Ferapont	Salem Ludwig
Anfisa	Tamara Daykarhanova

Right: Kim Stanley, Kevin McCarthy

Kim Stanley, Kevin McCarthy

THE OTHER SIDE OF MIDNIGHT

(20th CENTURY-FOX) Producer, Frank Yablans; Executive Producer, Howard W. Koch, Jr.; Director, Charles Jarrott; Screenplay, Herman Raucher, Daniel Taradash; Based on novel by Sidney Sheldon; Photography, Fred J. Koenekamp; Editors, Donn-Cambern, Harold F. Kress; Music, Michel Legrand; Design, John De Cuir; Costumes, Irene Sharaff; Assistant Director, Fred Brost; In DeLuxe Color; 165 minutes; Rated R; June release.

CAST

Noelle Page	Marie-France Pisier
Larry Douglas	John Beck
Catherine Douglas	Susan Sarandon
Constantin Demeris	Raf Vallone
Bill Fraser	Clu Gulager
Armand Gautier	Christian Marquand
Barbet	Michael Lerner
Lanchon	Sorrell Booke
Co-pilot Metaxas	Antony Ponzini
Demonides	Louis Zorich
Chotas	Charles Cioffi
Sister Teresa	Dimitra Arliss
Warden	Jan Arvan
Madame Rose	Josette Banzet
Doc Peterson	John Chappell
Female Guard	Eunice Christopher
Jacques Page	Roger Etienne

Right: John Beck, Susan Sarandon

Marie-France Pisier, Raf Vallone

56

**John Beck Top: Sorrell
Booke, Marie-France Pisier**

**Marie-France Pisier, and above
with Raf Vallone**

57

NEW YORK, NEW YORK

(UNITED ARTISTS) Producers, Irwin Winkler, Robert Chartoff; Director, Martin Scorsese; Screenplay, Earl MacRauch, Mardik Martin; Story, Earl MacRauch; Photography, Laszlo Kovacs; Design, Boris Leven; Associate Producer, Gene Kirkwood; Songs, John Kander, Fred Ebb; Choreography, Ron Field; Editors, Irving Lerner, Marcia Lucas, Tom Rolf, B. Lovitt; Art Director, Harry R. Kemm; In color; 155 minutes; Rated PG; June release.

CAST

Francine Evans	Liza Minnelli
Jimmy Doyle	Robert De Niro
Tony Harwell	Lionel Stander
Paul Wilson	Barry Primus
Bernice	Mary Kay Place
Frankie Harte	Georgie Auld
Nicky	George Memmoli
Palm Club Owner	Dick Miller
Horace Morris	Murray Moston
Artie Kirks	Lenny Gaines
Cecil Powell	Clarence Clemons
Ellen Flannery	Kathi McGinnis
Desk Clerk	Norman Palmer
Jimmy Doyle, Jr.	Adam David Winkler
Desk Clerk	Dimitri Logothetis
Eddie Di Muzio	Frank Sivera
Harlem Club Singer	Diahnne Abbott
Argumentative Woman	Margo Winkler
Record Producer	Steven Prince
Gilbert	Don Calfa
Justice of the Peace	Bernie Kuby
Wife of Justice of the Peace	Selma Archerd
Announcer in Moonlit Terrace	Bill Baldwin
Hat Check Girl in Meadows	Mary Lindsay

Robert DeNiro, Liza Minnelli

Top: Liza Minnelli (C)

Mary Kay Place Above: Robert DeNiro
Top: DeNiro, Liza Minnelli, William Tole

Liza Minnelli, also above with Robert
DeNiro Top: DeNiro, Barry Primus 59

HERBIE GOES TO MONTE CARLO

(BUENA VISTA) Producer, Ron Miller; Director, Vincent McEveety; Screenplay, Arthur Alsberg, Don Nelson; Based on characters created by Gordon Buford; Associate Producer, Jan Williams; Photography, Leonard J. South; Music, Frank De Vol; Art Directors, John B. Mansbridge, Perry Ferguson; Editor, Cotton Warburton; Assistant Directors, Paul "Tiny" Nichols, Win Phelps; Costumes, Chuck Keehne, Emily Sundby; In Technicolor; 105 minutes; Rated G; June release.

CAST

Jim Douglas	Dean Jones
Wheely Applegate	Don Knotts
Diane Darcy	Julie Sommars
Inspector Bouchet	Jacques Marin
Quincey	Roy Kinnear
Max	Bernard Fox
Bruno Von Stickle	Eric Braeden
Detective Fontenoy	Xavier Saint Macary
Monsieur Ribeaux	Francois Lalande
Emile	Alan Caillou
Duval	Laurie Main
Claude	Mike Kulcsar
Race Official	Johnny Haymer
Taxi Driver	Stanley Brock
Waiter	Gerard Jugnot
Doorman	Jean-Marie Proslier
Showroom M. C.	Tom McCorry
Truck Driver	Jean-Jacques Moreau
Girl Friend	Yveline Briere
Police Captain	Raoul Delfosse
Exhibit M. C.	Ed Marcus

and Lloyd Nelson (Mechanic), Sebastien Floche (Tourist), Madeleine Damien (Old Woman), Alain Janey (Man at cafe), Drivers: Richard Warlock, Kevin Johnston, Carey Loftkin, Bill Erickson, Gerald Brutsche, Bob Harris, Jesse Wayne, Reg Parton

Left: Don Knotts, Julie Sommars, Dean Jones

Dean Jones, Julie Sommars, Eric Braeden, Mike Kulcsar

Dean Jones, Julie Sommars, Don Knotts
Top: Dean Jones, Don Knotts

Katia Tchenko, Don Knotts, Dean Jones
Above: Dean Jones, Julie Sommars

61

EXORCIST II: THE HERETIC

(WARNER BROS.) Producers, John Boorman, Richard Lederer; Director, John Boorman; Screenplay, William Goodhart; Associate Producer, Charles Orme; Photography, William A. Fraker; Editor, Tom Priestley; Designer, Richard Macdonald; Music, Ennio Morricone; Assistant Director, Phil Rawlins, Victor Hsu; Art Director, Jack Collins; Costumes, Robert de Mora; In color; 117 minutes; Rated R; June release.

CAST

Regan	Linda Blair
Father Lamont	Richard Burton
Dr. Gene Tuskin	Louise Fletcher
Father Merrin	Max von Sydow
Sharon	Kitty Winn
The Cardinal	Paul Henreid
Older Kokumo	James Earl Jones
Edwards	Ned Beatty
Liz	Belinda Beatty
Spanish Girl	Rose Portillo
Mr. Phalor	Barbara Cason
Deaf Girl	Tiffany Kinney
Young Kokumo	Joey Green
Young Monk	Fiseha Dimetros
Abbot	Ken Renard
Conductor	Hank Garrett
Accident Victim	Lorry Goldman
Taxi Driver	Bill Grant
Tuskin Children	Shane Butterworth, Joely Adams

Linda Blair
Top: Richard Burton, Louise Fletcher

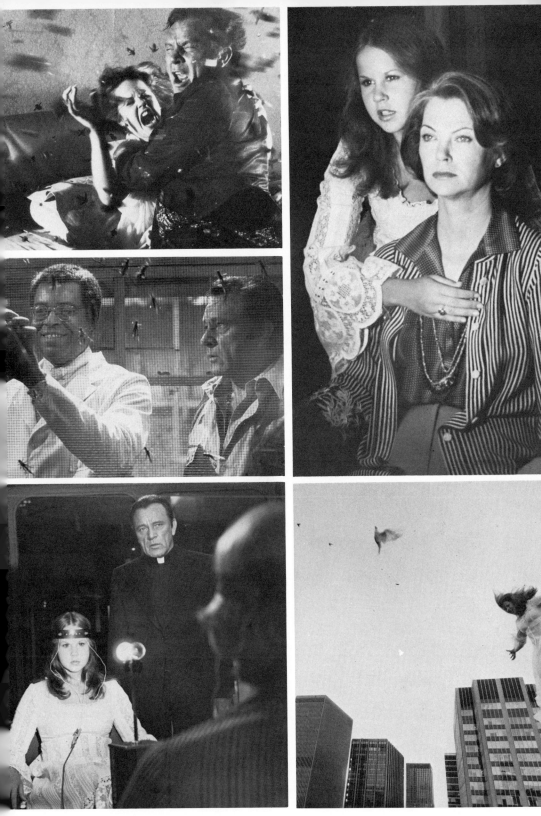

Linda Blair, Richard Burton Above: James
Earl Jones, Burton Top: Blair, Burton

Linda Blair Top: Linda Blair,
Louise Fletcher

63

SORCERER

(PARAMOUNT/UNIVERSAL) Producer-Director, William Friedkin; Screenplay, Walon Green; Baed on novel "The Wages of Fear" by Georges Arnaud; Editor-Associate Producer, Bud Smith; Photography, John M. Stephens, Dick Bush; Designer, John Box; Music, Tangerine Dream; Art Director, Roy Walker; Assistant Directors, Newton Arnold, Miguel Gil, Mark Johnson, Albert Shapiro; Costumes, Anthony Powell; In Panavision and Technicolor; 121 minutes; Rated PG; June release.

CAST

Scanlon/Dominguez	Roy Scheider
Victor Manzon/Serrano	Bruno Cremer
Nilo	Francisco Rabal
Kassem/Martinez	Amidou
Corlette	Ramon Bieri
Lartigue	Peter Capell
Marquez	Karl John
Carlos	Frederick Ledebur
Bobby Del Rios	Chico Martinez
Spider	Joe Spinell
Agrippa	Rosario Almontes
Billy White	Richard Holley
Blanche	Anne Marie Descott
Pascal	Jean-Luc Bideau
Lefevre	Jacques Francois
Guillot	Andre Falcon
Donnelly	Gerard E. Murphy
Boyle	Desmond Crofton
Murray	Henry Diamond
Ben	Ray Dittrich
Marty	Frank Gio
Vinnie	Randy Jurgensen
Carlo Ricci	Gus Allegretti

Roy Scheider, Randy Jurgenson
Above: Francisco Rabal Top: Scheider

64

Amidou, Ramon Bieri, Chico Martinez
Above: Bieri, Bruno Cremer, Scheider,
Amidou, Karl John

I NEVER PROMISED YOU A ROSE GARDEN

(NEW WORLD) Producer, Michael Hausman; Director, Anthony Page; Screenplay, Gavin Lambert; Photography, Bruce Logan; Designer, Toby Rafelson; Costume, Shadow; Editor, Garth Craven; An Imorh Production in color; 96 minutes; Rated R; July release.

CAST

Dr. Fried	Bibi Andersson
Deborah Blake	Kathleen Quinlan
Mr. Blake	Ben Piazza
Mrs. Blake	Lorraine Gary
Carla	Darlene Craviotto
Hobbs	Reni Santoni
Lee	Susan Tyrrell
Helene	Signe Hasso
McPherson	Norman Alden
Secret Wife of Henry VIII	Martin Bartlett
Anterrabae	Robert Viharo
Lactamaeon	Jeff Conaway
Dr. Halle	Dick Herd
Mrs. Forbes	Sarah Cunningham
The Spy	June C. Ellis
Sylvia	Diane Varsi
Kathryn	Patricia Singer
Eugenia	Mary Carver
Idat	Barbara Steele
Doctor in Ward D	Donald Bishop
Teacher in Ward D	Samantha Harper
Receptionist	Dolores Quentin
Student Nurse	Pamela Seaman
Nurses in Ward D	Cynthia Szigetti, Carol Androsky, Elizabeth Dartmoor, Cherry Davis
Women in Ward D	Lynn Stewart, Carol Worthington, Margo Burdichevsky, Gertrude Granor, Helen Verbit, Jan Burrell, Irene Roseen, Nancy Parsons, Leigh Curran

Top: Kathleen Quinlan

Bibi Andersson

MacARTHUR

(UNIVERSAL) Producer, Frank McCarthy; Director, Joseph Sargent; Screenplay, Hal Barwood, Matthew Robbins; Photography, Mario Tosi; Designer, John J. Lloyd; Music, Jerry Goldsmith; Editor, George Jay Nicholson; Assistant Directors, Scott Maitland, Donald E. Zepfel; In Panavision and Technicolor; 144 minutes; Rated PG; July release.

CAST

General Douglas MacArthur .... Gregory Peck
President Truman .... Ed Flanders
President Roosevelt.................................... Dan O'Herlihy
General Sutherland .... Ivan Bonar
General Marshall ....Ward Costello
Colonel Huff .... Nicolas Coster
Mrs. MacArthur .... Marj Dusay
The Secretary .... Art Fleming
Admiral King ....Russell D. Johnson
General Wainwright .... Sandy Kenyon
Representative Martin .... Robert Mandan
Colonel Diller .... Allan Miller
Colonel Whitney .... Dick O'Neill
Admiral Nimitz ....Addison Powell
General Sampson .... Tom Rosqui
General Eichelberger .... G. D. Spradlin
Admiral Halsey...................................Kenneth Tobey
General Walker .... Garry Walberg
General Marquat.................................... Lane Allan
TV Reporter .... Barry Coe
General Krueger .... Fverett Cooper
General Harding............................... Charles Cyphers
Prettyman .... Manuel De Pina
Castro .... Jesse Dizon
General Shepherd .... Warde Donovan
Emperor Hirohito ....John Fujioka
Aide.. Jerry Holland
Admiral Doyle ....Philip Kenneally
and John McKee (Adm. Leahy), Walter O. Miles (Gen. Kenney), Gerald S. Peters (Gen. Blamey), Eugene Peterson (Gen. Collins), Beulah Quo (Ah Cheu), Alex Rodine (Gen. Derevyanko), Yuki Shimoda (Prime Minister Shidehara), Fred Stuthman (Gen. Bradley), Harvey Vernon (Adm. Sherman), William Wellman, Jr. (Lt. Bulkeley).

Gregory Peck, also top
with Ivan Bonar

Gregory Peck, Kenneth Tobey
Above and Top: Gregory Peck

Ed Flanders, Gregory Peck
Top: Gregory Peck

THE LAST REMAKE OF BEAU GESTE

(UNIVERSAL) Executive Producers, Howard West, George Shapiro; Producer, William S. Gilmore; Director, Marty Feldman; Story, Marty Feldman, Sam Bobrick; Screenplay, Marty Feldman, Chris Allen; Photography, Gerry Fisher; Design, Brian Eatwell; Assistant Directors, Tom Joyner, Roberto Parra, Vincent Winter; Associate Producer, Bernard Williams; Costumes, May Routh; Editors, Jim Clark, Arthur Schmidt; Music, John Morris; Art director, Les Dilley; Choreography, Irving Davies; In Panavision and Technicolor; 85 minutes; Rated PG; July release.

CAST

Flavia Geste	Ann-Margret
Digby Geste	Marty Feldman
Beau Geste	Michael York
Markov	Peter Ustinov
Sheikh	James Earl Jones
Sir Hector	Trevor Howard
General Pecheur	Henry Gibson
Governor	Terry-Thomas
Boldini	Roy Kinnear
Crumble	Spike Milligan
Sheikh's Aide/Camel Salesman	Avery Schreiber
Judge	Hugh Griffith
Miss Wormwood	Irene Handl
Isabel Geste	Sinead Cusack
Captain Merdmanger	Henry Polic II
Blindman	Ted Cassidy
Father Shapiro	Burt Kwouk
Dostoevsky	Val Pringle
Lady in courtroom	Gwen Nelson
Beau at 6	Philip Bollard
Beau at 12	Nicholas Bridge
Digby at 12	Michael McConkey
Young Isabel	Bekki Bridge
Dr. Crippen	Roland MacLeod
Valentino	Martin Snaric
Henshaw	Stephen Lewis
Arab Horseman	Ed McMahon

Left: Marty Feldman, Ann-Margret

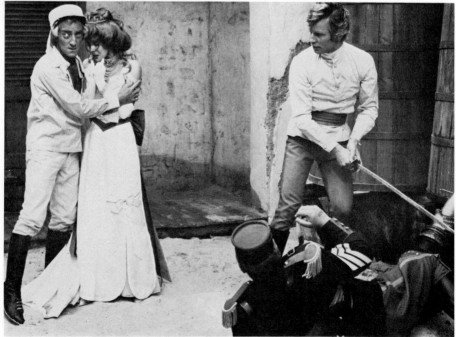

Marty Feldman, Ann-Margret, Michael York, Peter Ustinov

Peter Ustinov, and above with
Roy Kinnear Top: Chris Allen,
Marty Feldman

James Earl Jones Above: Avery Schreiber
Top: Ann-Margret, Roy Kinnear

THE BAD NEWS BEARS IN BREAKING TRAINING

(PARAMOUNT) Producer, Leonard Goldberg; Director, Michael Pressman; Screenplay, Paul Brickman; Based on characters created by Bill Lancaster; Photography, Fred J. Koenekamp; Editor, John W. Wheeler; Music, Craig Safan; Song Lyrics, Norman Gimbel; Art Director, Steve Berger; Costumes, Jack Martell; Assistant Director, Michael Daves; In Movielab Color; 99 minutes; Rated PG; July release.

CAST

Mike Leak	William Devane
Sy Orlansky	Clifton James
Kelly Leak	Jackie Earle Haley
Carmen Ronzonni	Jimmy Baio
Tanner Boyle	Chris Barnes
Ahmad Abdul Rahim	Erin Blunt
Agilar Boys	Jaime Escobedo, George Gonzales
Ogilvie	Alfred Lutter
Jimmie Feldman	Brett Marx
Rudi Stein	David Pollock
Timmy Lupus	Quinn Smith
Toby Whitewood	David Stambaugh
Mike Engelberg	Jeffrey Louis Starr
Caretaker	Fred Stuthman
Coach Manning	Dolph Sweet
Officer Mackie	Lane Smith
Coach Morrie Slaytor	Pat Corley

Jimmy Baio, William Devane
Top: George Gonzales, Jaime Escobedo

Above: William Devane

Top Row: Jeffrey Louis Starr, Erin Blunt, Alfred Lutter, David Stambaugh, David Pollock, Jackie Earle Haley, William Devane Kneeling: George Gonzales, Jimmy Baio, Chris Barnes, Jaime Escobedo, Brett Marx
Above Left: Lutter, Michelle Fruge, Leigh Manley

71

THE ISLAND OF DR. MOREAU

(AMERICAN INTERNATIONAL) Producers, John Temple-Smith, Skip Steloff; Executive Producers, Samuel Z. Arkoff, Sandy Howard; Director, Don Taylor; Screenplay, John Herman Shaner, Al Ramrus; From novel by H. G. Wells; Photography, Gerry Fisher; Ronnie Taylor; Editor, Marion Rothman; Music, Laurence Rosenthal; Design, Philip Jefferies; Costumes, Richard LaMotte, Emma Porteus, Rita Woods; Assistant Director, Bob Bender; In Movielab Color; 98 minutes; Rated PG; July release.

CAST

Dr. Moreau	Burt Lancaster
Braddock	Michael York
Montgomery	Nigel Davenport
Maria	Barbara Carrera
Sayer of the Law	Richard Basehart
M'Ling	Nick Cravat
Boarman	The Great John L.
Bullman	Bob Ozman
Hyenaman	Fumio Demura
Lionman	Gary Baxley
Tigerman	John Gillespie
Bearman	David Cass

Left: Burt Lancaster

GREASED LIGHTNING

(WARNER BROS.) Producer, Hannah Weinstein; Director, Michael Schultz; Screenplay, Kenneth Vose, Lawrence DuKore, Melvin Van Peebles, Leon Capetanos; Executive Producers, Richard Bell, J. Lloyd Grant; Associate Producer, James E. Hinton; Photography, George Bouillet; Editors, Bob Wyman, Christopher Holmes, Randy Roberts; Art Director, Jack Senter; Music, Fred Karlin; Assistant Directors, Terry Donnelly, Dwight Williams, Preston Holmes; Costumes, Celia Bryant; In Movielab Color; 96 minutes; Rated PG; July release.

CAST

Wendell Scott	Richard Pryor
Hutch	Beau Bridges
Mary	Pam Grier
Peewee	Cleavon Little
Sheriff Cotton	Vincent Gardenia
Woodrow	Richie Havens
Russell	Julian Bond
Beau Welles	Earl Hindman
Wendell's mother	Minnie Gentry
Hutch's wife	Lucy Saroyan
Billy Joe Byrnes	Noble Willingham

Top: Beau Bridges Below: Richie Havens, Cleavon Little, Richard Pryor, Pam Grier

Richard Pryor, and above with Pam Grier Top: Pryor

THE RESCUERS

(BUENA VISTA) Producer, Wolfgang Reitherman; Executive Producer, Ron Miller; Directors, Wolfgang Reitherman, John Lounsbery, Art Stevens; Suggested by "The Rescuers" and "Miss Bianca" by Margery Sharp; Story, Ken Anderson, Vance Gerry, David Michener, Burny Mattinson, Frank Thomas, Fred Lucky, Ted Berman, Dick Sebast; Directing Animators, Ollie Johnston, Frank Thomas, Milt Kahl, Don Bluth; Musical Score, Artie Butler; Songs sung by Shelby Flint; Art Director, Don Griffith; Assistant Directors, Jeff Patch, Richard Rich; Editors, James Melton, Jim Koford; A Walt Disney Production in Technicolor; 76 minutes; Rated G; July release.

VOICES OF:

Bob Newhart (Bernard), Eva Gabor (Miss Bianca), Geraldine Page (Mme. Medusa), Joe Flynn (Mr. Snoops), Jeanette Nolan (Ellie Mae), Pat Buttram (Luke), Jim Jordan (Orville), John McIntire (Rufus), Michelle Stacy (Penny), Bernard Box (Chairman), Larry Clemmons (Gramps), James Macdonald (Evinrude), George Lindsey (Rabbit), Bill McMillan (TV Announcer), Dub Taylor (Digger), John Fiedler (Owl)

**Penny, also top with
Bernard and Miss Bianca**

Madame Medusa   Bernard and Bianca

EMPIRE OF THE ANTS

(AMERICAN INTERNATIONAL) Producer-Director, Bert I. Gordon; Executive Producer, Samuel Z. Arkoff; Screenplay, Jack Turley; From story by H. G. Wells; Photography, Reginald Morris; Editor, Michael Luciano; Music, Dana Kaproff; Design, Charles Rosen; Costumes, Joanne Haas; Assistant Directors, David McGiffert, Mel Efros; In Movielab Color; 89 minutes; Rated PG; July release.

CAST

Marilyn Fryser	Joan Collins
Dan Stokely	Robert Lansing
Joe Morrison	John David Carson
Sheriff Kincade	Albert Salmi
Margaret Ellis	Jacqueline Scott
Coreen Bradford	Pamela Shoop
Larry Graham	Robert Pine
Charlie Pearson	Edward Power
Christine Graham	Brooke Palance
Sam Russell	Tom Fadden
Velma Thompson	Irene Tedrow
Harry Thompson	Harry Holcombe
Thomas Lawson	Jack Kosslyn
Mary Lawson	Ilse Earl
Ginny	Janie Gavin
Anson Parker	Norman Franklin
Phoebe Russell	Florence McGee

Left: Joan Collins, Robert Lansing

Jacqueline Scott, Joan Collins, Robert Pine, Pamela Shoop, Robert Lansing, John David Carson

Robert Lansing, John David Carson Top: John David Carson, Pamela Shoop, Robert Lansing

OUTLAW BLUES

(WARNER BROS.) Producer, Steve Tisch; Director, Richard T. Heffron; Screenplay, B. W. L. Norton; Executive Producers, Fred Weintraub, Paul Heller; Photography, Jules Brenner; Associate Producer, Eva Monley; Music, Charles Bernstein; Editors, Danford B. Green, Scott Conrad; Assistant Directors, Dennis Jones, Steve Lim; Art Director, Jack Marty; Costumes, Rosanna Norton; In Technicolor; 100 minutes; Rated PG; August release.

CAST

Bobby Ogden	Peter Fonda
Tina Waters	Susan Saint James
Buzz Cavenaugh	John Crawford
Garland Dupree	James Callahan
Hatch	Michael Lerner
Elroy	Steve Fromholz
Associate Warden	Richard Lockmiller
Billy Bob	Matt Clark
Cathy Moss	Jan Rita Cobler
Leon Warback	Gene Rader
Big Guy	Curtis Harris
Disc Jockey	Jerry Greene
Anchorman	Dave Helfert
Newsman	Jeffrey Friedman
Cop Chauffeur	James N. Harrel

Susan Saint James
Top: Peter Fonda, Susan Saint James

ONE ON ONE

(WARNER BROS.) Producer, Martin Hornstein; Director, Lamont Johnson; Screenplay, Robby Benson, Jerry Segal; Associate Producer, Ron Windred; Photography, Donald M. Morgan; Editor, Robbe Roberts; Art Director, Sherman Loudermilk; Music, Charles Fox; Lyrics, Paul Williams; Songs performed by Seals and Crofts; Assistant Directors, Chico Day, Anthony Brand, Gene De Ruelle, Thom Anable; Costumes, Donfeld; In Panavision and Technicolor; 98 minutes; Rated PG; August release.

CAST

Henry Steele	Robby Benson
Janet Hays	Annette O'Toole
Coach Moreland Smith	G. D. Spradlin
B. J. Rudolph	Gail Strickland
Hitchhiker	Melanie Griffith
Malcolm	James G. Richardson
Gonzales	Hector Morales
Tom	Cory Faucher

Annette O'Toole, Robby Benson
(also top right)

Robby Benson, Annette O'Toole

79

SIDEWINDER ONE

(AVCO EMBASSY) Producer, Elmo Williams; Director, Earl Bellamy; Screenplay, Thomas McMahon, Nancy Voyles Crawford; Photography, Dennis Dalzell; Art Directors, Tracy and Liz Bousman; Assistant Directors, Danny McCauley, Ernie Santell; In color; 97 minutes; Rated PG; August release.

CAST

Digger	Marjoe Gortner
J. W. Wyatt	Michael Parks
Chris Gentry	Susan Howard
Packard Gentry	Alex Cord
Mrs. Holt	Charlotte Rae
Willie Holt	Barry Livingston
Jerry Fleming	Bill Vint

Left: Marjoe Gortner, Michael Parks

**Barry Livingston, Charlotte Rae
Above: Alex Cord**

**Michael Parks, Susan Howard and above
with Alex Cord, Marjoe Gortner**

BOBBY DEERFIELD

(COLUMBIA) Producer-Director, Sydney Pollack; Screenplay, Alvin Sargent; Based on novel "Heaven Has No Favorites" by Erich Maria Remarque; Executive Producer, John Foreman; Photography, Henri Decae; Design, Stephen Grimes; Music, Dave Grusin; Editor, Fredric Steinkamp; Assistant Directors, Paul Feyder, Meyer Berreby; Art Director, Mark Frederix; In Panavision and Metrocolor; 124 minutes; Rated PG; September release.

CAST

Bobby	Al Pacino
Lillian	Marthe Keller
Lydia	Anny Duperey
The Brother	Walter McGinn
Uncle Luigi	Romolo Valli
Karl Holtzmann	Stephan Meldegg
Delvecchio	Jaime Sanchez
The Magician	Norm Nielsen
Tourists	Mickey Knox, Dorothy James
Priest in the garden	Guido Alberti
Catherine Modave	Monique Lejeune
Bertrand Modave	Steve Gadler
Flutist	Van Doude
Woman in the gas station	Aurora Maris
Carlos Del Montanara	Gerard Hernandez
Priest	Maurice Vallier
Musicians	Maurice Baquet, Tasso Adamopoulos, Claire Bernard, Jennifer Marks
Vincenzo	Antonio Faa'Di Bruno
Autograph Hound	Andre Vallardy
Tommy	Fedor Atkins
Mario	Patrick Floersheim
Head Mechanic	Bernie Pollack
Mechanic	Al Silvani
Nurse	Isabelle De Blonay
Man with dog	Franco Ressel
Reporter	Dominique Briand

Top: Al Pacino, Marthe Keller

Al Pacino

SHORT EYES

(PARAMOUNT) Producer, Lewis Harris; Director, Robert M. Young; Screenplay, Miguel Pinero from his play; Executive Producer, Marvin Stuart; Photography, Peter Sova; Associate Producers, Walker Stuart, Martin Hirsh; Editor, Edward Beyer; Music, Curtis Mayfield; Assistant Director, Robert Colesberry; Costumes, Paul Martino; Designer, Joe Babas; In color; 104 minutes; Rated R; September release.

CAST

Clark Davis	Bruce Davison
Juan	Jose Perez
Ice	Nathan George
El Raheem	Don Blakely
Paco	Shawn Elliott
Cupcakes	Tito Goya
Longshore	Joe Carberry
Omar	Kenny Steward
Mr. Nett	Bob Maroff
Mr. Brown	Keith Davis
Go Go	Miguel Pinero
Cha Cha	Willie Hernandez
Tony	Tony De Benedetto
Mr. Allard	Bob O'Connell
Mr. Morrison	Mark Margolis
Gomez	Richard Matamoros
Pappy	Curtis Mayfield
Johnny	Freddie Fender

Bruce Davison
Top: Jose Perez

Top: Curtis Mayfield
Below: Nathan George, Shawn Elliott

THE CHICKEN CHRONICLES

(AVCO EMBASSY) Producer, Walter Shenson; Director, Francis Simon; Screenplay, Paul Diamond; Associate Producer, Dan Allingham; Photography, Mathew Leonetti; Editor, George Folsey, Jr.; Assistant Director, Jack Baran; Art Director, Ray Markham; In color; 92 minutes; Rated PG; October release.

CAST

Max Ober	Phil Silvers
Mr. Nastase	Ed Lauter
David Kessler	Steven Guttenberg
Margaret	Lisa Reeves
Tracy	Meridith Baer
Mark	Branscombe Richmond
Weinstein	Wil Seltzer
Madalyn	Kutee
Charlie Kessler	Gino Baffa

Right: Phil Silvers, Steve Guttenberg, Kutee

Lisa Reeves, Steve Guttenberg, Meredith Baer
Above: Branscombe Richmond, Ed Lauter

Lisa Reeves, Steve Guttenberg
(also above)

LOOKING FOR MR. GOODBAR

(PARAMOUNT) Producer, Freddie Field; Adapted and Directed by Richard Brooks; Based on novel by Judith Rossner; Photography, William A. Fraker; Editor, George Grenville; Music, Artie Kane; Art Direction, Edward Carfagno; Costumes, Jodie Lynn Tillen; Assistant Director, David Silver; In Metrocolor; 135 minutes; Rated R; October release.

CAST

Theresa Dunn	Diane Keaton
Katherine Dunn	Tuesday Weld
James Morrissey	William Atherton
Mr. Dunn	Richard Kiley
Tony Lopanto	Richard Gere
Prof. Engle	Alan Feinstein
Gary Cooper White	Tom Berenger
Mrs. Dunn	Priscilla Pointer
Brigid Dunn	Laurie Prange
Barney	Joel Fabiani
Black Cat	Julius Harris
George	Richard Bright
Cap Jackson	LeVar Burton
Mrs. Jackson	Marilyn Coleman
Little Theresa	Elizabeth Cheshire

Left: Diane Keaton

Diane Keaton, Alan Feinstein

Diane Keaton (also above)

84

Diane Keaton, also top left with Richard Gere
Top Right: Richard Kiley, Tuesday Weld

JULIA

(20th CENTURY-FOX) Producer, Richard Roth; Executive Producer, Julian Derode; Director, Fred Zinnemann; Screenplay, Alvin Sargent; Based on story "Pentimento" by Lillian Hellman; Photography, Douglas Slocombe; Editor, Walter Murch; Music, Georges Delerue; Design, Gene Gallahan, Willy Holt, Carmen Dillon; Assistant Directors, Alain Bonnot, Anthony Waye; In DeLuxe Color; 116 minutes; Rated PG; October release.

CAST

Lillian Hellman	Jane Fonda
Julia	Vanessa Redgrave
Dashiell Hammett	Jason Robards
Johann	Maximilian Schell
Alan Campbell	Hal Holbrook
Dorothy Parker	Rosemary Murphy
Anne Marie	Meryl Streep
Train Passengers	Dora Doll, Elisabeth Mortensen
Sammy	John Glover
Young Julia	Lisa Pelikan
Young Lillian	Susan Jones
Grandmother	Cathleen Nesbitt
Undertaker	Maurice Denham
Passport Officer	Gerard Buhr
"Hamlet"	Stefan Gryff
Little Boy	Phillip Siegel
Woman	Molly Urquhart
Butler	Antony Carrick
Woman in Berlin station	Ann Queensberry
Man in Berlin Station	Edmond Bernard
Fat Man	Jacques David
Woman in green hat	Jacqueline Staup
Vienna Concierge	Hans Verner
Paris Concierge	Christian de Tiliere

86

Jane Fonda, Jason Robards
Top: Vanessa Redgrave, Jane Fonda

1977 Academy awards for Best Supporting Actor (Jason Robards), Supporting Actress (Vanessa Redgrave) and Best Screenplay (from another medium)

Maximilian Schell

Top: Jane Fonda, Vanessa Redgrave

Jason Robards

ROSELAND

(CINEMA SHARES INTERNATIONAL) Producer, Ismail Merchant; Director, James Ivory; Screenplay, Ruth Prawer Jhabvala; Photography, Ernest Vincze; Music, Michael Gibson; Editor, Humphrey Gibson; Executive Producers, Michael T. Murphy, Ottomar Rudolf; In color; 103 minutes; Rated PG; October release.

CAST

May	Teresa Wright
Stan	Lou Jacobi
Master of Ceremonies	Don De Natale
Marilyn	Geraldine Chaplin
Cleo	Helen Gallagher
Pauline	Joan Copeland
Russel	Christopher Walken
George	Conrad Janis
Rosa	Lilia Skala
Arthur	David Thomas
Ruby	Louise Kirtland
Bartender	Edward Kogan
Hustle Couple	Annette Rivera, Floyd Chisholm

Right: Christopher Walken, Geraldine Chaplin

Teresa Wright, Lou Jacobi

Lilia Skala, David Thomas
Above: Joan Copeland, Christopher Walken

Don DeNatale
Top: Joan Copeland, Helen Gallagher

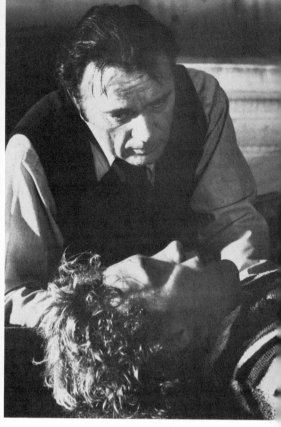

EQUUS

(UNITED ARTISTS) Producers, Elliott Kastner, Lester Persky; Director, Sidney Lumet; Screenplay, Peter Shaffer from his play; Design, Tony Walton; Photography, Oswald Morris; Music, Richard Rodney Bennett; Editor, John Victor-Smith; Associate Producer, Denis Holt; Assistant Director, David Tringham; Art Director, Simon Holland; In Panavision and color; 138 minutes; Rated R; October release.

CAST

Dr. Martin Dysart	Richard Burton
Alan Strang	Peter Firth
Frank Strang	Colin Blakely
Dora Strang	Joan Plowright
Harry Dalton	Harry Andrews
Magistrate Hesther Saloman	Eileen Atkins
Jill Mason	Jenny Agutter
The Horseman	John Wyman
Margaret Dysart	Kate Reid
Mr. Pearce	Ken James
Miss Raintree	Elva Mai Hoover
Mr. Davies	James Hurdle
Mary	Karen Pearson
Dr. Bennett	David Gardner
Hospital Patient	Patrick Brymer
First Child	Sheldon Rybowski
Second Child	Sufi Bukhari
Horse Trainer	Anita Van Hezewyck
Clown	Mark Parr
Ringmaster	Frazier Mohawk

Richard Burton, Joan Plowright
Top: Peter Firth (also Right) with Burton

Peter Firth, Jenny Agutter Above: Richard
Burton, Firth Top: Eileen Atkins, Burton

Richard Burton, Peter Firth Above: Burton,
Colin Blakely Top: Firth, Jenny Agutter   **91**

A PIECE OF THE ACTION

(WARNER BROS.) Producer, Melville Tucker; Director, Sidney Poitier; Screenplay, Charles Blackwell; Story, Timothy March; Photography, Donald M. Morgan; Music and Lyrics, Curtis Mayfield; Designer, Alfred Sweeney; Associate Producer-Editor, Pembroke J. Herring; Associate Producer, Kris Keiser; Songs performed by Mavis Staples; Assistant Directors, Dwight Williams, Craig Huston; Choreography, Arthur Mitchell; A First Artists Production in Metrocolor; 134 minutes; Rated PG; October release.

CAST

Manny Durrell	Sidney Poitier
Dave Anderson	Bill Cosby
Joshua Burke	James Earl Jones
Lila French	Denise Nicholas
Sarah Thomas	Hope Clarke
Nikki McLean	Tracy Reed
Bruno	Titos Vandis
Bea Quitman	Frances Foster
Ty Shorter	Jason Evers
Louie	Marc Lawrence
Nellie Bond	Ja'net Dubois

Left: Sidney Poitier, Bill Cosby

James Earl Jones
Above: Sidney Poitier

Denise Nicholas, Bill Cosby

FIRST LOVE

(PARAMOUNT) Producers, Lawrence Turman, David Foster; Director, Joan Darling; Screenplay, Jane Stanton Hitchcock, David Freeman; Based on story "Sentimental Education" by Harold Brodkey; Photography, Bobby Byrne; Editor, Frank Morriss; Design, Robert Luthardt; Assistant Director, Phil Rawlins; In Metrocolor; 91 minutes; Rated R; November release.

CAST

Elgin Smith	William Katt
Caroline	Susan Dey
David	John Heard
Shelley	Beverly D'Angelo
John March	Robert Loggia
Prof. Oxtan	Tom Lacy
Marsha	Swoosie Kurtz
Felicia	June Barrett
Zookeeper	Patrick O'Hara
Secretary	Judy Kerr
Girl in bar	Jenny Hill
Mrs. March	Virginia Leith
Cafeteria Boss	Billy Beck

Top: William Katt, Susan Dey
Below: William Katt, John Heard

John Heard, William Katt, Susan Dey
Above: Susan Dey, William Katt, also top

SEMI-TOUGH

(UNITED ARTISTS) Producer, David Merrick; Director, Michael Ritchie; Screenplay, Walter Bernstein; Based on novel by Dan Jenkins; Photography, Charles Rosher, Jr.; Designer, Walter Scott Herndon; Editor, Richard A. Harris; Music, Jerry Fielding; Costumes, Theoni V. Aldredge; Assistant Directors, Ken Swor, David Sosna; In DeLuxe Color and Panavision; 108 minutes; November release.

CAST

Billy Clyde Puckett	Burt Reynolds
Shake Tiller	Kris Kristofferson
Barbara Jane Bookman	Jill Clayburgh
Big Ed Bookman	Robert Preston
Friedrich Bismark	Bert Convy
Puddin	Roger E. Mosley
Clara Pelf	Lotte Lenya
Phillip Hooper	Richard Masur
Dreamer Tatum	Carl Weathers
T. J. Lambert	Brian Dennehy
Earlene	Mary Jo Catlett
Hose Manning	Joe Kapp
Vlada	Ron Silver
McNair	Jim McKrell
Interpreter	Peter Bromilow
Coach Parks	Norm Alden
Minister	Fred Stuthman
Dressmaker	Janet Brandt
Fitter	William Wolf
Stewardess	Jenifer Shaw
Puddin, Jr	Kevin Furry
Puddin's Wife	Ava Roberts

Kris Kristofferson, Jill Clayburgh, Burt Reynolds
Top: Brian Dennehy, Reynolds, Kristofferson

Kris Kristofferson, Jill Clayburgh, and above with Burt Reynolds Top: Robert Preston, Reynolds

Burt Reynolds, Jill Clayburgh Above: Kris Kristofferson, Clayburgh Top: Clayburgh, Robert Preston

THE TURNING POINT

(20th CENTURY-FOX) Producers, Herbert Ross, Arthur Laurents; Director, Herbert Ross; Screenplay, Arthur Laurents; Executive Producer, Nora Kaye; Music adapted and conducted by John Lanchbery; Photography, Robert Surtees; Editor, William Reynolds; Design, Albert Brenner; Assistant Director, Jack Roe; In DeLuxe Color; 119 minutes; November release.

CAST

Emma	Anne Bancroft
Deedee	Shirley MacLaine
Yuri	Mikhail Baryshnikov
Emilia	Leslie Browne
Wayne	Tom Skerritt
Adelaide	Martha Scott
Sevilla	Antoinette Sibley
Dahkarova	Alexandra Danilova
Carolyn	Starr Danias
Carter	Marshall Thompson
Michael	James Mitchell
Freddie	Scott Douglas
Arnold	Daniel Levans
Peter	Jurgen Schneider
Rosie	Anthony Zerbe
Ethan	Phillip Saunders
Janina	Lisa Lucas
Florence	Saax Bradbury
Sandra	Hilda Morales
Barney	Donald Petrie
Billy Joe	James Crittenden

and guest appearances by Lucette Aldous, Fernando Bujones, Richard Cragun, Suzanne Farrell, Marcia Haydee, Peter Martins, Clark Tippet, Marianna Tcherkassky, Martine Van Hamel, Charles Ward

Left: Shirley MacLaine, Ann Bancroft

Shirley MacLaine, Ann Bancroft, Tom Skerritt, Phillip Saunders

Shirley MacLaine, Anne Bancroft
Top: Leslie Browne, Mikhail Baryshnikov

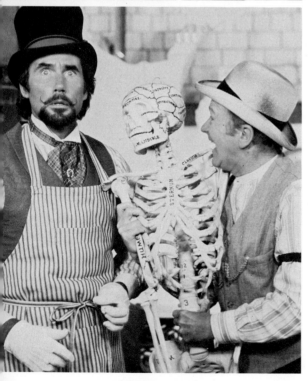

PETE'S DRAGON

(BUENA VISTA) Producers, Ron Miller, Jerome Courtland; Director, Don Chaffey; Screenplay, Malcolm Marmorstein; Based on story by Seton I. Miller, S. S. Field; Photography, Frank Phillips; Songs, Al Kasha, Joel Hirschhorn; Choreography, Onna White; Art Directors, John B. Mansbridge, Jack Martin Smith; Editor, Gordon D. Brenner; Costumes, Bill Thomas; Assistant Directors, Ronald R. Grow, John M. Poer; A Walt Disney Production in Technicolor; 134 minutes; Rated G; November release.

CAST

Nora	Helen Reddy
Dr. Terminus	Jim Dale
Lampie	Mickey Rooney
Hoagy	Red Buttons
Lena Gogan	Shelley Winters
Pete	Sean Marshall
Miss Taylor	Jane Kean
The Mayor	Jim Backus
Merle	Charles Tyner
Willie	Jeff Conaway
Grover	Gary Morgan
Paul	Cal Bartlett
Voice of Elliott	Charlie Callas
Captain	Walter Barnes
Store Proprietor	Robert Easton
Man with visor	Roger Price
Old Sea Captain	Robert Foulk
Egg Man	Ben Wrigley
Cement Man	Joe Ross
Fishermen	Al Checco, Henry Slate, Jack Collins

Jim Dale, Red Buttons
Top: Cal Bartlett, Helen Reddy

Top: Mickey Rooney, Helen Reddy, Sean Marshall

Gary Morgan, Charles Tyner, Shelley Winters, Jeff Conaway
Top: Sean Marshall, Elliott

103

THE GOODBYE GIRL

(WARNER BROS.) Producer, Ray Stark; Director, Herbert Ross; Screenplay, Neil Simon; Associate Producer, Roger M. Rothstein; Music, Dave Grusin; Title song written and performed by David Gates; Photography, David M. Walsh; Designer, Albert Brenner; Editor, John F. Burnett; Costumes, Ann Roth; Assistant Directors, Jack Roe, Edward Markley; In Metrocolor; 110 minutes; Rated PG; November release.

CAST

Elliott Garfield	Richard Dreyfuss
Paula McFadden	Marsha Mason
Lucy McFadden	Quinn Cummings
Mark	Paul Benedict
Donna	Barbara Rhoades
Mrs. Crosby	Theresa Merritt
Ronnie	Michael Shawn
Rhonda	Patricia Pearcy
Assistant Choreographer	Gene Castle
Dance Instructor	Daniel Levans
Linda	Marilyn Sokol
Mrs. Morganweiss	Anita Dangler
Mrs. Bodine	Victoria Boothby
Liquor Store Salesman	Robert Costanzo
Muggers	Poncho Gonzales, Jose Machado, Hubert Kelly
Cynthia	Dana Laurita
Drunk	Dave Cass
Strip Club Manager	Esther Sutherland
Strip Club Dancers	Loyita Chapel, Caprice Clarke
Critic	Clarence Felder
Japanese Salesmen	Kensuke Haga, Ryohei Kanokogi
Woman in audience	Ruby Holbrook
Gretchen	Kristina Hurrell
Furniture Movers	David Matthau, Milt Oberman
Painter	Eddie Villery

and Joseph Carberry, Eric Uhler, Ray Barry, Munson Hicks, Robert Kerman, Jeanne Lange, Robert Lesser, Fred McCarren, Nicholas Mele, Maureen Moore, Joseph Regalbuto, Peter Vogt, Wendy Cutler, Susan Elliot, Andy Goldberg, Paul Willson

Richard Dreyfuss received a 1977 Academy Award for Best Actor

Richard Dreyfuss, Marsha Mason
Top Right: Marsha Mason, Quinn Cummings

Marsha Mason, Richard Dreyfuss
Above Marsha Mason, Barbara Rhoades

Marsha Mason, Richard Dreyfuss, and above with Quinn Cummings Top: Dreyfuss, Cummings

Marsha Mason, Richard Dreyfuss, and at top Above: Quinn Cummings, Marsha Mason

CLOSE ENCOUNTERS OF THE THIRD KIND

(COLUMBIA) Producers, Julia and Michael Phillips; Direction and Screenplay, Steven Spielberg; Photography, Vilmos Zsigmond, Douglas Trumbull, William A. Fraker, Douglas Slocombe, John Alonzo, Laszlo Kovacs, Richard Yurcich, Dave Stewart, Robert Hall, Don Jarel, Dennis Muren; Editor, Michael Kahn; Music, John Williams; Design, Joe Alves; Art Direction, Dan Lomino; Costumes, Jim Linn; Assistant Director, Chuck Myers; In Metrocolor; 135 minutes; November release.

CAST

Roy Neary	Richard Dreyfuss
Claude Lacombe	Francois Truffaut
Ronnie Neary	Teri Garr
Jilian Guiler	Melinda Dillon
Barry Guiler	Cary Guffey
Interpreter Laughlin	Bob Balaban
Project Leader	J. Patrick McNamara
Wild Bill	Warren Kemmerling
Farmer	Roberts Blossom
Jean Claude	Philip Dodds
Neary Children	Shawn Bishop, Adrienne Campbell, Justin Dreyfuss
Robert	Lance Hendricksen
Team Leader	Merrill Connally
Major Benchley	George Dicenzo

Richard Dreyfuss, also above

1977 Academy Award for Best Cinematography

Francois Truffaut

Melinda Dillon

THE GAUNTLET

(WARNER BROS.) Producer, Robert Daley; Director, Clint Eastwood; Screenplay, Michael Butler, Dennis Shryack; Photography, Rexford Metz; Editors, Ferris Webster, Joel Cox; Art Director, Allen E. Smith; Music, Jerry Fielding; Associate Producer, Fritz Manes; Assistant Directors, Richard Hashimoto, Lynn Morgan, Peter Bergquist, Al Silvani; A Malpaso Company Production in Panavision and DeLuxe Color; 110 minutes; Rated R; December release.

CAST

Ben Shockley	Clint Eastwood
Gus Mally	Sondra Locke
Josephson	Pat Hingle
Blakelock	William Prince
Constable	Bill McKinney
Feyderspiel	Michael Cavanaugh
Waitress	Carole Cook
Jail Matron	Mara Corday
Bookie	Douglas McGrath
Desk Sergeant	Jeff Morris
Bikers	Samantha Doane, Roy Jenson, Dan Vadis

Left: Clint Eastwood, Sondra Locke

Pat Hingle, Clint Eastwood

Clint Eastwood, Sondra Locke
(also at top)

Clint Eastwood, and top
with Sondra Locke

THE CHOIRBOYS

(UNIVERSAL) Producers, Merv Adelson, Lee Rich; Executive Producers, Pietro Bregni, Mario Bregni, Mark Damon; Director, Robert Aldrich; Screenplay, Christopher Knopf; Based on novel by Joseph Wambaugh; Photography, Joseph Biroc; Editors, Maury Winetrobe, William Martin, Irving Rosenblum; Music, Frank DeVol; Design, Bill Kenney; Assistant Director, Malcolm Harding; In Technicolor; 119 minutes; Rated R; December release.

CAST

Whalen	Charles Durning
Motts	Louis Gossett, Jr.
Slate	Perry King
Tanaguchi	Clyde Kusatsu
Van Moot	Stephen Macht
Roscoe Rules	Tim McIntyre
Proust	Randy Quaid
Sartino	Chuck Sacci
Lyles	Don Stroud
Bloomguard	James Woods
Scuzzi	Burt Young
Riggs	Robert Webber
Fanny	Jeanie Bell
Mrs. Lyles	Blair Brown
Ora Lee Tingle	Michele Carey
Yanov	Charles Haid
Hod Carrier	Joe Kapp
Hadley	Barbara Rhodes
Capt. Drobeck	Jim Davis
Foxy/Gina	Phyllis Davis
Luther Quigley	Jack DeLeon
Lt. Grimsley	George Di Cenzo
Lt. Finque	David Spielberg
Pete Zoony	Vic Tayback
Blaney	Michael Wills
Sabrina	Susan Batson
Carolina Moon	Claire Brennen

Charles Durning, Louis Gossett, Jr., Robert Webber Above: Barbara Rhoades, Chuck Sacci

Top: Charles Durning, Louis Gossett, Jr., Perry King, Clyde Kusatsu, Stephen Macht, Tim McIntire, Randy Quade, Chuck Sacci, Don Stroud, James Woods

HIGH ANXIETY

(20th CENTURY-FOX) Producer-Director, Mel Brooks; Screenplay, Mel Brooks, Ron Clark, Rudy DeLuca, Barry Levinson; Photography, Paul Lohmann; Editor, John C. Howard; Designer, Peter Wooley; Music, John Morris; Costumes, Patricia Morris; Assistant Director, Jonathan Sanger; A Crossbow Production in Deluxe Color; 94 minutes; December release.

CAST

Richard Thornydyke	Mel Brooks
Victoria Brisbane	Madeline Kahn
Nurse Diesel	Cloris Leachman
Dr. Charles Montague	Harvey Korman
Brophy	Ron Carey
Professor Lilloman	Howard Morris
Dr. Wentworth	Dick Van Patten
Desk Clerk	Jack Riley
Cocker Spaniel	Charlie Callas
Zachary Cartwright	Ron Clark
Killer	Rudy DeLuca
Bellboy	Barry Levinson
Norton	Lee Delano
Dr. Baxter	Richard Stahl
Dr. Eckhardt	Darrell Zwerling
Piano Player	Murphy Dunne
Man who is shot	Al Hopson
Flasher	Bob Ridgely
Arthur Brisbane	Albert J. Whitlock

Right: Mel Brooks

Howard Morris, Harvey Korman, Cloris Leachman, Mel Brooks, Madeline Kahn, Ron Carey

TELEFON

(UNITED ARTISTS) Producer, James B. Harris; Director, Don Siegel; Screenplay, Peter Hyams, Stirling Silliphant; Based on novel by Walter Wager; Music, Lalo Schifrin; Photography, Michael Butler; Designer, Ted Haworth; Editor, Douglas Stewart; Art Director, William F. O'Brien; In Panavision and Metrocolor; 103 minutes; Rated PG; December release.

CAST

Grigori Borzov	Charles Bronson
Barbara	Lee Remick
Nicolai Dalchimsky	Donald Pleasence
Dorothy Putterman	Tyne Daly
Colonel Malchenko	Alan Badel
General Strelsky	Patrick Magee
Marie Wills	Sheree North
Harley Sandburg	Frank Marth

Left: Charles Bronson, Lee Remick

Patrick Magee, Charles Bronson, Alan Badel

**Charles Bronson Above: Frank Marth, Tyne Daly,
Alan Case Top: Bronson, Roy Jenson**

Lee Remick, Charles Bronson
(also above)

113

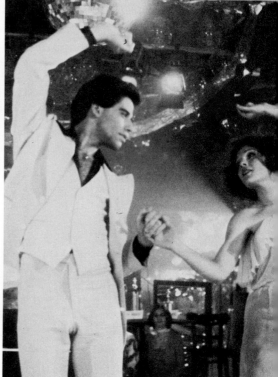

SATURDAY NIGHT FEVER

(PARAMOUNT) Producer, Robert Stigwood; Director, John Badham; Screenplay, Norman Wexler; Based on story by Nik Cohn; Photography, Ralf D. Bode; Editor, David Rawlins; Musical numbers staged and choreographed by Lester Wilson; Additional Music and Adaptation, David Shire; Original Music, Barry Robin, Maurice Gibb; In color; 120 minutes; Rated R; December release.

CAST

Tony Manero	John Travolta
Stephanie	Karen Lynn Gorney
Bobby C.	Barry Miller
Joey	Joseph Call
Double J	Paul Pape
Annette	Donna Pescow
Gus	Bruce Ornstein
Flo	Julie Bovasso
Frank, Jr.	Martin Shakar
Fusco	Sam J. Coppola
Grandmother	Nina Hansen
Linda	Lisa Peluso
Doreen	Denny Dillon
Pete	Bert Michaels
Paint Store Customer	Robert Costanza
Becker	Robert Weil
Girl in disco	Shelly Batt
Connie	Fran Drescher
Jay Langhart	Donald Gantry
Haberdashery Salesman	Murray Moston
Detective	William Andrews
Pizza Girl	Ann Travolta
Deejay	Monti Rock III
Frank, Sr.	Val Bisoglio

John Travolta, also above and Top

Top: John Travolta, Karen Lynn Gorney

Karen Lynn Gorney, John Travolta

THE WORLD'S GREATEST LOVER

(20th CENTURY-FOX) Produced, Directed and Written by
Gene Wilder; Co-Producer/Production Design, Terence Marsh;
Co-Producer/Editor, Chris Greenbury; Photography, Gerald
Hirschfeld; Music, John Morris; Art Director, Steve Sardanis;
Assistant Director, Mel Dellar; In DeLuxe Color; 89 minutes;
December release.

CAST

Rudy Valentine	Gene Wilder
Annie	Carol Kane
Zitz	Dom DeLuise
Hotel Manager	Fritz Feld
Cousin Buddy	Cousin Buddy
Maid	Hannah Dean
Anne Calassandro	Candice Azzara
Uncle Harry	Carl Ballantine
Rudolph Valentino	Matt Collins
Mr. Kipper	Lou Cutell
Room Clerk	James Gleason
Director	Ronny Graham
Barber	Michael Huddleston
Aunt Tillie	Florence Sundstrom

Right: Gene Wilder

Gene Wilder

Carol Kane, Gene Wilder

THE DAY THE MUSIC DIED (Atlantic Releasing Corp.) Producer-Director-Screenplay, Bert Tenzer; Executive Producers, Thomas Coleman, Michael Rosenblatt; Editor, Chris Andrives; In Technicolor; Rated R; January release. CAST: Mel Winkler (J.J.), Murray the K (Himself), Jackie Ziman (Samantha), Arthur York (White Radical Leader), Jimi Hendrix, Country Joe and the Fish, Marvin Gaye, Dr. John, Little Anthony and the Imperials, Van Morrison, The Ronnettes, Phil Ochs, New York Rock and Roll Ensemble, The Temptations, Elephant's Memory, The Beatles, Jim Morrisson and the Doors, Herman's Hermits, Jan and Dean, Gary Lewis and the Playboys, Mountain, Johnny Rivers, Steppenwolf, Dionne Warwick, Otis Redding

POINT ME TOWARD TOMORROW Produced by Francis Ellie; In color; January release; Rated X; No other credits available. CAST: Lew Seager, Lee Richards, Rodger Schultz, Charlie Black, Giuseppe Welch, Dan Raymond, Mark Hamilton

HER LAST FLING (Hollywood International) Producer, Merino Fortes; Director, Bruce Van De Buren; Screenplay, Edgar Warren; Editor-Assistant Director, Anthony Rossi; Music Editor-Production Manager, Sharon Thorpe; Photography, Fernand Fortes; Sound, Roger Bergmann; Executive Producers, Mike Merino, Troy Benny; A Diamond Films Presentation; 75 minutes; January release. CAST: Sandy Feldman, Sue Yu, Peter Ace, Roger Dickson, Marilyn Martin, Doris Gray, Iris Medina, Richard Robinson, Serrena Hall, Bettina Mia

HARLAN COUNTY, U. S. A. (Cabin Creek) Producer-Director, Barbara Kopple; Photography, Hart Perry, Kevin Keating, Phil Parmet, Flip McCarthy, Tom Hurwitz; Editors, Nancy Baker, Mary Lampson, Lora Hays, Mirra Bank; Music, Hazel Dickens, Merie Travis; 103 minutes; Rated PG; January release. A documentary on the year-long strike by the miners in Eastern Kentucky.

PUMPING IRON (Cinema 5) Producers, George Butler, Jerome Gary; Directors, George Butler, Robert Fiore; Conceived by George Butler; From the book "Pumping Iron" by Charles Gaines and George Butler; Title Song and Music, Michael Small; Editors, Larry Silk, Geof Bartz; Photography, Robert Fiore; In color; 85 minutes; Rated PG; January release. CAST: Arnold Schwarzenegger, Louis Ferrigno, Matty Ferrigno, Victoria Ferrigno, Mike Katz, Franco Columbu, Ed Corney, Ken Waller, Serge Nubret, Robin Robinson, Marianne Claire

THE AMAZING DOBERMANS (Golden) Producer, David Chudnow; Executive Producer, Don Reynolds; Director, Byron Chudnow; Screenplay, Michael Kraike, William Goldstein, Richard Chapman; Story, Michael Kraike, William Goldstein; Photography, Jack Adams; Editor, James Potter; Music, Alan Silverstri; In color; 96 minutes; Rated G; January release. CAST: Fred Astaire (Daniel Hughes), James Franciscus (Lucky), Barbara Eden (Justine), Jack Carter (Solly), Billy Barty (Clown), Parley Baer (Circus Owner)

A LABOR OF LOVE (Flaxgold) Produced and Directed by Robert Flaxman, Daniel Goldman; Editor, Daniel Goldman; Photography, Robert Flaxman; Associate Producers, Jack Behrend, John Titis; In color; 70 minutes; Rated X; January release. CAST: Henry Chebarhaschi, Deborah Dan, Ronald Dean, Peter Selden, Len Ozwald, Jerry Goodman, Anna Welch, Alex Boas

GOD BLESS DR. SHAGETZ (L-T Films) Producers, Peter S. Traynor, William D. Sklar; Directors, Edward Collins, Peter S. Traynor, Larry Spiegel; Screenplay, Larry Spiegel, Richard Benson; Story, Royce Applegate; Music, Charles Bernstein; A Centaur Film in Eastmancolor; Rated PG; January release. CAST: Dean Jagger, James Keach, Michele Marsh, Robert Walker, Doria Cook, Dabbs Greer, Lurene Tuttle, Regis Toomey

THE EDGE (Mountain States) Direction and Screenplay, Roger C. Brown; Producers, Barry Corbet, Thomas Hubbard; In color; 100 minutes; Rated PG; January release. A documentary on dangerous sports.

THERE IS NO THIRTEEN (Film Ventures International) Producer, Robert Boggs; Direction and Screenplay, William Sachs; Executive Producers, William Sachs, Alan M. Harris; Music, Riz Ortolani; In Movielab Color; 91 minutes; Rated R; January release. CAST: Mark Damon (George), Margaret Markov (Number 11), Harvey Lembeck (Older George), Jean Jennings (Number 12), Lee Moore (Dr. Hunnicutt), Reuben Schafer (Mr. A), Bonnie Inch (Rosa)

Franco Columbu
in "Pumping Iron"

THE WETTER THE BETTER (Volcano) Produced, Directed and Written by Eric George; In color; Rated X; January release. CAST: Jennifer Jordan, Andrea True, Eric Edwards, Alan Marlow, Helen Madigan

DEEP TANGO (Cunard) In Eastmancolor; Rated X; No other credits available; January release. CAST: Mona Watson, Annette Haven, Keith Henderson

LIONS FOR BREAKFAST (Goldstone) In DeLuxe Color; Rated G; No other Credits available; January release. CAST: Jim Henshaw, Sue Petrie, Jan Rubes, Paul Bradley

CRASH (Group I) Producer-Director, Charles Band; Screenplay, Marc Marais; Music, Andrew Belling; In Panavision and DeLuxe Color; 78 minutes; Rated PG; January release. CAST: Jose Ferrer (Mark), Sue Lyon (Kim), John Ericson (Greg), Leslie Parrish (Kathy), John Carradine (Dr. Edwards), Jerome Guardino (Lt. Pegler)

NIGHT AFTER NIGHT (Independent) Directed and Edited by Gary Kahn; In color; Rated X; January release. CAST: Darby Lloyd Rains, Jamie Gillis, Kim Pope, Alan Marlow, Eric Edwards, Helen Madigan

TEENAGE MADAM (Aventura) Director, Rik Taziner; In Eastmancolor; Rated X; January release. CAST: John C. Holmes, Desiree

FALSE FACE (United International) Producers, Joseph Weintraub, John Grissmer; Director, John Grissmer; Screenplay, Mr. Grissmer from story by Mr. Weintraub; Design, William DeSeta; Music, Robert Cobert; 95 minutes; In color; Rated R; January release. CAST: Robert Lansing (Dr. Reynolds), Judith Chapman (Hester/Jane), Arlen Dean Snyder (Uncle Bradley), David Scarroll (Dr. Dean), Sandy Martin (Sandy), Bruce Atkins (Plumber)

Arnold Schwarzenegger, Franco Columbu
in "Pumping Iron"

Marlo Thomas, Mercedes McCambridge
in "Thieves"

ECSTASY IN BLUE (Independent) In Eastmancolor; Rated X; No other credits available; January release. CAST: Terri Hall, Marc Stevens, C. J. Laing, Annie Sprinkle

SEX ON THE GROVE TUBE (Newport) Formerly "Case of the Full Moon Murders"; Directors, Sean S. Cunningham, Bud Talbot; 65 minutes; Rated R; January release. CAST: Sheila Stuart, Cathy Walker, Fred Lincoln, Ron Browne, Harry Reems, Jean Jennings, Liz Argo

AMERICAN SEX FANTASY (Anonymous Releasing Triumvirate) Executive Producer, Beula Brown; Producer, Jim Holiday; Director, Beau Buchanan; Art Director, Chuck Lawrence; Editor, Jim Holiday; Music, Kenny Armstrong, Joseph Gallello; Lyrics, Joseph Gallello; In color; Rated X; 85 minutes; February release. CAST: Toni Roam, Shelly Dinah Myte, Peony Jones, Jeniffer Jordan, Susan Barret, Kevin Andre, Jackie Beardsley, Bert Blake, Chad Davis, Wirlyn Dervich, Dean Edwards, John Fraser, Jamie Gillis, Grover Griffith, Jake Hudson, Micky Humm, Chris Walton, Harry Watson

THE TOWN THAT DREADED SUNDOWN (American International) Producer-Director, Charles B. Pierce; Screenplay, Earl E. Smith; Narrator, Vern Stierman; Photography, Jim Roberson; Editor, Tom Boutross; Associate Producer, Tom Moore; Music, Jaime Mendoza-Nava; Art Directors, Myrl Teeter, Grant Sinclair; In Movielab Color; Rated R; 90 minutes; February release. CAST: Ben Johnson (Capt. J. D. Morales), Andrew Prine (Deputy Norman Ramsey), Dawn Wells (Helen), Jimmy Clem (Sgt. Griffin), Charles B. Pierce (Patrolman Benson), Cindy Butler (Peggy), Earl E. Smith (Dr. Kress), Christine Ellsworth (Linda Mae), Mike Hackworth (Sammy), Jim City (Police Chief), Robert Aquino (Sheriff Barker), Misty West (Emma Lou), Rick Hildreth (Buddy), Steve Lyons (Roy), Bud Davis (Phantom Killer)

Marlo Thomas, Charles Grodin
in "Thieves"

THIEVES (Paramount) Producer, George Barrie; Director, John Berry; Screenplay, Herb Gardner, based on his play of the same title; Photography, Arthur J. Ornitz, Andrew Lazlo; Editor, Craig McKay; Music, Jule Styne, Mike Miller, Shel Silverstein; Design, John Robert Lloyd; Art Director, Robert Gundlach; Sound, Dick Vorisek, Jack C. Jacobsen, James A. Perdue; Assistant Director, Burt Bluestein; Costumes, Albert Wolsky, Max Solomon, Beverly Cycon; A Brut Production in Technicolor; Rated PG; 103 minutes; February release. CAST: Marlo Thomas (Sally Cramer), Charles Grodin (Martin Cramer), Irwin Corey (Joe Kaminsky), Hector Elizondo (Man Below), Mercedes McCambridge (Street Lady), John McMartin (Gordon), Gary Merrill (Street Man), Ann Wedgeworth (Nancy), Larry Scott (Carlton), Bob Fosse (Mr. Day), Norman Matlock (Mr. Night)

F FOR FAKE (Speciality Films) Direction, Screenplay, Master of Ceremonies, Orson Welles; Production Coordinator, Francois Reichenback; No other credits available. February release. A documentary on fakery, forgery, swindling and art.

UNION MAIDS (New Day Distribution Co-op) Produced and Directed by Julia Reichert, James Klein, Miles Mogulescu; Editors, James Klein, Julia Reichert; Photography, Sherry Novick, Tony Heriza; 55 minutes; In black and white; February release. A documentary on trade-unionism, and particularly about Kate Hyndman, Stella Nowicki and Sylvia Woods.

ON THE LINE (Distribution Co-op) Producer-Director, Barbara Margolis, Marc N. Weiss; Narrated by Rip Torn; In color; 60 minutes; February release. A documentary on cooperative social action.

SUNDANCE AND THE KID (Film Ventures International) Director, Arthur Pitt; Presented by Edward L. Montoro; In color; Rated PG; February release. CAST: John Wade, Karen Blake, Robert Neuman

MORE (Leo De Leon) Direction and Screenplay, Ralph Ell; Rated X; In color; February release. CAST: Harry Reems, Gloria Haddit, DeLaine Young, Harry Valentine, Bobby Astyr

BLONDE VELVET (Video Box Films) Director, Dexter Eagle; In color; Rated X; February release. CAST: Jennifer Welles, Richard Bolla, Sharon Mitchell, Bobby Astyr, Susan McBain, Jake Teague, David Innis, Alexandra, Sarah Nicholson, Roger Caine, Eva Henderson, Jeanette Sinclair

DEVIL TIMES FIVE (Seymour Borde) Director, Sean MacGregor; Associate Producer, Albert Cole; Screenplay, John Durren; Story, Dylan Jones; Executive Producer, Jordan M. Wink; Music, William Loose; In DeLuxe Color; 87 minutes; Rated R; February release. CAST: Sorrell Booke (Harvey), Gene Evans (Papa Doc), Taylor Lacher (Rick), Shelley Morrison (Ruth), Carolyn Stellar (Lovely), Joan McCall (Julie), John Durren (Ralph), Tierre Turner (Brian), Leif Garrett (David), Gail Smale (Sister Hannah), Dawn Lynn, Tia Robene, Henry Beckman

ONCE OVER NIGHTLY (A. B. Enterprises) Director, Andrea True; In color; Rated X; February release. CAST: Terri Hall, Andrea True, Annie Sprinkle

MISS KINSEY'S REPORT (Independent) An Eric Edwards Film; In color; Rated X; February release. CAST: Susan McBain, Paul Hues, John Laurence, David Del

DOGS (R. C. Riddell) Producers, Bruce Cohn, Allan F. Bodoh; Director, Burt Brinckerhoff; Screenplay, O'Brian Tomalin; Executive Producer, Michael Leone; A Mar Vista Production; In color; Rated R; February release. CAST: David McCallum, George Wyner, Eric Server, Sandra McCabe

MARY! MARY! (Scope) Produced, Directed and Written by Bernard Morris; Music, B. F. Sharp; A Linda Production; In color; 80 minutes; Rated X; February release. CAST: Constance Money (Mary), John Leslie (Ned), Sharon Thorpe (Jane), Jerry Smith (Eric), Sandi Reagan (Bonnie), Angela Haze (Kate), Ken Scudder (Policeman), Andre (Arranger), Ed Pastram (Charlie)

ODYSSEY (Asom) Produced, Directed and Written by Gerard Damiano; In color; 86 minutes; Rated X; February release. CAST: Susan McBain, Richard Bolla, Nancy Dare, Sandy Long, Michael Gaunt, Celia Dargent, Gloria Leonard, Samantha Fox, Linda Maidstone, Sue Bright, Leonie Mars, Paul Hues, Philip Marlowe, Valerie Adami, C. J. Laing, Gil Perkins, Wade Nichols, Bobby Astyr, Vanessa Del Rio, Pepe, Terri Hall, Eva Henderson, Sharon Mitchell, Ellyn Grant, Tony Mansfield

TEENAGE BRIDE (Boxoffice International) Director, Gary Troy; In Movielab Color; February release. CAST: Sharon Kelly, Don Summerfield, Cyndee Summers, Jane Louise, Ron Presson, Elmer Klump, Cheri Man

A WHALE OF A TALE (Luckris) Producer-Director, Ewing M. Brown; Executive Producer, Chris Christenson; Music, Jonathan Cain; In Eastmancolor; Rated G; February release. CAST: William Shatner, Marty Allen, Abby Dalton, Andy Devine, Richard Arlen, Scott Kolden

MY WIFE, THE HOOKER (Pacific Coast) Director, Sparky Shayne; In color; Rated X; February release. CAST: Justina Lynne, Elke Torena

LET MY PUPPETS COME (Asom) Producer-Director, Gerard Damiano; In color; Rated X; February release. CAST: Penny Nicholls, Lynette Sheldon, Viju Krem, Little Louis, Al Goldstein

EMMA MAE (Pro-International) Produced, Directed and Written by Jamaa Fanaka; Photography, Stephen Posey; Editor, Robert Fitzgerald; Music, H. B. Barnum; Art Director, Adel Mazen; Assistant Director, Henry Sanders; In Metrocolor; 100 minutes; Rated R; February release. CAST: Jerri Hayes (Emma Mae), Ernest Williams II (Jesse), Charles David Brooks III (Zeke), Eddie Allen (James), Robert Slaughter (Devo), Malik Carter (Big Daddy), Teri Taylor (Dara), Leopoldo Mandeville (Chay), Gammy Burdett (Daisy), Laetitia Burdett (Melik), Eddy Dyer (Huart), Synthia James (Ulika), Jewell Williams (Maddie)

CHATTERBOX (American International) Producer, Bruce Cohn Curtis; Director, Tom De Simone; Screenplay, Mark Rosin, Norman Yonemoto; Story, Tom De Simone; Associate Producer, John Williams; Photography, Tak Fujimoto; Music, Fred Karger; Editor, William Martin; Songs, Michael Hazelwood; In color; 73 minutes; Rated R; February release. CAST: Candice Rialson (Penelope), Larry Gelman (Dr. Pearl), Jane Kean (Eleanor), Perry Bullington (Ted), Arlene Martell (Marlene), Michael Taylor (Dick), Cynthia Hoppenfield (Linda-Ann), Robert Lipton (Jon David), Rip Taylor (Mr. Jo), Irwin Corey (Himself), Sandra Gould (Mrs. Bugatawski), Trent Dolan (Frank)

GUARDIAN OF THE WILDERNESS (Sunn Classic Pictures) Producer, Charles E. Sellier; Director, David O'Malley; Screenplay, Casey Conlon; Photography, Henning Schellerup; Music, Robert Summers; Editor, Sharon Miller; Art Director, Paul Staheli; In color; Rated G; 112 minutes; February release. CAST: Denver Pyle (Galen), John Dehner (John), Ken Berry (Zachary), Cheryl Miller (Kathleen), Don Shanks (Teneiya), Cliff Osmond (McCollough), Jack Kruschen (Madden), Prentiss Rowe (Forebes), Ford Rainey (Lincoln), Brett Palmer, Melissa Jones (Grandchildren)

PAUL, LISA & CAROLINE (Belladonna Films) Executive Producer, Alberto Fasana; Producer-Director Editor, Peter Balakoff; Screenplay, Peter and Belinda Balakoff; Photography, Roy Snowden; Art Direction, Pierre Bardot; Sound, John Clarke; In color; 107 minutes; Rated X; March release. CAST: Gena Lee (Caroline), Tovia Borodyn (Paul), Diane Miller (Lisa), Margaret Monroe (Belinda), William Margold (Peter), John Boland (Bill), Ann Webster (Nancy), Tomy (Millie), Jana Knox (Polly), Karla Garrett (Jan), Hillary Scott (Fran), Charles Gabriels (Lew), Jacques Girard (Fred), Richard Aaron (Tom), Robert Monday (Mark), Eileen Leese (Helga), Carol Romo (Margot), Mary Fraga (Gloria), George Monagham (Artist), Mickle Scott (Director), Ron LaSauce (Bruce), James Rain (Hank), Kalifa (Beth), Honey West (Stripper), Bruce Allan Brown (Comic)

THE GREAT TEXAS DYNAMITE CHASE (New World) Producer, David Irving; Executive Producers, Marshall Backlar, Marshall Whitfield, Karen Whitfield; Director, Michael Pressman; Screenplay, David Kirkpatrick, Mark Rosin; Photography, Jamie Anderson; Editor, Millie Moore; Music, Craig Safran; Rated R; March release. CAST: Claudia Jennings (Candy), Jocelyn Jones (Ellie Jo), Johnny Crawford (Slim), Chris Pennock (Jake), Tara Strohmeier (Pam)

KNOCKOUT (A Turn of the Century Fights, Inc.) Producer, Bill Cayton; Director, Jim Jacobs; Editor, Steve Lott; Narration, Kevin Kennedy; 104 minutes; Rated G; March release. A collection of scenes from boxing history.

NEW GIRL IN TOWN (New World) Produced and Written by Peter J. Oppenheimer; Director, Gus Trikonis; Photography, Irv Goodnoff; Editor, Jerry Cohen; Music, Kim Richmond; 90 minutes; Rated R; March release. CAST: Monica Gayle (Jamie), Glenn Corbett (Jeb), Roger Davis (Kelly), Johnny Rodriguez (Himself), Jesse White (C. Y. Ordell), Marcie Barkin (Alice)

"Jackie Starr—X Reporter"

PORN FLAKES (RFD) formerly "Bang Bang"; Director, Chuck Vincent; Screenplay, Chuck Vincent, Christopher Covino; Photography, Pierre Schwartz; Editor, Mark Ubell; In Eastmancolor; 81 minutes; Rated X; March release. CAST: C. J. Laing, Jeffrey Hurst, Jennifer Jordan, Brenda Basse, Lynn Bishop, Jaymie Bloom, John Christopher, Michael Datorre, Erica Eaton, Marlow Ferguson, Cecelia Gardner, Misty Grey, Lance Knight, Wade Nichols, David Savage, Annie Sprinkle, Tracy West, Marlene Willoughby

SUPER VAN (Empire) Producers, Sal A. Capra, Sandy Cohen; Executive Producer, Nolan Russell Bradford; Director, Lamar Gard; Screenplay, Neva Friedenn, Robert Easter; Based on story by John Arnoldy; Photography, Irv Goodnoff; Editor, Steve Butler; Music, Andy DeMartino, Mark Gibbons, Bob Stone; In color; 91 minutes; Rated PG; March release. CAST: Mark Schneider (Clint), Katie Saylor (Karen), Morgan Woodward (T.B.), Len Lesser (Banks), Skip Riley (Vince), Bruce Kimball (Sarge), Tom Kindle (Boseley), Ralph Seeley (Clint's Father), Richard Sobek (Grinder)

JACKIE STAR—X REPORTER (Anonymous Releasing Triumvirate) Director, Milton Vickers; Music, Torino; In color; Rated X; 70 minutes; March release. CAST: Kim Pope (Jackie Starr). No other details available.

ABAR—THE FIRST BLACK SUPERMAN (Mirror) Producer, J. P. Joshua; Executive Producer, James Smalley; In color; Rated PG; March release. CAST: J. Walter Smith, Tobar Mayo, Roxie Young, Gladys Lum, Rubert Williams, Tina James, Art Jackson, Tony Rumford, Odell Mack

THE CHILD (Boxoffice International) Producer, Robert Dadashian; Director, Robert Voskanian; Screenplay, Ralph Lucas; Music, Rob Wallace; Photography, Mori Alavi; Executive Producer, Harry Novak; A Panorama Film in Eastmancolor; Rated R; March release. CAST: Laurel Barnett (Elise), Rosalie Cole (Rosalie), Frank Janson (Father), Richard Hanners (Len), Ruth Ballen (Mrs. Whitfield), Slosson Bing Jong (Gardener)

Gena Lee, Tovia Borodyn
in "Paul, Lisa and Caroline"

Valerie Perrine, Terence Hill
in "Mr. Billion"

SANDSTONE (Don Henderson) Produced and Directed by Jonathan Dana, Bunny Peters Dana; Photography, Patrick Darrin, Robert Primes; Editors, Mr. Darrin, Mr. and Mrs. Dana; Music, Dennis Dragon; 80 minutes; Rated X; March release. A documentary about new styles of sexual relationships.

OFF THE EDGE (Pentacle) Producer-Director, Michael Firth; Photography, Geoff Cocks, Tony Lilleby, Jeff Stevens, Michael Firth; Editor, Michael Economon; Music, Richard Clements; In Eastmancolor; 77 minutes; Rated PG; March release. A documentary.

THE FARMER (Columbia) Producer, Gary Conway; Director, David Berlatsky; Screenplay, Janice Colson-Dodge, John Carmody, Patrick Regan, George Fargo; Story, George Fargo; Photography, Irv Goodnoff; Music, Hugo Montenegro; Executive Producer, Peter B. Mills; Editor, Richard Weber; Associate Producers, Richard Bridges, Eric Weston, Lang Elliott, Chick Simmons; Art Director, Charlie Hughes; In Panavision and color; 98 minutes; Rated R; March release. CAST: Gary Conway (Kyle), Angel Tompkins (Betty), Michael Dante (Johnny O), George Memmoli (Passini), Timothy Scott (Weasel), Jack Waltzer (Doc Valentine), Ken Renard (Gumshoe), John Popwell (Connors), Stratton Leopold (Laundry Sam), Sonny Shroyer (Corrigan), Eric Weston (Lopie), Don Payne (Mr. Moore), Bill Moses (Bank Representative), Roy Tatum (Soldier), Laura Whyte (Waitress), Wayne Stewart (Sergeant), Ray McIver (Train Bartender), Lewell Akins (Conductor), Louis C. Pessolano (Bartender), Dave Craig (2nd Soldier), Judge Parker, Saturday Session (Banjo Players)

DEVIL'S EXPRESS (Howard Mahler) Director, Barry Rosen; Producers, Niki Patton, Steve Madoff; In Panavision and Technicolor; 82 minutes; Rated R; March release. CAST: Warhawk Tanzania, Larry Fleishman, Sam DeFazio, Wilfredo Roldan, Elsie Roman, Sarah Nyrick

SLIPPERY WHEN WET (Evart) Director, Karl Andersson; In color; Rated X; March release. CAST: C. J. Laing, Annie Sprinkle, Christa Anderson, Hope Stockton, Mike Jeffries, Sonny Landham, Jeff Hurst, Ursula Austin

"Raggedy Ann & Andy"

THE CRATER LAKE MONSTER (Crown International) Producer-Director, William R. Stromberg; Screenplay, William R. Stromberg, Richard Cardella; Photography, Paul Gentry; In Fantamation and color; 85 minutes; Rated PG; March release. CAST: Richard Cardella, Glenn Roberts, Mark Siegel, Kacey Cobb, Richard Garrison, Michael Hoover, Bob Hyman, Suzanne Lewis

SHARON (Asom) Director, Navred Reef; In color; Rated X; March release. CAST: Sharon Sanders, Jean Jennings, Zebedy Colt, David Christopher, Paul Hues, Bobby Astyr

MIDNIGHT HUSTLE (Dynamite) Produced, Directed and Written by Steve Brown; In color; Rated X; March release. CAST: Marilyn Zukor, Juliette Orwell, John Seeman, Turk Lyon, Ken Scudder, Joan Devlon, Tyler Reynolds

LITTLE ORPHAN SAMMY (Variety Films) Producer, Michael Roberts; Director, Arlo Schiffin; Screenplay, Ron Wertheim; Photography, Pierre Schwartz; In color; 80 minutes; Rated X; March release. CAST: Jennifer Wells (Hata Mari), Rocky Millstone (Sammy), Lin Flanagan (Daddy Sawbucks), Andrea True (Bellydancer), Jamie Gillis (Da), Kim Pope (Miss Take), C. J. Laing (Maid), Sarah Nicholson (Marian), Helen Madigan (Doctor), Nicki Hilton (Nurse), Al Levitsky (Repairman)

MEATCLEAVER MASSACRE (Group I) Director, Evan Lee; Executive Producer, Steven L. Singer; In color; 82 minutes; Rated R; March release. CAST: Larry Justin, Bob Mead, Bob Clark, Jim Habif, Christopher Lee, Sandra Crane, Evelyn Ellis, Jonathan Grant

JOHNNY VIK (Sun Dog) Direction and Screenplay, Charles Nauman; In color; rated G; March release. CAST: Warren Hammack

OVERNIGHT SENSATIONS (Essex) Produced and Directed by Robert Benjamin, Rico Manzini, Al Jarry; Music, Peter March; Photography, Gerry Bone, Robert Benjamin; Editor, Christopher Nils; In color; Rated X; March release. CAST: Sharon Thorpe, John Leslie Dupre, Annette Haven, Tahoe Jonathan, Joe Civera, Victoria Starr

JOEY (Dimension) Produced, Directed and Written by Horace B. Jackson; Executive Producers, Clarence Avant, Larry Woolner; In DeLuxe Color; 96 minutes; rated PG; March release. CAST: Danny Martin, Marie O'Henry, Renny Roker, Juanita Moore, Candi Keath, Cal Haynes, Mile Sims, Marc Hannibal, Marcie Williams

LOVE LIPS (Art Mart) Produced, Directed and Written by Dale J. Martin; In color; Rated X; March release. CAST: Sharlin Alexander, Turk Lyon, Mark McIntire, T. J. Youngblood, Patricia Lee, Abigail Clayton, John Seeman, Joe Severa, Ken Scudder

BANG, BANG, YOU GOT IT (RFD) Title changed to "Porn Flakes"; Director, Chuck Vincent; Screenplay, Chuck Vincent, Christopher Covino; Photography, Pierre Schwartz; In Eastmancolor; 81 minutes; Rated X; March release. CAST: C. J. Laing, Jeffrey Hurst, Jennifer Jordan, Brenda Basse, Lynn Bishop, Jaymie Bloom, John Christopher, Michael Datorre, Erica Eaton, Marlow Ferguson, Cecelia Gardner, Misty Grey, Lance Knight, Wade Nichols, David Savage, Annie Sprinkle, Tracy West, Marlene Willoughby

MR. BILLION (20th Century-Fox) Formerly "The Windfall"; Producers, Steven Bach, Ken Friedman; Executive Producer, Gabriel Katzka; Director, Jonathan Kaplan; Screenplay, Ken Friedman, Jonathan Kaplan; Photography, Matthew F. Leonetti; Editor, O. Nicholas Brown; Music, Dave Grusin; Art Director, Richard Berger; Assistant Director, Peter Bogart; In DeLuxe Color; 91 minutes; Rated PG; March release. CAST: Terence Hill (Guido), Valerie Perrine (Rosi), Jackie Gleason (John), Slim Pickens (Duane), William Redfield (Leopold), Chill Wills (Col. Winkle), Dick Miller (Bernie), R. G. Armstrong (Sheriff), Dave Cass (Boss Kidnapper), Sam Laws (Pops), John Ray McGhee (Carnell), Kate Heflin (Lucy), Leo Rossi (Italian Kidnapper), Bob Minor (Black Kidnapper), Frances Heflin (Mrs. Apple Pie), Ralph Chesse (Anthony)

RAGGEDY ANN AND ANDY (20th Century-Fox) Producer, Richard Horner; Supervised and Directed by Richard Williams; Screenplay, Patricia Thackray, Max Wilk; Based on stories and characters created by Johnny Gruelle; Designer, Corny Cole; Music, Joe Raposo; In color; 84 minutes; Rated G; March release. An animated feature using the voices of Claire Williams, Didi Conn, Mark Baker, Fred Stuthman, Niki Flacks, George S. Irving, Arnold Stang, Joe Silver, Alan Sues, Marty Brill, Paul Dooley, Mason Adams, Allen Swift, Hetty Galen, Sheldon Harnick, Ardyth Kaiser, Margery Gray, Lynn Stuart

Mary Woronov
in "Hollywood Boulevard"

John Ryan, Sharon Farrell
in "It's Alive"

WELCOME TO L. A. (United Artists) Producer, Robert Altman; Direction and Screenplay, Alan Rudolph; Photography, Dave Myers; Music and Songs, Richard Baskin; Editor, William A. Sawyer, Tom Walls; In color; 106 minutes; Rated R; March release. CAST: Keith Carradine (Carroll), Sally Kellerman (Ann), Geraldine Chaplin (Karen), Harvey Keitel (Ken), Luren Hutton (Nona), Viveca Lindfors (Susan), Sissy Spacek (Linda), Denver Pyle (Carl), John Considine (Jack), Richard Baskin (Eric)

11 × 14 (Benning) Producer-Director, James Benning; No other credits; In color; 81 minutes; Not rated; April release. CAST: Serafina Bathrick (Woman), Paddy Whannel (Man), Harvey Taylor (Young Man), Ted Brady (Man's Son), Tim Welsh, Rick Goodwin (Boys), Barbara Frankel, Bette Gordon (Woman's Friends)

HOLLYWOOD BOULEVARD (New World) Producer, Jon Davison; Directors, Joe Dante, Allan Arkush; Screenplay, Patrick Hobby; Music, Andrew Stein; Photography, Jamie Anderson; Associate Producer, Terri Schwartz; Editors, Amy Jones, Allan Arkush, Joe Dante; Art Director, Jack DeWolfe; Costumes, Jane Rum; In Metrocolor; Rated R; 83 minutes; April release. CAST: Candice Rialson (Candy), Mary Woronov (Mary), Rita George (Bobbi), Jeffrey Kramer (Patrick), Dick Miller (Walter), Richard Doran (P. G.), Tara Strohmeier (Jill), Paul Bartel (Erich), John Kramer (Duke), Jonathan Kaplan (Scotty), George Wagner (Camerman), W. L. Luckey (Rico), David Boyle (Kid), Glen Shimada (Filipino), Joe McBride (Drive-in rapist), Barbara Pieters (Drive-in mother), Sean Pieters (Drive-in kid), Sue Veneer (Dyke), Charles B. Griffith (Mark), Miller Drake (Mutant), Godzina (Herself), Roberta Dean, Milt Kahn (Reporters), Todd McCarthy (Author), Commander Cody & The Lost Planet Airmen

YOUNG, HOT 'N' NASTY TEENAGE CRUISERS (Raunchy Tonk) Produced, Directed and Written by Martin Margulies and Tom Denucci; In color; Rated X; 80 minutes; April release. CAST: Serena, Tony Conn, Christine Shaffer, Johnny Legend, John Holmes, William Margold

IT'S ALIVE (Warner Bros.) Produced, Directed and Written by Larry Cohen; Executive Producer, Peter Sabiston; Co-Producer, Janelle Cohen; Photography, Fenton Hamilton; Editor, Peter Honess; Music, Bernard Herrmann; In Technicolor and Panavision; 91 minutes; Rated PG; April release. CAST: John Ryan (Frank), Sharon Farrell (Lenore), Andrew Duggan (Professor), Guy Stockwell (Clayton), James Dixon (Lt. Perkins), Michael Ansara (Capt.), Robert Emhardt (Executive), William Wellman, Jr. (Charlie), Shamus Locke (Doctor), Mary Nancy Burnett (Nurse), Diana Hale (Secretary), Daniel Holzman (Boy), Patrick Macallister, Gerald York, Jerry Taft, Gwil Richards, W. Allen York (Expectant Fathers)

AMERICAN TICKLER (Spectrum) Formerly "The Winner of 10 Academy Awards"; Producer, Robbin Cullinen; Director, Chuck Vincent; Executive Producer, Burrill W. Heller; Photography, James McCalmont; Art Director, Falco Maltese; Costumes, Eddie Heath; Editors, Mark Ubell, R. X. Acosta; Screenplay, Christopher Covino, Robbin Cullinen, Bert Goodman, Richard Helfer, Chuck Vincent, Straw Weisman; Music, Peter McKenzie, Pisces Music; Assistant Director, Christopher Covino; In Cineffects Color; Rated R; 77 minutes; April release. CAST: Joan Sumner, Marlow Ferguson, W. P. Dremak, Jeff Alin, Leta Binder, David Hausman, Joe Piscopo, Jane Dentinger, Bev Lubin, Tyrone Quinn, Michael Dattore, Luis DeJesus, Carole Field, Pat Finnegan, Kathy Hickman, Kurt Mann, Allen Dawson, Arthur Epstein, Suzanne Filipovna, Edward French, William Karnovsky, Michael Masone, Nan Penman, Pailette Sanders, Joan Shangold, Zuleyka Reyes, David Savage, David Buckley, Paul Giacobbe, Lidde Kroner, Norman Garrett, Derik Hausman, Martha Ubell

SHINING STAR (Marvin) Producer-Director, Sig Shore; Story and Screenplay, Robert Lipsyte; Photography, Alan Mstzger; Editor, Bruce Witkin; Score composed and performed by Earth, Wind and Fire; 100 minutes; Rated PG; April release. CAST: Harvey Keitel (Coleman), Ed Nelson (Carlton), Cynthia Bostick (Velour), Bert Parks (Franklyn), Jimmy Boyd (Gary), Michael Dante (Mike), Maurice White (Early), Earth, Wind and Fire (The Group)

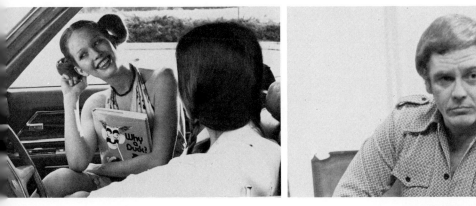

Serena
in "Teenage Cruisers"

Guy Stockwell
in "It's Alive"

"Wizards"

WIZARDS (20TH CENTURY-FOX) Produced, Directed and Written by Ralph Bakshi; Editor, Donald W. Ernst; Photography, Ted C. Bemiller; Music, Andrew Belling; Layout, John Sparey; Sequence Animation, Irven Spence; In DeLuxe Color; 80 minutes; Rated PG; April release. Voices of Bob Holt, Jesse Wells, Richard Romanus, David Proval, James Connell, Steve Gravers, Barbara Sloane, Angelo Grisanti, Hyman Wien, Christopher Tayback, Mark Hamil, Peter Hobbs, Tina Bowman

TRACKS (Trio) Producers, Howard Zucker, Irving Cohen, Ted Shapiro; Direction and Screenplay, Henry Jaglom; Photography, Paul Glickman; Executive Producer, Bert Schneider; Editor, George Folsey, Jr.; In color; 90 minutes; April release. CAST: Dennis Hopper (Sergeant), Taryn Power (Stephanie), Dean Stockwell (Mark), Topo Swope (Chloe), Michael Emile (Emile), Zack Norman (Gene), Alfred Ryder (Man)

CHERRY HILL HIGH (Cannon) Producer-Director, Alex E. Goitein; Story and Screenplay, William Shears, Wylie White; Photography, Werner Hlinka; In Metrocolor; Rated R; April release. CAST: Linda McInerney, Nina Carson, Lynn Hastings, Stephanie Lawlor, Carrie Olson, Gloria Upson

DELORA (Troma) Director, Kenneth Lane; Presented by Lloyd Kaufman; April release. CAST: Chryse Maile, Kenneth Lane

CINDERELLA 2000 (Independent International) Producer-Director, Al Adamson; Screenplay, Bud Donnelly; Music, Sparky Sugarman; Choreography, John Appleton, Eddie Garetti; Photography, Louis Horvath; Executive Producers, Samuel M. Sherman, Dan Q. Kennis; In Todd-AO 35 and Metrocolor; 95 minutes; Rated X; April release. CAST: Catharine Erhardt (Cindy), Jay B. Larson (Fairgodfather), Vaughn Armstrong (Tom), Erwin Fuller (Controller), Rena Harmon (Stepmother), Bhurni Cowans (Bella), Adina Ross (Stella), Eddie Garetti (Robot), Olivia Michelle, Art Cacaro, Sherri Coyle, John Appleton

ECSTASY (Essex) Produced, Directed and Written by Billy Thornberg; In color; April release. CAST: John C. Holmes, Barbara Barton, Jenny Sue Logan, Kathy Reilly

JUST BE THERE (American Films) Director, David Feldshuh; Screenplay, Kathy Fehn; In color; Rated PG; April release. CAST: Michael Montgomery, Lynn Baker, Charley McCarty

THE TAKING OF CHRISTINA (Unique) Producer, Jason Russell; Direction and Screenplay, Armand Weston; In color; 90 minutes; Rated X; April release. CAST: Bree Anthony, Al Levitsky, Eric Edwards, Terri Hall, Chris Jordan, C. J. Laing, Leila

BABYFACE (Key) Producer-Director, Alex de Renzy; Screenplay, John Milligan; In color; 103 minutes; Rated X; April release. CAST: Cuddles Malone, Dan Roberts, Amber Hunt, Linda Wong, Paul Thomas, Patricia Lee, Kathryn Reid, Joe Civera, Angela Grant, Carla Harwood, Sandy Pinney, Molly Seagrim, Khristine Hellar, John Leslie, Ken Scudder, Turk Lyon, Otis Sistrunk

PORTRAIT OF SEDUCTION (Essex) Producer, J. Louis Fantoni; Director, Anthony Spinelli; Screenplay, Stanley Woods; Photography, Neil Wagner; In color; Rated X; 76 minutes; April release. CAST: Vicky Lyon (Kelly), Jeffrey Stern (Terry), Robert Cole (Jeb), Monique Cardin (Val), Rita Stone (Mother)

THE VAN (Crown International) Producer, Paul Lewis; Director, Sam Grossman; Screenplay, Robert Rosenthal, Celia Susan Cotelo; Photography, Irv Goodnoff; Songs composed and performed by Sammy Johns; In color; 90 minutes; Rated R; April release. CAST: Stuart Getz, Deborah White, Harry Moses, Marcie Barkin, Bill Adler, Stephen Oliver, Connie Lisa Marie, Danny DeVito

FIGHTING BLACK KINGS (New Line) In Technicolor; Rated PG; No other credits available; April release. CAST: William Oliver, Charles Martin, Willie Williams, Mas Oyama

THE ABDUCTION OF LORELEI (Rank) Producer-Director, Richard Rank; In Eastmancolor; Rated X; April release. CAST: Jenn Gillian, John Galt, Monique Perris, Charles Neal

CHRISTOPHER STREET BLUES (A Francis Ellie Production) In color; Rated X; April release. CAST: Lee Richards, Giuseppe Welch, Lew Seager, Mark Hamilton, Dan Raymond

DESIRES WITHIN YOUNG GIRLS (Leisure Time Booking) Producer, Harold Lime; Director, Ramsey Karson; Screenplay, Harold Lime, Ramsey Karson; Photography, Mike O'Hara; In color; 104 minutes; Rated X; April release. CAST: Georgina Spelvin (Mattie), Clair Dia (Penny), Annette Haven (Sissy), John Leslie (Mark), John Seeman (chauffeur), Joan Devlon (Baroness), Bonnie Holiday (Model), Paul Thomas (John), Stacy Evans (Suzy), Abigail Clayton (Gail), Sabrina (Dominique), Turk Lyon (Charles), Frank Hollowell (Dasher), Robert Metz (Chris), Carl Irwin (Clark)

TOMCATS (Dimension) Producers, Wayne Crawford, Andrew Lane; Director, Harry E. Kerwin; Music, R. O. DeCordre; An American General Production presented by Mickey Zide; In color; Rated R; April release. CAST: Chris Mulkey, Polly King, Scott Lawrence

TEENAGE CRUISERS (Raunchy Tonk) A Martin Margulies-Tom Denucci film in color; Rated X; April release. CAST: Serena, Christine Shaffer, John C. Homes, William Margold, Tony Conn, Rick Cassidy

PELVIS (Funky Films) Producer, Lew Mishkin; Director/Editor, R. T. Megginson; Screenplay, Straw Weisman; Photography, Lloyd Freidus; In color; 84 minutes; Rated R; April release. CAST: Luther Bud Whaney (Pelvis), Mary Mitchell (Betty), Cindy Tree (Susie), Billy Padgett (Rev.), Bobby Astry (Snake), Jai Oscar St. John (Pimp), Chris Thomas (Candy), Carole Baxter (Skate), Mike DeMarco, Patricia John, Rick Endelson, Amazing Dorian

COUNT THE WAYS (Evolution Enterprises) Produced, Directed and Written by Ann Perry; Music, Dan Samuels; Photography, Ken Gibb; In Eastmancolor; 84 minutes; Rated X; May release. CAST: Tyler Horne, Yvonne Green, Charla, Desiree, Joe Summer, Jason Wells, Cissy Davenne

**Dennis Hopper
in "Tracks"**

**Jesse Vint, Karen Carlson
in "Black Oak Conspiracy"**

**Carroll Baker, Perry King
in "Andy Warhol's Bad"**

BLACK OAK CONSPIRACY (New World) Producers, Jesse Vint, Tom Clark; Director, Bob Kelljaw; Screenplay, Hugh Smith, Jesse Vint; Story, Hugh Smith; Music, Don Peake; Executive Producer, Gail Clark; Associate Producer, Richard Franchot; Assistant Director, Dennis Jones; Photography, Chris Ludwig; Editor, Sam Shaw; Costumes, Gerry Puhara; "Jingo's Song" written and performed by Phil Everly; In Movielab Color: 92 minutes; Rated R; May release. CAST: Jesse Vint (Jingo), Karen Carlson (Lucy), Albert Salmi (Sheriff), Seymour Cassel (Homer), Douglas V. Fowley (Bryan), Robert F. Lyons (Harrison), Mary Wilcox (Beulah), James Gammon (Deputy), Janus Blyth (Melba), Will Hare (Doc Rondes), Jeremy Foster (Billie Bob), Peggy Stewart (Virginia), Jo Anne Strauss (Sadie), Vic Perrin (Finch), Darby Hinton (Miner in cafe), Dana Derfus (Miner), Bill Cross (Stunt Gaffer), Rock Walker, Buff Brady (Policemen)

DAY OF THE ANIMALS (Film Ventures International) Producer, Edward L. Montoro; Director, William Girdler; Screenplay, William Norton, Eleanor E. Norton; Story, Edward L. Montoro; Music, Lalo Schifrin; Editors, Bub Asman, Jim Mitchell; Photography, Robert Sorrentino; In Todd-AO 35 and DeLuxe Color; 97 minutes; Rated PG; May release. CAST: Christopher George, Leslie Nielsen, Linda Day George, Richard Jaeckel, Michael Ansara, Ruth Roman

THE ULTIMATE PLEASURE (Diamond Films) Produced and Photographed by Merino Fortes; Director, Bruce Van Buren; Screenplay, Edgar Warren; In color; Rated X; May release. CAST: John Holmes, Nina Fause, Iris Medina, Vicky Kauffmann, Dolores Couburn, Peter Dubois, Sheela Derby, Marilyn Martin, Doris Gray, Peter Ace

EATEN ALIVE (Virgo International) Formerly "Death Trap"; Producer, Mardi Rustam; Director, Tobe Hooper; Co-Producer, Alvin Fast; Executive Producer, Mohammed Rustam; Associate Producers, Larry Huly, Samir Rustam, Robert Kantor; A Mars Production; In color; Rated R; May release. CAST: Neville Brand, Mel Ferrer, Carolyn Jones, Marilyn Burns, William Finely, Stuart Whitman

ANDY WARHOL'S BAD (New World) Producer, Jeff Tornberg; Director, Jed Johnson; Screenplay, Pat Hackett, George Abagnalo; Photography, Allan Metzger; Music, Mike Bloomfield; 105 minutes; Rated R; May release. CAST: Carroll Baker (Mrs. Aiken), Perry King (LT), Susan Tyrrell (Mary Aiken), Stefania Cassini (PG), Cyrinda Foxe (RC), Mary Boylan (Grandmother), Charles MacGregor (Detective), Tere Tereba (Ingrid), Brigid Polk (Estelle), Susan Blond (Young Mother), Gordon Oasheim (Aiken), Maria Smith (Marsha), Geraldine Smith (Glenda), Lawrence Tierney (O'Reilly), Joe Lamba (Russel), John Starke (Joe), Renee Paris (Mrs. Leachman)

THE BIG BOUNCE Director, Jan Anders; In Eastmancolor; No other credits available; May release. Starring Uschi Digard

69 MINUTES (N. B. Releasing) Producer-Director, Ian Morrison; Executive Producer, Jack Poessiger; Associate Producer, Joe Leahy; A Naughty Boys Production in Deluxe Color; 75 minutes; Rated R; May release. CAST: Joe Leahy, John Chambers, Cindy Allison, Twila Pollard, Bill Williams, Michael Davenport, Vic Jolley

THE YOUNG STUDENTS (Art Mart) In Eastmancolor; Rated X; No other credits available; May release. CAST: Susie Muffet, Linda Wong, Joe Severa, Vicki Lindsey

SWEET PUNKIN' Producer, Robert Michaels; Director, Robert Norman; In color; 80 minutes; Rated X; May release. CAST: C. J. Laing, Tony Perez, John C. Holmes, Jeff Hurst, Eric Edwards, Crystal Sync, Jennifer Jordan, Tootsie Robusto, Dance Warren, Tony Dee, Marlene Willoughby

THE FUN HOUSE (L. B. S. Productions) Producer, Norman F. Kaiser; Director, Victor Janos; Screenplay, Brian Lawrence; In color; Rated R; May release. CAST: Steven Morrison, Dennis Crawford, Lawrence Bornman, Janet Sorley, Paul Phillips, Elaine Norcross, Alex Kregar, Franklin Statz, Barbara Amusen, Geraldine Sanders

**Albert Salmi
in "Black Oak Conspiracy"**

"Day of the Animals"

123

Chuck Norris, George Murdock in "Breaker! Breaker!"

BREAKER! BREAKER! (American International) Producer-Director, Don Hulette; Executive Producers, Samuel Schulman, Bernard Tabakin; Screenplay, Terry Chambers; Photography, Mario DiLeo; Editor, Steven Zaillian; Music, Don Hulette; Art Director, Thomas Thomas; Assistant Director, Doron Kauper; A Paragon Films Production in color; 86 minutes; Rated PG: May release. CAST: George Murdock (Judge Trimmings), Terry O'-Connor (Arlene Trimmings), Don Gentry (Sgt. Strode), Chuck Norris (J. D. Dawes), John DiFusco (Arney), Ron Cedillos (Deputy), Michael Augenstein (Billy), Dan Vandergrift (Wilfred), Douglas Stevenson (Drake)

TEENAGE GRAFFITI (Allied Artists) Producer, Sheldon Tromberg; Director, Christopher C. Casler; Executive Producer, Stephen M. Trattner; In color; Rated PG; May release. CAST: Michael W. Driscoll, Jeanetta Arnetta, Alden Sherry

TEMPTATIONS (Video Box Films) Producer, Dexter Eagle; Director, Louis F. Antonero; Screenplay, John T. Hansen; In color; 80 minutes; Rated X; May release. CAST: Jennifer Welles, Jake Teague, Marlene Willoughby, John Leslie Dupre, Alexandria, Roger Caine, Hope Stockton, Vanessa Del Rio, Rocky Millstone, Gloria Leonard, David Innis

PORTRAITS OF PLEASURE (Sunset) Director, Bo Koup; In Eastmancolor; Rated X; May release. CAST: Susan McBain, Sharon Mitchell, Jon Black

THE DEVIL INSIDE HER (Leisure time) Direction and Screenplay, Zebedy Colt; In color; 70 minutes; Rated X; May release. CAST: Terri Hall, Jody Maxwell, Rod Dumont, Dean Tate, Zebedy Colt, Nancy Dare, Annie Sprinkle, Renee Sanz, Chad Lambert

ERUPTION (Cal-Vista) Producer-Director, Stanley Kurlan; Screenplay, Juston Welton; Photography, Jack Mathews; In color; 85 minutes; Rated X; May release. CAST: John C. Holmes (Pete), Leslie Bovee (Sandra), Suzan Hart (Angie), Eric Evol (Scott), Gene Clayton (Harry), Wynne Colburn

Jennifer Doyle, Marilyn Corwin, Cheryl Smith, Yana Nirvana in "Cinderella"

PEACH FUZZ (Command Cinema) Producer, Michael Bernard; Direction and Screenplay, Cecil Howard; Theme song, Mike Greenberg, Buddy Lambert; Photography, Anna Riva; In color; Rated X; May release. CAST: Jean Dalton, Hope Stockton, Michele Damon, Jeffrey Hurst, Zebedy Colt, Marc Ubell

JABBERWALK (I.T.M.) Produced, Directed and Written by Romano Vanderbes; Music, Emmanuel Vardi; Narrator, Norman Rose; In color; Rated R; May release. A documentary about bizarre and unusual practices in the U.S.

CINDERELLA (Group I) Producer, Charles Band; Director, Michael Pataki; Screenplay, Frank Ray Perilli; Music, Andrew Belling; Lyrics, Lee Arries; Photography, Joseph Mangine; Choreography, Russell Clark; Executive Producers, Lenny Shabes, Ronald Domont; Editor, Laurence Jacobs; In Panavision and DeLuxe Color; 94 minutes; Rated X; May release. CAST: Cheryl Smith (Cinderella), Kirk Scott (Lord Chamberlain), Brett Smiley (Prince), Sy Richardson (Fairygodmother), Yana Nirvana (Drucella), Marilyn Corwin (Marbella), Jennifer Doyle (Stepmother), Buckley Norris (King), Pamela Stonebrook (Queen), Shannon Korbel (Nymphomaniac)

DEATH GAME (Levitt-Pickman) Executive Producers, Mel Bergman, William Duffy; Producers, Larry Spiegel, Peter Traynor; Screenplay, Anthony Overman, Michael Ronald Ross; Photography, David Worth; Music, Jimmie Haskell; In color; 89 minutes; Rated R; May release. CAST: Sondra Locke (Jackson), Colleen Camp (Donna), Seymour Cassel (George), Beth Brickell (Karen), Michael Kalmansohn (Deliveryboy), Ruth Warshawsky (Mrs. Grossman)

FOREVER YOUNG, FOREVER FREE (Universal) Producer, Andre Pieterse; Executive Producer, Philo C. Pieterse; Direction and Screenplay, Ashley Lazarus; Story, Andre Pieterse; Photography, Arthur J. Ornitz; Music, Lee Holdridge; Song, Rod McKuen, Lee Holdridge; Editor, Lionel Selwyn; Art Director, Wendy Malan; Assistant Director, Jannie Wienand; In color; 87 minutes; Rated G; May release. CAST: Jose Ferrer (Father Alberto), Karen Valentine (Carol Anne), Bess Finney (Sister Marguerita), Muntu Ndebele (Tsepo), Norman Knox (Jannie), Bingo Mbonjeni (Cash General), Simon Sabela (Rakwaba)

YOUTHQUAKE (World Wide) Producer-Director, Max B. Miller; Executive Producer, Carl A. Albert; Associate Producer, Marvin Young; Photography, Bob Grant; In Eastmancolor; 90 minutes; Rated PG; May release. A documentary study of rock and religion.

YOUNG LADY CHATTERLEY (PRO International) Executive Producer, William Silberkleit; Producers, Alan Roberts, David Winters; Screenplay, Steve Michaels; Photography, Bob Brownell; Music, Don Bagley; Editor, Soly Bina; Art Director, Gale Peterson; Costumes, Lennie Barin; Assistant Director, Danny Biederman; In Metrocolor; 100 minutes; Rated X; May release. CAST: Harlee McBride (Cynthia), Peter Ratray (Paul), William Beckley (Philip), Ann Michelle (Gwen), Joi Staton (Mary), Mary Forbes (Lady Frances), Patrick Wright (Flashback Gardner)

MOONSHINE COUNTY EXPRESS (New World) Producer, Ed Carlin; Director, Gus Trikonis; Screenplay, Hubert Smith, Daniel Ansley; Photography, Gary Graver; Editor, Gene Ruggiero; Music, Fred Werner; Assistant Directors, Nicole Scott, Jack Bohrer, Gerald Olson; Art Director, Peter Jamison; In Movielab Color; 95 minutes; Rated PG; June release. CAST: John Saxon (J. B. Johnson), Susan Howard (Dot), William Conrad (Starkey), Morgan Woodward (Sweetwater), Claudia Jennings (Betty), Jeff Corey (Preacher Hagen), Dub Taylor (Uncle Bill), Maureen McCormick (Sissy), Albert Salmi (Sheriff), Len Lesser (Scoggins), Bruce Kimball (Harley), Candice Rialson (Mayella), E. J. Andre (Lawyer), Fred Foresman (Pap Hammer), Dick Esterly (Hackberry), Tom Deaton (Tiny), Rick Langston (Gabe), William Luckey (Hood), Lenka Novak (Manicurist), Dean Christianson (Leroy), Still Guards: Terry Pittsford, Stanley Creamer, Jim Springer, Mel Shahan, Starkey's Men: Richard Wood, Stephen Dach, Roland Meyer, James Morales, John Young, Gene Livermore, Dave Brewer

VISIONS (Chuck Vincent) Producer, Chuck Vincent; Direction and Screenplay, Feliz Miguel Arroyo; Photography, Anna Riva; Editor, Mark Ubell; Art Director, Falco Maltese; Costumes, Eddie Heath; In color; 70 minutes; Rated X; June release. CAST: Wade Nichols, Suzanne McBain, Victoria Corsaut, Peter Andrews, David Christopher, Kurt Mann, W. P. Dremak, Harriet Hart, Susaye London, Tony Mansfield, Sharon Mitchell, G. G. Palma, Betty Brooks, Dominic Dominguez, Greg Hart, Jill Haven, Maxwell Maximum, Paul Morton

Evel Knievel, Lauren Hutton, Eric Olson
in "Viva Knievel!"

"Sinbad and the Eye of the Tiger"

VIVA KNIEVEL! (Warner Bros.) Producer, Stan Hough; Director, Gordon Douglas; Screenplay, Antonio Santillan, Norman Katkov; Story, Antonio Santillan; Executive Producer, Sherrill C. Corwin; Photography, Fred Jackman; Music, Charles Bernstein; Designer, Ward Preston; Editor, Harold Kress; Costumes, Paul Zastupenvich; Assistant Directors, Malcolm Harding, Cheryl Downey, Louis Muscate; In Panavision and Technicolor; 106 minutes; Rated PG; June release. CAST: Evel Knievel (Himself), Gene Kelly (Will Atkins), Lauren Hutton (Kate Morgan), Red Buttons (Ben Andrews), Leslie Nielsen (Stanley Millard), Frank Gifford (Himself), Sheila Allen (Sister Charity), Cameron Mitchell (Barton), Eric Olson (Tommy Atkins), Albert Salmi (Cortland), Dabney Coleman (Ralph Thompson), Ernie Orsatti (Norman Clark), Sidney Clute (Andy), Robert Tafur (Gov. Garcia), Marjoe Gortner (Jessie)

JOYRIDE (American International) Executive Producers, Hal Landers, Bobby Roberts; Producer, Bruce Cohn Curtis; Director, Joseph Ruben; Screenplay, Joseph Ruben, Peter Rainer; Editor, Bill Butler; Photography, Stephen M. Katz; Co-Producer, Eugene Mazzola; Music, Jimmie Haskell; Assistant Director, Chuck Russell; In color by Movielab; 92 minutes; Rated R; June release. CAST: Desi Arnaz, Jr. (Scott), Robert Carradine (John), Melanie Griffith (Susie), Anne Lockhart (Cindy), Tom Ligon (Sanders), Cliff Lenz (Henderson), Robert Loper (Simon), Diana Grayf (Rhonda), Diane O'Mack (Debbie), Susan Ludlow (Personnel Lady), Ted D'Arms (Site Manager), Gail Rosella (Cashier), Richard Mazzola (Car Salesman), Michael O'Neill (Henderson's Assistant), Duncan Maclean (Diner Owner), Richard Riehle (Bartender), Richard Tietjen (Sam), Paul Fleming (Big Ed)

SATAN'S CHEERLEADERS (World Amusement) Producer, Alvin L. Fast; Director, Greydon Clark; Screenplay, Greydon Clark, Alvin L. Fast; Music, Gerald Lee; Executive Producer, Michael MacFarland; In Movielab Color; Rated R; June release. CAST: John Ireland, Yvonne DeCarlo, Jack Kruschen, John Carradine, Sydney Chaplin, Jacquelin Cole, Kerry Sherman, Hillary Horan, Alisa Powell, Sherry Marks

SINBAD AND THE EYE OF THE TIGER (Columbia) Producers, Charles H. Schneer, Ray Harryhausen; Director, Sam Wanamaker; Screenplay, Beverley Cross; Story, Beverley Cross, Ray Harryhausen; Photography, Ted Moore; Music, Roy Budd; Editor, Roy Watts; Design, Geoffrey Drake; Art Directors, Fernando Gonzales, Fred Carter; Costumes, Cynthia Tingey; Assistant Director, Miguel A. Gil, Jr.; In Metrocolor; Rated G; June release. CAST: Patrick Wayne (Sinbad), Taryn Power (Dione), Margaret Whiting (Zenobia), Jane Seymour (Farah), Patrick Troughton (Melanthius), Kurt Christian (Rafi), Nadim Sawaiha (Hassan), Damien Thomas (Kassim), Bruno Barnabe (Balsora), Bernard Kay (Zabid), Salami Coaker (Maroof), David Sterne (Aboo-Seer)

BAD GEORGIA ROAD (Dimension) Producer-Director, John C. Broderick; Screenplay, Jeffrey Bernini, John C. Broderick; Music, Don Peake; Associate Producer, Victoria Levee; In DeLuxe Color; 86 minutes; Rated R; June release. CAST: Gary Lockwood, Carol Lynley, Royal Dano, John Wheeler, John Kerry, Cliff Emmich, Tom Kibbe, Glynn Rubin, Mary Woronov, George Flowers

FANTASTIC ANIMATION FESTIVAL (Cinema Shares International) Concept Director, Christopher Padilla; Executive Director, Dean A. Berko; A Voyage Production; In color; 103 minutes; Rated PG; June release. An anthology of animated films.

REFLECTIONS (Stu Segall) Produced and Written by William Dancer; Director, Michael Zem; Photography, Rahn Vickery; In color; 81 minutes; Rated X; June release. CAST: Annette Haven, Paul Thomas, Khristine Hellar, Linda Wong, Bonnie Holiday, Dave Penney, John Leslie, Heather Grant, Sandi Pinney, Chris Surili, Joe Nassivera, Ray Wells, Bob Miglietta

THE ELECTRIC CHAIR (Orrin Pictures) Producer-Director, Pat Patterson; A Hugh Rollings Production; In color; Rated R; June release. CAST: Nita Patterson, Katherine Cortez, Barry Bell, Don Cummins, Martin McDonald

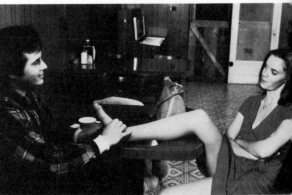

"Moonshine County Express"

Desi Arnaz, Jr., Anne Lockhart
in "Joyride"

Nancy Morgan, Ron Howard
in "Grand Theft Auto"

Fiona Lewis, Robert Forster
in "Stunts"

GRAND THEFT AUTO (New World) Producer, Jack Davison; Executive Producer, Roger Corman; Director, Ron Howard; Screenplay, Rance Howard, Ron Howard; Associate Producer, Rance Howard; Photography, Editor, Joseph Dante; Art Director, Keith Michaels; Assistant Directors, Cal Naylor, Linda Civitello, Tom Jacobson; In Metrocolor, 89 minutes; Rated PG; June release. CAST: Ron Howard (Sam), Nancy Morgan (Paula), Marion Ross (Vivian), Pete Isacksen (Sparky), Barry Cahill (Bigby), Hoke Howell (Preacher), Lew Brown (Jack), Elizabeth Rogers (Priscilla), Rance Howard (Ned), Don Steele (Curly Q.), Paul Linke (Collins), Leo Rossi (Sal), Robby Weaver (Harold), Clint Howard (Ace), Jim Ritz (Officer), Bill Conklin (Engle), Ken Lerner (Benny), Jack Perkins (Shadley), Rev. Bobs Watson (Minister), Gary K. Marshall (Underworld Boss), Karen Kaysing (Bride), Paul Bartel (Groom), Rick Seaman (Max), Tom Waters (Lester), Ancel Cook (Dink), Vic Rivers (Muskovitz), Cal Naylor (Car Salesman), Jim Costigan (Hiram), Reed Chenault (Rex), Phyliss Citas (Lupe), Leo Michelson (Farmer), Jim Begg (Businessman), Jimi Fox (Engineer), Gisella Blake (Accordionist), Larry Cruikshank (Elder Spokesman), Gene Hartline (Gas Station Attendant), George Wagner (Camera Operator), Bill Denochelle, Eddie Mulder (Derby Drivers), Wayne Goodwin (Mysterious Man), Lars Fredriksen (Stony), Glen Towery (Tony), Todd McCarthy (Reporter)

THE THOROUGHBREDS (Pan American) Director, Henry Levin; Executive Producer, Mario Crespo, Jr.; In color; Rated G; June release. CAST: Vera Miles, Stuart Whitman, Sam Groom, Pat Renella

FOR THE LOVE OF BENJI (Mulberry Square Productions) Producer, Ben Vaughn; Direction and Screenplay, Joe Camp; Story, Ben Vaughn, Joe Camp; Executive Producer, Joe Camp; Music, Euel Box; Photography, Don Reddy; Editor, Leon Seith; In color; 85 minutes; Rated G; June release. CAST: Patsy Garrett (Mary), Cynthia Smith (Cindy), Allen Fluzat (Paul), Ed Nelson (Chandler), Art Vasil (Stellos), Peter Bowles (Ronald), Bridget Armstrong (Elizabeth), Mihalis Lambrinos (Baggage Room Man)

STUNTS (New Line) Executive Producers, Peter S. Davis, Robert Shaye; Producers, Raymond Lofaro, William Panzer; Director, Mark L. Lester; Story, Raymond Lofaro; Screenplay, Dennis Johnson, Barney Cohen; Music, Michael Kamen; Associate Producer, Mark Fleischman; In color; 90 minutes; Rated PG; June release. CAST: Robert Forster, Fiona Lewis, Joanna Cassidy, Darrell Fetty, Bruce Glover, Jim Luisi, Richard Lynch, Candace Rialson, Malachi Throne, Ray Sharkey, Phil Adams, Dick Butler, Joie Chitwood, Deanne Coleman, Gary Davis, Larry Dunn, Ted Duncan, Bud George, Beau Gilbson, Lee Pulford, Dar Robinson, Chuck Tamburro

THE GRATEFUL DEAD (Monarch/Noteworthy) Producer, Eddie Washington; Editors, Susan Crutcher, Jerry Garcia; Executive Producer, Ron Rakow; Animation, Gary Gutierrez; 131 minutes; Not rated; June release. A documentary on the rock group The Grateful Dead.

JOURNEY INTO THE BEYOND (Burbank International) Producer, Rudolf Kalmowicz; Directed and Created by Rolf Olsen; Photography, Franz Lererle; Written by Paul Ross; Editors, Alfred Srp, Ric Eisman; Music, Don Great; In color, black and white; 95 minutes; Rated R; June release. A "journey" into the supernatural narrated by John Carradine.

BLACK FIST (Worldwide) Producers, William Larrabure, Richard Kaye; Director, Timothy Galfas; Screenplay, Tim Kelly; Executive Producer, Charles L. Hamilton; Editor, Andrew Maisner; In color; 94 minutes; Rated R; June release. CAST: Richard Lawson, Annazette Chase, Philip Michael Thomas, Dabney Coleman, Robert Burr, Denise Gordy, Richard Kaye, Ed Rue, John Wesley Rodgers, Ron Carson, Al Checco, Joseph Ruskin, Carolyn Calcote, Morris Buchanan, Stephanie Faulkner, H. B. Haggerty, Eddie Crawford

MY SEX RATED WIFE (Melody) Producer, Louis Su; Director, David Stitt; Photography, Lloyd Kaufman; In color; Rated X; June release. CAST: Sharon Mitchell, Wade Nichols, Terri Hall, Gloria Leonard, Michael Carter, Sue Denim, Mike Shea, Roger Caine, Gregory Costas

Ed Nelson, Benji
in "For the Love of Benji"

"Journey into the Beyond"

**Alan Arkin, Anjanette Comer, Byron Stewart
in "Fire Sale"**

**Vincent Gardenia, Kay Medford
in "Fire Sale"**

THE HONEY CUP (Independent) Director, John Parkham; In color; Rated X; June release. CAST: Eric Edwards, Rose Merl, Crystal Sync, Nancy Dare, Sonny Landham, Stephanie Dennis, Richard Bolla, Marlene Willoughby

HARD SOAP, HARD SOAP (Freeway) Producer, Richard Aldrich; Director, Robert Chinn; Screenplay, John T. Chapman; Based on his novel "Milkmen Get Up Early"; Photography, Vilmos Varisek; Executive Producer, Damon Christian; A Golden Gate Production; In Eastmancolor; 76 minutes; Rated X; June release. CAST: Laurien Dominique (Penny), Candice Chambers (Lou), John C. Holmes (Doctor), Joan Devlin (Patty), Charles Law (Milkman), Jeffrey Stern (Willard), Paul Thomas (Janitor), Dale Meador (Priest), Ken Scudder (Fred), Cindy Barron, Blair Morris, Sabrina, Barbara Ericson, John Seeman, Joe Civera

REUNION (Mature) Director, Jay West; In Eastmancolor; 72 minutes; Rated X; June release. CAST: Bree Anthony, Tony Richards, Nancy Love, Alan Login, Vanessa Del Rio, Taylor Young, Marlene Willoughby

THE VIOLATION OF CLAUDIA (Lustig) Produced, Directed and Edited by Billy Bagg; Screenplay, Sally McKinley, Travis Webb; Story, Billy Bagg; Photography, Rob Lindsay; Music, Michael Karp; In Technicolor; Rated X; June release. CAST: Sharon Mitchell, Jamie Gillis, Don Peterson, Waldo Short, Crystal Sync, Victor Hines, Gandi Sanders, Cheri Baines, Jack Jeffries, Justine Fletcher, Long Jeanne Silver, Guido D'Alisa, Andrew Bellina

2076 OLYMPIAD (Aragon) Produced, Directed and Written by James R. Martin; Photography, Mannuel Whitaker; Art Director, Suzanne M. Steiner; Music, Lawrence J. Ponzak; In color; 90 minutes; June release. CAST: Jerry Zafer (Jeff), Sandy Martin (Shiela), Dean Bennett (Judd), Joel Camphausen (Herman), Joann Secunda (Jody), Alan Kirk (Glen), Sigrid Heath (Diana), Meredith Rile (Joan), J. R. Martin (Newscaster), Robert Boxco (Marvin), Gene Shay (Sam), Gladys Williams (Agatha), John LaMotta (Boris)

FIRE SALE (20th Century-Fox) Producer, Marvin Worth; Director, Alan Arkin; Screenplay, Robert Klane from his novel; Editor, Richard Halsey; Music, Dave Grusin; Designer, James H. Spencer; Photography, Ralph Woolsey; Assistant Directors, Tom Lofaro, Ed Markley, Bruce Satterlee; In DeLuxe Color; 88 minutes; Rated PG; June release. CAST: Alan Arkin (Ezra), Rob Reiner (Russel), Vincent Gardenia (Benny), Anjanette Comer (Marion), Kay Medford (Ruth), Barbara Dana (Virginia), Sid Caesar (Zabbar), Alex Rocco (Al), Byron Stewart (Captain), Oliver Clark (Blossom), Richard Libertini, MacIntyre Dixon (Painters), Augusta Dabney (Mrs. Cooper), Don Keefer (Banker), Bill Henderson (Psychiatrist), John Horn (Louis), Sally K. Marr (Jackie), Speedy Zapata (Janitor), Kimelle Anderson (Nurse), Selma Archerd (Ellie), Bob Leslie (Van Driver), John Hudkins (Wheelchair Patient), Viola Harris (Helen), Marvin Worth (Milton)

NAKED RIVER (EMC) Producer, John Lange; Director, William Diehl, Jr.; Screenplay, Raymond Marlowe, Jr.; Music, Paul Jarvis; In color; Rated R; June release. CAST: Gerald Richards (Big Jim), Edmund Genest (Sam), Linda Cook (Melody), Johnny Popwell (Barney), Philip Pleasants (Sid), Stuart Culpepper (Harry), Edie Kramer (Sharon), April Johnson (Fancy), Bill Moses (John)

CRACKING UP (American International) Producers, C. D. Taylor, Rick Murray; Executive Producer, Joe Roth; Directors, Rowby Goren, Chuck Staley; Art Director, C. D. Taylor; Editor, Roger Parker; Music, Ward Jewel, The Tubes; In color; 69 minutes; Rated R; July release. CAST: Phil Proctor (Walter Concrete), Peter Bergman (Barbara Halters), Michael Mislove, Fred Willard, Paul Zegler, Steve Bluestein, The Credibility Gap, Harry Shearer, Michael McCane, David Lander, The Graduates, Jim Fisher, Jim Staahl, Gino Insana, "Kansas City" Bob McClurg, Leslie Ackerman, Rowby Goren, Neil Isreal, Rick Murray, C. D. Taylor, Edie McClurg, Mary McCusker, Cris Pray, Ron Prince, Lynn Marie Stuart, Steven Stucker, Kurt Taylor, Paul Willson, Fee Waybill

"Cracking Up"

"Cracking Up"

**Gary Levinson
in "Shock Waves"**

SHOCK WAVES (Joseph Brenner) Formerly "Death Corps"; Producer, Reuben Trane; Director, Ken Weiderhorn; Screenplay, John Harrison, Ken Weiderhorn; Photography, Reuben Trane; Music, Richard Einhorn; No other credits available; Rated PG; July release. CAST: Peter Cushing (Scar), John Carradine (Ben), Brooke Adams (Rose), Fred Buch (Chuck), Jack Davidson (Norman), Luke Halpin (Keith), D. J. Sidney (Beverly), Don Stout (Dobbs), Death Corps Members: Tony Moskal, Gary Levinson, Jay Maeder, Bob Miller, Talmadge Scott, Bob White

ORCA (Paramount) Producer, Luciano Vincenzoni; Director, Michael Anderson; Screenplay, Luciano Vincenzoni, Sergio Donati; Photography, Ted Moore, Vittorio Dragonetti; Editors, Ralph E. Winters, John Bloom, Marion Rothman; Music, Ennio Morricone; Song Lyrics, Coro Conners; Design, Mario Garbuglia; Art Directors, Boris Juraga, Ferdinando Giovannoni; Costumes, Jost Jakob, Philippe Pickford; Assistant Director, Brian Cook; Underwater Director, Folco Quilici; In color; Presented by Dino De Laurentiis; 92 minutes; Rated PG: July release. CAST: Richard Harris (Nolan), Charlotte Rampling (Rachel), Will Sampson (Umilak), Bo Derek (Annie), Keenan Wynn (Novak), Robert Carradine (Ken), Scott Walker (Swain), Peter Hooten (Paul), Wayne Heffley (Priest), Vincent Gentile (Gas Station Man), Don "Red" Barry (Dock Worker)

DISCO 9000 (Choice Inc./Cosmo Inc.) Producers, Demetris Johnson, Robert Paul Ross; Director, D'Urville Martin; Screenplay, Roland S. Jefferson; A Long Star and Yellow Rose Production; In color; Rated PG; July release. CAST: John Poole, Jeanie Bell, Harold Nicholas, Cal Wilson, Nicholas Lewis, Beverly Anne, Shirley Washington, Harold Daniels, Johnnie Taylor, Lucius Allen, Ricky Bell, Gary Jeter, Brad Pye, Jr.

THE HILLS HAVE EYES (Vanguard) Producer, Peter Locke; Direction and Screenplay, Wes Craven; Music, Don Peake; Photography, Eric Saarinen; In color; Rated R; July release. CAST: Susan Lanier, Robert Houston, Martin Speer, Dee Wallace, Russ Grieve, John Steadman, Michael Berryman, Virginia Vincent, James Whitworth, Brenda Marinoff, Cordy Clark, Janus Blythe, Lance Gordon, Arthur King, Ron Stein

**Richard Harris, Charlotte Rampling
in "Orca"**

THE BEACH BUNNIES (S.C.A.) Producer-Director, A. C. Stephen; In color; Rated R; July release. CAST: Wendy Cavanough, Brenda Fogerty, Linda Gildersleeve, Mariwin Roberts

CREME RINSE Producer-Director, R. J. Doyle; In Eastmancolor; Rated X; July release. CAST: John Holmes, Rene Bond, Misty Adams, George Chase

WHISKEY MOUNTAIN (Celestial) Producer-Director, William Grefe; Screenplay, Nicholas E. Spanos; Executive Producer, Richard W. A. Davis; Music and lyrics written and performed by Charlie Daniels; In color; Rated PG; July release. CAST: Christopher George, Preston Pierce, Linda Borgeson, Roberta Collins, Robert Leslie, John Davis Chandler

BADGE 69 Director, Thomas Mock; Music, The Scorpios; In Eastmancolor; Rated X; July release. CAST: Lynn Stevens, Dori West, Marc Stevens, Susan Kevins

PUNK ROCK (Gail) Director, Carter Stevens; Screenplay, Al Hazrad; In color; Rated X; July release. CAST: Wade Nichols, Susaye London, Jeanie Sanders, Randi Coppasquatto, Richard Bolla, Nancy Dare, Paula Morton, Bobby Astyr, Eric Edwards, Elda, Stiletto, Peter Andrews, Roger Caine

BABY ROSEMARY (Essex) Producer, Bill Steele; Director, Howard Perkins; Screenplay, Ruth Price, Virgil Rom; In color; 80 minutes; Rated X; July release. CAST: Sharon Thorpe (Rosemary), John Leslie Dupre (John), Leslie Bovee (Unis), Ken Cotten (Mick), John Seeman (Undertaker), Semantha King, Candida Royale

LONG JEANNE SILVER (Stu Segall) Director, Alex de Renzy; In color; Rated X; July release. CAST: Long Jeanne Silver, Laurie Wilson, Troy Stein, Joe Civera, Amber Hunt, Sandy Pinney, Paul Thomas, Laura Greer

THE JADE PUSSYCAT (Freeway) Direction and Screenplay, Bob Chinn; In color; Rated X; July release. CAST: John C. Holmes, Georgina Spelvin, Linda Wong, Jessica Temple Smith, Christina Sarver, Mimi Zuber, Bonnie Holiday, Lyle Stewart, Timi Lee, Danny Hussong, Steve Balint

INSIDE JENNIFER WELLES (Evart) Producer, Howard B. Howard; Director, Jennifer Welles; Photography, James Hammermill; In Technicolor; 107 minutes; Rated X; July release. CAST: Jennifer Welles, James Chin, Ed Chin, Steve Mitchell, Richard Bolla, Cheri Baines, Ken Anderson, Peter Andrews, Pepe, Manny Duran, Marlene Willoughby, G. G. Palma, Teddy Ngai, David Innis, Mike DeMarco, Joji Tani, Moory Yank Park, David Shaker, Bobby Niles, Mike Dattore, Dave Ruby, David Del

TAKE TIME TO SMELL THE FLOWERS (International Cinema) Producer-Director, Chris Caras (Karas); Music, Chris Shrantakis, Gerald Liebmann; In color; Rated X: July release. CAST: Viju Krem, David Anthony, Ellen Irons, Greta Hartog, Harrington Smith, Elizabeth Martin

GIZMO (New Line) Producer-Director, Howard Smith; Executive Producer, Francois de Menil; Narration written by Kathleen Cox, Nicholas Hollander, Clark Whelton; Editor, Terry Manning; Music, Dick Lavsky; In black and white and color; 79 minutes; Rated PG; July release. A documentary.

HAUNTS (Intercontinental) Producers, Herb Freed, Burt Weisbourd; Director, Herb Freed; Screenplay, Anne Marisse, Herb Freed; Photography, Larry Secrist; Assistant Director, David McGiffert; In Eastmancolor; 98 minutes; Rated PG: July release. CAST: May Britt (Ingrid), Aldo Ray (Sheriff), Cameron Mitchell (Carl), William Gray Espy (Frankie), Susan Nohr (Nel), Ben Hammer (Vicar), E. J. Andre (Doc), Kendall Jackson (Loretta)

THE PEOPLE THAT TIME FORGOT (American International) Producer, John Dark; Director, Kevin Connor; Screenplay, Patrick Tilley; Based on novel by Edgar Rice Burroughs; Photography, Alan Hume; Editors, John Ireland, Barry Peters; Music, John Scott; Designer, Maurice Carter; Art Directors, Bery Davey, Fernando Gonzalez; Assistant Director, Bryan Coates; Costumes, Brenda Dabbs; In Movielab Color; 90 minutes; Rated PG; July release. CAST: Patrick Wayne (Ben), Doug McClure (Bowen), Sarah Douglas (Charly), Dana Gillespie (Ajor), Thorley Walters (Norfolk), Shane Rimmer (Hogan), Tony Britton, John Hallam, Dave Prowse, Gaylord Reid, Kiran Shah, Richard Parmentier, Jimmy Ray, Tony McHale

Didi Conn, Joe Silver
in "You Light Up My Life"

Mary Woronov, Lynn Lowry
in "Sugar Cookies"

AXE (Boxoffice International) Producer, J. G. Patterson; Direction and Screenplay, Frederick R. Friedel; Music, George Newman Shaw, John Willhelm; In color; Rated R; July release. CAST: Jack Canon, Ray Green, Frederick R. Friedel, Leslie Lee, Douglas Powers, Frank Jones, Carol Miller, Hart Smith, George J. Monaghan, Scott Smith

LOOSE ENDS (Bauer International) Producer, Victoria Wozniak; Director, David Burton Morris; Screenplay, David Burton Morris, Victoria Wozniak; Photography, Gregory M. Cummins; Editor, G. M. Cummins; Music, John Paul Hammond; Art Director, Ann Morris; Sound, Jay Booth; In black and white; 103 minutes; August release. CAST: Chris Mulkey (Billy), John Jenkins (Eddie), Linda Jenkins (Jen)

YOU LIGHT UP MY LIFE (Columbia) Produced, Directed, Written and Music by Joseph Brooks; Associate Producers, Nick Grippo, Edwin Morgan; Editor, Lynzee Klingman; Photography, Eric Saarinen; Art Director and Designer, Tom Rasmussen; Assistant Directors, Ed Morgan, Sandy Knoopf; In Technicolor; 90 minutes; Rated PG; August release. CAST: Didi Conn (Laurie), Joe Silver (Si), Michael Zaslow (Cris), Stephan Nathan (Ken), Melanie Mayron (Annie), Jerry Keller (Conductor), Lisa Reeves (Carla), John Gowans (Charley), Simmy Bow (Granek), Bernice Nicholson (Mrs. Granek), Ed Morgan (Account Executive), Joe Brooks (Creative Director), Amy Letterman (Laurie as a child), Marty Zagon (Nussbaum), Martin Gish (Harold), Arnold Weiss (Usher), Bruan Byers (Singer), Terry Brannen (Usher), Tom Gerard (Best Man), Barry Godwin, John Miller, Stephan Tice (Ushers), Eileen Dietz, Lindsey Jones, Kasey Ciszk, Greta Ronnegun, Lisa Nicholson (Bridesmaids), Ruth Manning (Mrs. Rothenberg), Rosemary Lovell, Judy Novgrad (Receptionists), Jeffrey Kramer (Background Singer), Frank Conn (Stage Manager), Mary Kwan, Edward Steefe, Cynthia Szigeti (Cousins), Sparky Watts (Uncle Fritz), Robin O'Hara (Aunt Emma), Ken Olfson, Richmond Shepard (Commercial directors), Aurora Roland (Gail), Thelma Pelish (Rachel), John Millerburg (Studio Musician), Nancy Chadwick (Producer), Matt Hyde, Jerry Barnes (Engineers), Bob Manahan (Assistant Engineer)

SUGAR COOKIES (Troma) Producers, Lloyd Kaufman, Ami Artzi; Director, Theodore Gershuny; Screenplay, Lloyd Kaufman, Theodore Gershuny; Music, Gershon Kingsley; In Eastmancolor; 92 minutes; Rated R; August release. CAST: Mary Woronov, George Shannon, Lynn Lowry, Monique Van Vooren, Jennifer Welles, Maureen Byrnes

THE KENTUCKY FRIED MOVIE (United Film Distribution Co.) Producer, Robert K. Weiss; Executive Producer, Kim Jorgensen; Director, John Landis; Screenplay, David Zucker, Jim Abrahams, Jerry Zucker; Photography, Stephen M. Katz; Music, Igo Kantor; A Ned Topham Presentation; In color, black and white; 90 minutes; Rated R; August release. CAST: Marilyn Joi (Cleopatra), Saul Kahan (Schwartz), Marcy Goldman (Housewife), Joe Medalis (Paul), Barry Dennem (Claude), Rich Gates (Boy), Tara Strohmeir (Girl), Neil Thompson (Newscaster), George Lazenby (Architect), Henry Gibson, Bill Bixby (Themselves), Donald Sutherland (Clumsy), Evan Kim (Loo), Derek Murcott (Pennington), Master Bong Soo Han (Dr. Klahn)

TENTACLES (American International) Executive Producer, Ovidio Assonities; Producer, Enzo Doria; Director, Oliver Hellman; Screenplay, Jerome Max, Tito Carpi, Steve Carabatsos; Photography, Roberto D'Ettore Piazzoli; Music, S. W. Cipriani; In color; Rated PG; 90 minutes; August release. CAST: John Huston (Ned), Shelley Winters (Tillie), Bo Hopkins (Will), Henry Fonda (Whitehead), Cesare Danova (Corey), Alan Boyd (Mike), Claude Akins (Capt. Robards)

RUBY (Dimension) Executive Producer, Steve Krantz; Producer, George Edwards; Director, Curtis Harrington; Screenplay, George Edwards, Barry Schneider; Photography, William Mendenhall; Editor, Bill McGee; Music, Don Ellis; In color; Rated R; 84 minutes; August release. CAST: Piper Laurie (Ruby), Stuart Whitman (Vince), Roger Davis (Dr. Keller), Janit Baldwin (Leslie), Crystin Sinclaire (Lila), Paul Kent (Louie), Len Lesser (Barney), Jack Perkin (Avery), Edward Donno (Jess), Sal Vecchio (Nicki), Fred Kohler (Jake)

Sarah Douglas, Patrick Wayne, Doug McClure,
Dana Gillespie in "People That Time Forgot"

Amy Letterman
in "You Light Up My Life"

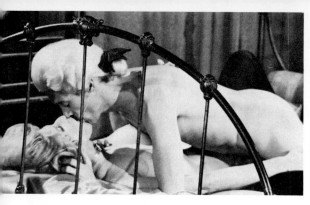

Jane Goodman, John Holmes in "The New Erotic
Adventures of Casanova"

Bo Svenson
in "Final Chapter-Walking Tall"

THE NEW EROTIC ADVENTURES OF CASANOVA (Hollywood International) Executive Producer, Miguel Merino; Screenplay, Edgar G. Warren; Photography, Fernando Fortes; Director, John Holmes; Editors, Louis Hermman, Giuseppe Gordeano; Assistant Director, Mando Sharp; A Diamond Films Presentation; In color; 90 minutes; Rated X; August release. CAST: John Holmes (Casanova/John), Susan Silver (Dr. Sharpe), Peter Johns (Paul), Jane Goodman (Lady Angie), Will Verdi (Col. Zatzki), Rock Steady (Swordsman), Dave Reagan (Swordsman), Cathy Linger (Swordsgirl), Bridgette Felina (Gypsy Girl), Bob Dwyer (Dr. Moreau), Diane Bills (Louise), Sue Susser (Gratia), Nancy Hoffman (Miriam), Iris Medina (Maid), Tory Jeffery (Pawnshop man), Eileen Dover (Ann), Tracy O'Neil (Jane), Justine Taylor (Joyce), Christian Sarver (Marge), David Blair (George), Georgette Peters (Rose)

POLK COUNTY POT PLANE (Westco) Producer-Director, Jim West; In color; Rated PG; August release. CAST: Bob Watson, Don Watson, Paul Benefield, Debbie Washington, Jan Jones, Randy Mewbourn, Winona Myles

CHERRY HUSTLERS (Gail) Director, Art Ben; In color; Rated X; August release. CAST: Vanessa Del Rio, Roger Caine, Jennifer Jordan, Alan Login, Bobby Astyr, Brooke Young, Taylor Young

SISTERS OF DEATH (First American) Producers, Gustaf Unger, Gary Messenger; Director, Joseph Mazzuca; Screenplay, Elwyn Richards, Burt Hansen; In color; Rated PG; August release. CAST: Arthur Franz, Cheri Howell, Paul Carr, Claudia Jennings

BARBARA BROADCAST (Crescent) Producer, L. Sultana; Director, Henry Paris; Screenplay, Jake Barnes; Photography, Chico Carter; In color; 80 minutes; Rated X; August release. CAST: Annette Haven (Barbara), C. J. Laing (Roberta), Constance Money (Slave), Suzanne McBain (Cynthia), Jamie Gillis (Curly), Shirley Peters (Joyce), Alan Marlow, Bobby Astyr, Wade Nichols, Peter Andrews, Zebedy Colt, Sharon Mitchell, Loren Michaels, Camille Farrell, Helen Wolf, Michael Dattore

FINAL CHAPTER—WALKING TALL (American International) Producer, Charles A. Pratt; Director, Jack Starrett; Screenplay, Howard B. Kreitsek, Samuel A. Peeples; Photography, Robert B. Hauser; Editor, Houseley Stevenson; Music, Walter Scharf; Art Director, Joe Altadonna; Costumes, Michael W. Hoffman, Chris Zamiara; Assistant Director, Carl Olsen; In Deluxe Color; 112 minutes; Rated R; August release. CAST: Bo Svenson (Buford), Margaret Blye (Luan), Forrest Tucker (Buford's Father), Lurene Tuttle (Buford's Mother), Morgan Woodward (The Boss), Libby Boone (Secretary), Leif Garrett, Dawn Lyn (Buford's children), Bruce Glover (Deputy), Taylor Lacher (Martin), Sandy McPeak (Lloyd), Logan Ramsey (John), Robert Phillips (Johnny), Clay Tanner (O. Q.), David Adams (Robbie), Vance Davis (Aaron), H. B. Haggerty (Bulo), John Malloy (Producer)

RACE FOR YOUR LIFE, CHARLIE BROWN (Paramount) Producers, Lee Mendelson, Bill Melendez; Director, Bill Melendez; Co-Director, Phil Roman; Screenplay, Charles Schultz from his "Peanuts" comic strip characters; Editors, Chuck McCann, Roger Donley; In color; 75 minutes; Rated G; August release. An animated feature using the voices of Duncan Watson, Greg Felton, Stuart Brotman, Gail Davis, Liam Martin, Kirk Jue, Jordan Warren, Jimmy Ahrens, Melanie Kohn, Tom Muller, Bill Melendez, Fred Van Amburg

ORIENTAL BABYSISTER (Essex) Director, Leonard Burke; In color; Rated X; August release. CAST: Linda Wong, Mary Quint, Connie Peters, David Brooks, Michael Zarilla

THE BLACK PEARL (Diamond) Producer-Director, Saul Swimmer; Screenplay, Victor B. Miller, Rodney Sheldon; Based on novel by Scott O'Dell; Music, Deodato; A William Cash/Saul Swimmer Production; In color; Rated PG; August release. CAST: Gilbert Roland, Carl Anderson, Mario Custodio

END OF THE WORLD (Irwin Yablans) Producer, Charles Band; Director, John Hayes; Screenplay, Frank Ray Perilli; Photography, John Huneck; Music, Andrew Belling; In DeLuxe Color; 82 minutes; Rated PG; August release. CAST: Christopher Lee, Sue Lyon, Kirk Scott, Lew Ayres, Macdonald Carey, Dean Jagger

BREAKER BEAUTIES (Stu Segall) Produced, Directed and Written by Steven Barry; In color; Rated X; August release. CAST: Alexandra, Richard Bolla, Jean Dalton, Bobby Astyr, Vanessa Rel Rio, Wade Nichols, Don Peterson, Mary Beth Johnson, Victoria Corsaut, Sharon Mitchell

ANGELA THE FIREWORKS WOMAN (Essex) Direction and Screenplay, Abe Snake; In color; 78 minutes; Rated X; August release. CAST: Sarah Nicholson, Eric Edwards, Helen Madigan, Erica Eaton, Ellis Deigh, Lefty Cooper

HEAT WAVE (Command Cinema) Producer, Michael Bernard; Director, Cecil Howard; In color; Rated X; August release. CAST: Susan McBain, Sharon Mitchell, Gloria Leonard, Ming Toy, Fanny Wolfe, Mal Dane Cross, Ursula Austin, John Leslie, Dupre, Richard Bolla, Terry Flame, Nina

LURE OF THE DEVIL'S TRIANGLE Producer, Robert Argove; Director, Philip Ronald; In color; Rated X; August release. CAST: Patricia Rivers, Mike Cone, Scott Daniels, Victoria Le

"Race For Your Life, Charlie Brown"

130

"Race For Your Life, Charlie Brown"   "Dynasty"

CAN I DO IT ... TILL I NEED GLASSES (National-American) Producer, Mike Callie; Director, I. Robert Levy; Screenplay, Mike Callie, Mike Price; Music, Bob Jung; In color; Rated R; August release. CAST: Roger Behr, Debra Klose, Noose Carlson, Walter Olkewicz, Jeff Doucette, Roger Peltz, Victor Dunlop, Saba, Patrick Wright

UNDERAGE Director, Walter D. Roberts; In color; Rated X; August release. CAST: Justine Fletcher, Paula Morton, Cheri Baines, Marlene Willoughby, Wade Nichols, Lyna Manstone

BIG TIME (World Wide) Producers, Christopher Joy, Leon Isaac, Andrew Georgias, Louis Gross; Director, Andrew Georgias; Executive Producer, William "Smokey" Robinson; Music composed and performed by Smokey Robinson; In color; 96 minutes; Rated PG; August release. CAST: Christopher Joy (Eddie), Tobar Mayo (Harold), Jayne Kennedy (Shana), Art Evans (Murdock), Roger E. Mosley (J. J.), Tina Dixon (Fat Woman), Milt Kogan, Vic Martorano, Richard Kennedy, Jinaki, Ernest Sarracino, Ella Edwards

DYNASTY (Cinema Shares International) Producer, Frank Wong; Director, Mei Chung Chang; Photography, Zon Su Chang; In Technicolor; 94 minutes; Rated R; No other credits available; September release. CAST: Bobby Ming, Pai Ying, Lin Ta Shing

DIRTY DUCK (New World) Producer, Jerry Good; Directed, Written, Animated and Designed by Charles Swenson; Songs, Mark Volman, Howard Kaylan; A Murakami Wolfe Production in color; 75 minutes; Rated X; September release. Voices of Mark Volman, Robert Ridgeley, Walker Edmiston, Cynthia Adler, Janet Lee, Lurene Tuttle, Jerry Good, Howard Kaylan

THE HAPPY HOOKER GOES TO WASHINGTON (Cannon) Producer-Director, William A. Levey; Executive Producer, Alan C. Marden; Screenplay, Robert Kaufman; Photography, Robert Caramico; Editor, Lawrence Marinelli; Art Director, Robin Royce, B. B. Neel; Costumes, John David Ridge, Gail Viola; Assistant Director, John Patterson; In Movielab Color; 86 minutes; Rated R; September release. CAST: Joey Heatherton (Xaviera), George Hamilton (Ward), Ray Walston (Senator Sturges), Jack Carter (Senator Caruso), Phil Foster (Senator Krause), David White (Senator Rawlings)

SAN FRANCISCO GOOD TIMES Produced, Directed and Edited by Allan Francovich, Eugene Rosow; In black and white; 90 minutes; Not rated; September release. CAST: The Good Times Commune, Timothy Leary, Bill Graham, Peter Townshend, Magic Floating Lotus Opera Company, Berkeley Astrology Guild. A documentary about the underground newspaper Good Times.

ROAD OF DEATH (Re-Mart International) Producer, Joseph Fink; Direction and Screenplay, Rene Martinez, Jr.; In color; Rated R; September release. CAST: Carol Connors, Joe Banana, Jack Birch, Lea Vivot

BARE KNUCKLES (Intercontinental) Producer-Director, Don Edmonds; Photography, Dean Cundey; In color; 90 minutes; Rated R; September release. CAST: Robert Viharo, Sherry Jackson, Gloria Hendry, Michael Heit, John Daniels

LOVE AND THE MIDNIGHT AUTO SUPPLY (I.P.A.) Direction and Screenplay, James Polakof; Executive Producer, Beverley Johnson; In color; Rated PG; September release. CAST: Michael Parks, Scott Jacoby, Linda Crystal, Colleen Camp, George McCallister, Monica Gayle, Bill Adler, Rory Calhoun, Rod Cameron, John Ireland

DEVIL'S ECSTASY (Unique) Director, Brandon G. Carter; Music, Bill Phyx; Photography, Eric R. Graydon; In color; Rated X; September release. CAST: Deborah Whitney, Tara Blair, John McNight, David Lamont

BLOWDRY (Great Exploitations) Producer, Joey Vincent; Director, Laser Sceptor; Screenplay, Sam Kitt; Music, Bill Dern, Joel Mofsenson; In DeLuxe Color; 75 minutes; Rated X; September release. CAST: Pepe, Helen Madigan, Peonies Jong, Michael Gaunt, Ultra Max, Richard Bolla, Crystal Sync, Marie Roberts, Jamie Gillis

NIGHTMARE COUNTY (Intercontinental) Producer, Maurice Smith; Direction and Screenplay, Sean McGregor; In color; Rated R; September release. CAST: Sean McGregor, Gayle Hemingway

CONFESSIONS (Essex) Director, Leonard Burke; In color; Rated X; September release. CAST: Cindy Johnson, John Leslie, Karen Custick, Ron Rogers, Eric Marin, Joe Civera, Sonny Lustig, Terrence Scanlon

THE GUY FROM HARLEM (International Cinema) Director, Rene Martinez, Jr.; In color; Rated R; September release. CAST: Loye Hawkins, Cathy Davis, Patricia Fulton, Wanda Starr

TEENAGE PAJAMA PARTY No credits available; In color; Rated X; September release. CAST: C. J. Laing, Terri Hall, Sharon Mitchell, Susaye London, Barbi James, Priscilla Major, Pamela Grimes, Gary Cook, Wade Nichols, Richard Bolla

HOOCH (Omni) Producer, Thierry Pathe; Direction and Screenplay, Ed Mann; Music, H. M. Saffer, Paul Solovay; Executive Producer, Joel Goldstein; In color; Rated PG; September release. CAST: Gil Gerard, Erika Fox, Melody Rogers

DROP OUT WIFE (S. C. A.) Producer-Director, A. C. Stephen; In Eastmancolor; September release. CAST: Angela Carnon, Terri Johnson, Lynn Harris, Kathy Hilton, Forman Shane

DEATH DRIVER (Omni) Producer, Earl Owensby; Director, Jimm Huston; Screenplay, Elizabeth Upton; Music, Arthur Smith, Clay Smith; In Technicolor; Rated PG; September release. CAST: Earl Owensby, Mike Allen, Patty Shaw, Mary Ann Hearn

JOY (Mature) Producer, Derek Davidson; Director, Harley Mansfield; Screenplay, Mr. Davidson, Mr. Mansfield; Music, Martin Lewinter; Photography, Keith McGovern; In color/ 75 minutes; Rated X; September release. CAST: Sharon Mitchell (Joy), Jake Teague (Handcock), Richard Bolla (Fred), Melinda Marlowe (Burgler), Jay Pierce (Rick), Jesse Wilson (Officer), Marco, Paul Hues, Robert Hill, Gloria Leonard, Frank Kenwood, Tony Turco, Ellen Williams, Justine Fletcher, Ursula Brooke, Bobby Astyr, Eric Edwards, Mike Jefferson, Paula Morton, Neil Lansing

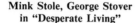
Mink Stole, George Stover
in "Desperate Living"

"Cheering Section"

HIGH VELOCITY (First Asian Films of California) Producer, Takashi Ohashi; Director, Remi Kramer; Executive Producer, Joseph Wolf; Associate Producer, Michael J. Parsons; Screenplay, Remi Kramer, Michael J. Parsons; Music, Jerry Goldsmith; In color; 106 minutes; Not rated; September release. CAST: Ben Gazzara (Clifford), Britt Ekland (Mrs. Andersen), Paul Winfield (Watson), Keenan Wynn (Andersen), Alejandro Rey (Alejandro), Victoria Racimo (Dolores)

DESPERATE LIVING (New Line) Produced, Directed, Written by John Waters; Photography, Thomas Loizeaux; Editor, Charles Roggero; Music, Chris Lobinger, Allen Yarus; Design, Vincent Peranio; Costumes, Van Smith; In color; 90 minutes; Rated X; October release. CAST: Liz Renay (Muffy), Mink Stole (Peggy), Susan Lowe (Mole), Edith Massey (Queen Carlotta), Mary Vivian Pearce (Princess Coo-Coo), Jean Hill (Grizelda), Cookie Mueller (Flipper), Marina Melin (Shina), Sharon Niesp (Shotsie), Ed Peranio (Lt. Wilson), Steve Butow (Lt. Grogan), Channing Wilroy (Lt. Williams), George Stover (Bosley Gravel), Turkey Joe (Motorcycle Cop), Roland Hertz (Muffy's husband), Pirie Woods (Babysitter), H. C. Kliemisch (Big Jimmy Dong), George Figgs (Herbert), Pat Moran (Pervert), Dolores Deluxe (Nurse), Goons: Peter Koper, Steve Parker, Chuck Yeaton, Pete Denzer, Ralph Crocker, David Klein

THE CHALLENGE (New Line) Produced, Directed and Written by Herbert Kline; Narrated by Orson Welles; Photography, Derrett Williams, Arnold Eagle; In color; 104 minutes; October release. A documentary covering nearly a century of modern art.

THE LINCOLN CONSPIRACY (Sunn Classic) Producers, Charles E. Sellier, Jr., Rayland D. Jensen; Director, James L. Conway; Screenplay, Jonathan Cobbler; Photography, Henning Schellerup; Editor, Martin Dreffke; Art Director, William Cornford; Music, Bob Summers; In color; 90 minutes; rated G; October release. CAST: Bradford Dillman (John Wilkes Booth), Robert Middleton (Edward Stanton), John Anderson (Abraham Lincoln), John Dehner (Colonel of National Detective Police Service), Whit Bissell, James Greene

CHEERING SECTION (Dimension) Producer, Wayne Crawford; Director, Harry E. Kerwin; Screenplay, Mr. Kerwin, Mr. Crawford; In color; Rated R; October release. CAST: Rhonda Foxx, Tom Leindecker, Greg D'Jah, Patricia Michelle, Jeff Lain

FOXY LADY (Rosewood) Producer-Director, Jack Mathews; Music, Dody Mitchell; Photography, Jack Bristel; In color; Rated X; October release. CAST: Valerie Driskell, John Leslie, Sand Pinney, Finlay McGuire, Kim Yoko, Seth Wagner, Lee Foster, Paul Crandall

VIRGIN DREAMS (Stu Segall) Direction and Screenplay, Zebedy Colt; In color; Rated X; October release. CAST: Jean Jennings, Wade Nichols, Gloria Leonard, Terri Hall, Susan McBain, Zebedy Colt, Philip Marlowe, Bill Carl, Ralph Stevens, Gary Cooke

JOINT VENTURE (Adventure) Presented by Gerard Damiano; In color; Rated X; October release. CAST: Vanessa Del Rio, Sharon Mitchell, Bobby Astyr, Michael Dattore, Gerard Damiano, Paula Morton, Bibi Wayne, Marilyn Long, Marie Dee, Jennifer Right

MANIAC (New World) Formerly "Assault on Paradise"; Producer, James V. Hart; Director, Richard Compton; Screenplay, John C. Broderick, Ron Silkosky; Executive Producer, Patrick S Ferrell; Photography, Charles Correll; Music, Don Ellis; In color; Rated PG; October release. CAST: Oliver Reed, Deborah Raffin, Stuart Whitman, Jim Mitchum, John Ireland, Paul Koslo

HOW'S YOUR LOVE LIFE? Produced, Directed and Written by Russell Vincent; In color; Rated X; October release. CAST: Russ Vincent, Leslie Brooks, Rick Cooper, John Agar, Mary Beth Hughes

REDNECK MILLER (Nu-South) Director, John Clayton; Producer, W. Henry Smith; Screenplay, W. Henry Smith, Joseph A Alvarez; Photography, Austin McKinney; In color; Rated R; October release. CAST: Geoffrey Land, Sydney Rubin, Pat Walsh, Marcel Cobb, Paulette Gibson, Steve Jones, Lou Walker

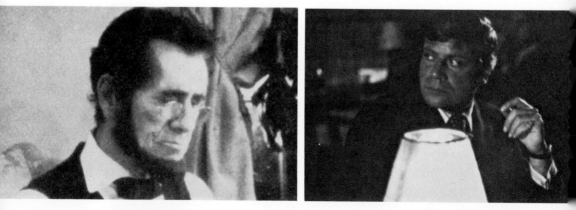

132

John Anderson
in "The Lincoln Conspiracy"

Oliver Reed
in "Maniac"

Jan-Michael Vincent, Paul Winfield
in "Damnation Alley"

Monique Cardin
in "The Secret Dreams of Mona Q"

SYLVIA (Stu Segall) Produced, Directed and Written by Armand Peters; Music, Horace Diaz; In color; Rated X; 92 minutes; October release. CAST: Joanna Bell, Penny Servant, Helen Madigan, Marc Stevens, Sonny Landham, Helen Devine, Joe Fisher

A COMING OF ANGELS (Artemis) Producer-Director, Joel Scott; Screenplay, Gary Stevens, Robin Marks; Music-Lyrics, Scott Mansfield; In color; 85 minutes; Rated X; October release. CAST: Leslie Bovee (Robin), Abigail Clayton (Jennifer), Annette Haven (Carrie), Jamie Gillis (Mark), Amber Hunt (Sherry), Susan McBain (Andrea), John Leslie (Robert), Eric Edwards (Andy)

POCO . . . LITTLE DOG LOST (Cinema Shares International) Producer-Director, Dwight Brooks; Screenplay, William E. Carville; In color; rated G; October release. CAST: Chill Wills, Michelle Ashburn, Clint Ritchie, Sherry Bain

DEMON LOVER (Wolf Lore) Produced, Directed and Written by Donald G. Jackson, Jerry Younkins; In color; Rated R; October release. CAST: Christmas Robbins, Val Mayerick, Gunnar Hansen, Tom Hutton, Dave Howard, Susan Bullen, Phil Foreman, Linda Conrad, Ron Hiveley

TAKE ONE (Reel to Reel) Producer-Director, Wakefield Poole; Photography, Edd Dundas, Wakefield Poole; Music, Tommy Talley; In color; Rated X; 98 minutes; October release. CAST: Jeff Addison, Philip Borden, Tony Franco, Sal Guange, Richard Locke, Bill O'Connell, Dick Ogden, Guillermo Ricardo

DAMNATION ALLEY (20th Century-Fox) Producers, Jerome M. Zeitman, Paul Maslansky; Executive Producers, Hal Landers, Bobby Roberts; Director, Jack Smight; Screenplay, Alan Sharp, Lukas Heller; From novel by Roger Zelanzny; Photography, Harry Stradling, Jr.; Editor, Frank J. Urioste; Music, Jerry Goldsmith; Design, Preston Ames; Art Director, William Cruse; Assistant Director, Donald Roberts; In DeLuxe Color; 95 minutes; Rated PG; October release. CAST: Jan-Michael Vincent (Tanner), George Peppard (Denton), Dominique Sanda (Janice), Paul Winfield (Keegan), Jackie Earle Haley (Billy), Kip Niven (Perry)

THE REUNION (World Wide Films) Produced, Directed and Written by Mike Talbot; Executive Producer, Sumner T. McKnight II; Presented by Sierra Productions; In CFI Color; Rated PG; October release. CAST: Mike Talbot, Peter Isacksen, Danny J. Sheflin, William Wisher, Joanne Hicks, Louise Foster, Mike Villani

THE SECRET DREAMS OF MONA Q (Troma) Producers, Lloyd Kaufman, Charles Kaufman, David Stitt; Director, Charles Kaufman; Photography, Lloyd Kaufman; Editor, Dan Loenthal, Lars Lindstrom; Screenplay, Rolf Schonfeld; Costumes, Joan Puma, Nina Fina; Music, John Flagg, Steve Fox Band; A Duty Productions/Saga Films Presentation; In color; Rated X; November release. CAST: Monique Cardin (Mona), Wade Nichols (Bob), Tom Bauer (Priest/Witchdoctor/Rabbi), Ushi Inger (Rebecca), Swen Kringel (Jim), Inga Bjorg (Delores), Jim Conroi (Jonas), Secretaries: Alexandra, Rose Taft, Pixies: Bob Astyr, Michael Shea, Nymphs: Helga Unster, Eva Haarlan, Sharon Mitchell, Liz Rock

HEROES (Universal) Producers, David Foster, Lawrence Turman; Director, Jeremy Paul Kagan; Screenplay, James Carabatsos; Photography, Frank Stanley; Music, Jack Nitzsche; Designer, Charles Rosen; Editor, Patrick Kennedy; Assistant Directors, John Andersen, Louis Muscate; In Technicolor; 119 minutes; Rated PG; November release. CAST: Henry Winkler (Jack), Sally Field (Carol), Harrison Ford (Ken), Val Avery (Bus Driver), Olivia Cole (Jane), Hector Elias (Dr. Elias), Dennis Burkley (Gus), Tony Burton (Chef), Michael Cavanaugh (Peanuts), Helen Craig (Bus Depot Manager), John P. Finnegan (Munro), Betty McGuire (Mrs. Munro), John O'Leary (Ticket Clerk), Rom Rosqui, Ben Fuhrman (Patrolmen), Fred Stuthman (Nathan), Caskey Swain (Frank), Earle Towne (Leo), Kenneth Augustine (Charles), Rick Blanchard (Andy), Louis Carello (Stokes), Robert Kretschmann (Robert), Alex Tinne (Bridegroom), Dick Ziker (Artie), William Ackridge (Starter), Gary Bertz, James W. Gavin (Pilots), Susan Bredhoff (Nurse), Bill Burton, David Ellis (Bar Patrons), Pat Hustis (Car Driver), Bennie Moore (Adcox)

Jackie Earle Haley, Dominique Sanda, Jan-Michael
Vincent, George Peppard in "Damnation Alley"

Henry Winkler, Sally Field
in "Heroes"

Richard Pryor
in "Which Way Is Up?"

William Shatner
in "Kingdom of the Spiders"

SUMMERDOG (Salisbury Associates) Producer-Director, John Clayton; Screenplay, George and Sherry LaFollette-Zabriskie; Photography, Bil Godsey; Editor, Julie Tanser; Music, Michael Gibson; A Film Foundry Production; 90 minutes; Rated G; November release. CAST: James Congdon (Peter), Elizabeth Eisenman (Carol), Oliver Zabriskie (Adam), Tavia Zabriskie (Becky), Don Rutledge (Caleb), Estelle Harris (Mrs. Baleeka), Tony Capra (Mr. Baleeka)

WHICH WAY IS UP? (Universal) Producer, Steve Krantz; Associate Producer, Michael Chinich; Director, Michael Schultz; Screenplay, Carl Gottlieb, Cecil Brown; Adapted from the film "The Seduction of Mimi" by Lina Wertmuller; Photography, John A. Alonzo; Music, Paul Riser, Mark Davis; Editor, Danford B. Greene; Designer, Lawrence G. Paull; Assistant Directors, Scott Maitland, Donald Zepfel; Title Song, Norman Whitfield; Sung by Stargard; In Panavision and Technicolor; 94 minutes; Rated R; November release. CAST: Richard Pryor (Leroy/Rufus/Reverend), Lonette McKee (Vanetta), Margaret Avery (Annie Mae), Morgan Woodward (Mann), Marilyn Coleman (Sister Sarah), Bebe Drake-Hooks (Thelma), Gloria Edwards (Janelle), Ernesto Hernandez (Jose), DeWayne Jessie (Sugar), Morgan Roberts (Henry), Diane Rodriguez (Estrella), Dolph Sweet (Boss), Timothy Thomerson (Tour Guide), Danny Valdez (Chuy), Luis Valdez (Ramon), Marc Alaimo (Frankie), Tony Alvarenga (Errand Boy), Victor Argo (Angel), Pat Ast (Hooker), Blair Burrows (Goon), Kathy Cronkite, Ron Cummins (Photographers), Evelyn J. Dutton (Receptionist), Carmen Filpi (Wino), Darrell Giddens (Man at picnic), Cheryl Harvey, Julie Dorman, Louise Johnson, Yvonne Mooney (Congregation ladies), Sidney Lanier (Rossi), Tanya Lee (Althea), Terrence Locke (Assassin), Ted Markland, Ralph Montgomery, Hank Robinson, Bob Terhune (Goons), Paul Mooney (Inspector), Shane Mooney (Alvin), Harry Northup (Chief Goon), Korla Pandit (Hindu), Cliff Pellow (White Boss), Mark Robin, Dennis O'Flaherty (Reporters), Eddie Smith (Man at picnic), Spo-de-odee (Cripple), Carol Trost (Ms. Collins), Joseph Turkel (Harry), Angela Wilson (Dawn), Hank Worden (Flunky), El Teatro Campesino

KINGDOM OF THE SPIDERS (Dimension) Producers, Igo Kanter, Jeffrey M. Sneller; Director, John Cardos; Executive Producer, Henry Fownes; Screenplay, Richard Robinson, Alan Caillou; Photography, John Morrill; Editor, Steve Zaillian, Igo Kantor; Assistant Director, Larry Kostroff; In Eastmancolor; 94 minutes; Rated PG; November release. CAST: William Shatner (Rack), Tiffany Bolling (Diane), Woody Strode (Walter), Lieux Dressler (Emma), Altovise Davis (Birch), David McLean (Sheriff), Natasha Ryan (Linda), Marcy Rafferty (Terry), Joe Ross (Vern), Adele Malis (Betty), Roy Engel (Mayor)

CHINA DE SADE (Stu Segall) Director, Charles DeSantos; Music, Fred Hogus; In color; Rated X; November release. CAST: Linda Wong, Tracy O'Neil, Kelley O'Day, Ari Adler, Jewell Bryght, Dale Meador, Mark Anthony, Richard Strong, Lance Hunt

STOCKCAR! Victory) No credits available; Rated PG; November release. CAST: Richard Petty, Cale Yarborough, David Pearson, Buddy Baker, Bobby Allison, Bennie Parsons, Janet Guthrie, The Winston Grand National Drivers

HEROWORK (NBS) Producers, Dirk Petersmann, Michael Adrian; Direction and Screenplay, Michael Adrian; Music, Don Peake; Associate Producer, Edward Khmara; In Panavision and color; Rated PG; November release. CAST: Rod Browning, Robert Chapel, Tabi Cooper, Nancy Kandal, Milt Kogan, Hugh Gillin

INSIDE BABY SISTER (Aventura) Directed and Written by Rik Taziner; In color; Rated X; November release. Starring Kristine Hellar

PETEY WHEATSTRAW (Generation International) Producer, Theodore Toney; Associate Producer, Rudy Ray Moore; Executive Producer, Burt Steiger; Direction and Screenplay, Cliff Roquemore; Photography, Nickolas Von Sternberg; In color; Rated R; November release. CAST: Rudy Ray Moore, Jimmy Lynch, Leroy & Skillet, Eboni Wryte, Wildman Steve, G. Tito Shaw

Richard Pryor in "Which Way Is Up?"

Will Geer
in "Billion Dollar Hobo"

David Carradine
in "Thunder and Lightning"

THE BILLION DOLLAR HOBO (International Picture Show) Producer, Lang Elliott; Director, Stuart McGowan; Photography, Irv Goodnoff; In DeLuxe Color; Rated G; November release. CAST: Tim Conway, Will Geer, Eric Weston

CHARGE OF THE MODEL-T'S (Ry-Mac Films) Produced, Directed and Written by Jim McCullough; Executive Producer, W. Lewis Ryder; Photography, Dean Cundey; Music, Euel Box; In Panavision and color; Rated G; November release. CAST: Louis Nye, John David Carson, Herb Edelman, Carol Bagdasarian, Arte Johnson, Jim McCullough, Jr., Bill Thurman

THUNDERCRACK (Thomas Bros.) Producers, John Thomas, Charles Thomas; Directed, Photographed and Edited by Curt McDowell; Screenplay, George Kuchar; Music, Mark Ellinger; In black and white; 150 minutes; rated X; November release. CAST: Marion Eaton (Mrs. Hammond), George Kuchar (Bing), Melinda McDowell (Sash), Mookie Blodgett (Chandler), Moira Benson (Roo), Rick Johnson (Toydy), Ken Scudder (Bond), Maggie Pyle

THE FINAL SIN (Command) Producer, Michael Bernard; Director, Cecil Howard; In color; Rated X; November release. CAST: Linda Wong, Melba Walsh, Mick Jones, Ursula Brandwin, Richard Strong, Paul Thomas

GAME SHOW MODELS (Independent International) Produced, Directed and Written by David Neil Gottlieb; In Metrocolor; 90 minutes; Rated R; November release. CAST: John Vickery, Rae Sperling, Thelma Houston, Diane Sommerfield, Gilbert De Rush, Sid Melton, Dick Miller, Willie Bobo

THUNDER AND LIGHTNING (20th Century-Fox) Producer, Roger Corman; Director, Corey Allen; Screenplay, William Hjortsberg; Editor, Anthony Redman; Music, Andy Stein; Photography, James Pergola; In color; 95 minutes; Rated PG; November release. CAST: David Carradine (Harley), Kate Jackson (Nancy Sue), Roger C. Carmel (Ralph Jr.), Sterling Holloway (Hobe), Ed Barth (Rudi), Ron Feinberg (Bubba), George Murdock (Jake), Pat Cranshaw (Taylor), Charles Napier (Jim Bob), Hope Pomerance (Mrs. Hunnicutt), Malcolm Jones (Rainey)

FANTASM (Filmways Australasian) Producer, Anthony I. Ginnane; Director, Richard Franklin; Screenplay, Ross Dimsey; In color; 85 minutes; November release. CAST: John Bluthal, Dee Dee Levitt, Sue Doloria, Maria Arnold, Rene Bond, Bill Margold, Uschi Digart, Gene Allan Poe, Mary Gavin, Serena, John C. Holmes, Mara Lutra, Gretchen Gayle, Maria Welton

SEX MAGIC Directed by Jack DeVeau; In color; Rated X. November release. CAST: Jack Wrangler, Roger, Bill Eld, Mandingo, Jayson MacBride, Tom Trooper

ERASERHEAD (Independent) Produced, Directed, Written and Edited by David Lynch; Photography, Fred Elms, Herbert Cardwell; Music, Fats Waller; In black and white; 100 minutes; November release. CAST: Jack Nance (Henry), Charlotte Stewart (Mary X), Jeanne Bates (Mrs. X), Allen Josephs (Mr. X), Judith Anna Roberts (Girl), Laurel Near (Lady), Jean Lange (Grandmother), V. Phipps-Wilson (Landlady), Jack Fisk (Man)

CADILLAC NAMED DESIRE (Blue Movie Productions) Producer, John Janovic; Screenplay, Oliver Nalreh; In color; Rated X; November release. CAST: Sharon Thorpe, Lou Mann, Jesse McKinna, Justina Lynne

FEELINGS (Kemal Enterprises) Producer-Director, Kemal Horulu; Screenplay, Jack Parre; Photography, Joe Mann; Music, Selma Marks; In color; 93 minutes; Rated X; November release. CAST: Lesllie Bovee, Jamie Gillis, Terri Hall, Ras Kean, Eva Henderson, Bobby Astyr, Nancy Dare, Helen Madigan, Richard Bolla, Edward B. Davis, Lee Dupree

DIRTY LILLY (Baja) Director, Marc Ubell; Photography, Robert Michael; Editor, John Christopher; Costumes, Eddie Heath; In color; 75 minutes; Rated X; December release. CAST: Beth Anne (Lilly), Marlow Ferguson (Daddy), Molly Malone (Mother), Eric Edwards (Lawyer), Caroline Sidney (Secretary), Kurt Mann (Director), Richard Bolla (Male Star), Sharon Mitchell (Female Star), C. J. Lang (Ginger), Roger Cane (Muscleman), Marlene Willoughby (S & M Girl), Witches: Dave Ruby, Peter Andrews, W. P. Dremak

George Murdock, David Carradine
in "Thunder and Lightning"

"Thunder and Lightning"

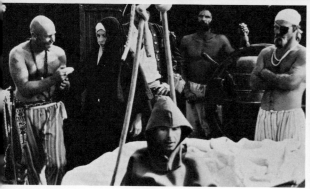

"Captain Lust and the Pirate Women"

Iron Eyes Cody, Lana Wood, Ben Johnson
in "Grayeagle"

INVASION OF THE LOVE DRONES (Drones) A Sensory Man Production; Screenplay, Jerome Hamlin, Conrad Baunz, Michael Gury, John Phillips; Photography and Editing, Jerome Hamlin; In color; 72 minutes; Rated X; November release. CAST: Eric Edwards, Viveca Ash, Bree Anthony, Tony Blue, Sarah Nicholson, Jamie Gillis

CAPTAIN LUST (Anonymous Releasing Triumvirate) Producer-Director, Beau Buchanan; Screenplay, Steven Barry, Beau Buchanan; Photography, Joe Mangine; Editor, B. E. Bangsberg; Music, Fred Schminke; Costumes, Madeline O'Connor; In color; 82 minutes; Rated X; December release. CAST: Wade Nichols (Handsome Jack), Bobby Astyr (Brother Nuncompus), Jake Teague (Capt. Lust), Beau Buchanan (Rip), Sharon Mitchell (Sweet Anne), Verri Knotty (Cuntessa), Jamie Gillis (Capt. Surecock), Nancy Dare (Esmeralda), Justine Fletcher (Sister Inferior), Margarita Promponas (Mama Tushy), Ming Toy (Poon), Barbara Buryiak (French Wench), Ed Scheibly (Old Monk), Suzanne Sugarman (Waitress), Geniveve Spyderkooky (Candy), Luanne Esposito (Penelope), Harvey Cowan (Harvey), Michael Rooney (Dog), Christopher Cable (Helmsman), Vito Sackville-West (Lookout), William Tanke (1st Watchman), Jan P. Bush (2nd Watchman), Solange Shannon (Terry), Pirates: Bill Berry, Jacob Brooke, Calypso, Roy Carlton, Joe Cocoran, Philip De Hatte, Jeffrey B. Dunn, David Grossman, Rick Holiday, Joshua King, Patrick King, Joel Leffert, Tim Maggee, Rick Smith, Richard Steuber, Mark Vincent, Patrisha Daugsiewicz, Joyce Early, Margaret Flanagan, Susaye London, Jackie Wright

MR. MEAN (Lone Star & Po'Boy) Producer-Director, Fred Williamson; Screenplay, Jeff Williamson; Associate Producer, Lee Thornberg; Photography, Maurizio Maggi; In color; Rated R; December release. CAST: Fred Williamson, Lou Castel, Raimund Harmstorf, Crippy Yocard, Anthony Maimone, Rita Silva, Pat Brocato, David Mills, Angela Doria

GRAYEAGLE (American International) Produced, Directed and Written by Charles B. Pierce; Associate Producer, Tommy Clark; Photography and Editing, Jim Roberson; Music, Jaime Mendoza-Nava; Assistant Director, Bud Davis; Art Director, John Ball; In color; 104 minutes; Rated PG; December release. CAST: Ben Johnson (Colter), Iron Eyes Cody (Standing Bear), Lana Wood (Beth), Jack Elam (Trapper), Paul Fix (Running Wolf), Alex Cord (Grayeagle), Jacob Daniels (Scar), Jimmy Clem (Abe), Cindy Butler (Ida), Charles B. Pierce (Bugler), Blackie Wetzel (Medicine Man)

A HERO AIN'T NOTHIN' BUT A SANDWICH (New World) Producer, Robert B. Radnitz; Director, Ralph Nelson; Screenplay, Alice Childress from her novel; Photography, Frank Stanley; Editor, Fred Chulack; Music, Tom McIntosh; Design, Walter Scott Herndon; Costumes, Nedra Watt; Assistant Director, Reuben Watt; In CFI Color; 105 minutes; Rated PG; December release. CAST: Cicely Tyson (Sweets), Paul Winfield (Butler), Larry B. Scott (Benjie), Helen Martin (Mrs. Bell), Glynn Turman (Nigeria), David Groh (Cohen), Kevin Hooks (Tiger), Kenneth Green (Jimmy Lee), Harold Sylvester (Doctor), Erin Blunt (Carwell), Claire Brennen (Social Worker), Arthur French (Guard), Bill Cobbs (Bartender), Sheila Wills (Admission Clerk), Arnold Johnson (Patient), Barbara Alston (Girl Friend), Keny Long (Male Nurse), Hartwell Simms (Minister)

THE INCREDIBLE MELTING MAN (American International) Producer, Samuel W. Gelfman; Direction and Screenplay, William Sachs; Photography, Willy Curtis; Music, Arlon Ober; Art Director, Michael Levesque; In color; 86 minutes; Rated R; December release. CAST: Alex Rebar (The Incredible Melting Man), Burr DeBenning (Dr. Nelson), Myron Healey (Gen. Perry), Michael Alldredge (Sheriff), Ann Sweeny (Judy), Lisl Wilson (Dr. Loring), Rainbeaux Smith (Model), Julie Drazen (Carol), Stuart Edmond Rodgers, Chris Whitney (Little Boys), Edwin Max (Harold), Dorothy Love (Helen), Janus Blythe (Nell), Jonathon Demme (Matt)

Larry B. Scott, Cicely Tyson, Paul Winfield
in "A Hero Ain't Nothin' But A Sandwich"

Alex Rebar
in "The Incredible Melting Man"

FAYE DUNAWAY
in "Network"
1976 ACADEMY AWARD FOR BEST ACTRESS

JASON ROBARDS
in "All the President's Men"
144 *1976 ACADEMY AWARD FOR BEST SUPPORTING ACTOR*

BEATRICE STRAIGHT
in "Network"
1976 ACADEMY AWARD FOR BEST SUPPORTING ACTRESS

BLACK AND WHITE IN COLOR

(ALLIED ARTISTS) Producers, Arthur Cohn, Jacques Perrin, Giorgio Silvagni; Director, Jean-Jacques Annaud; Screenplay, Jean-Jacques Annaud, Georges Conchon; Photography, Claude Agostini; Associate Producer, Jean-Michel Nakache; Art Director, Max Douy; Coordinators, Gerard Crosnier, Timite Bassori; Music, Pierre Bachelet; Editor, Francoise Bonnot; In color; Presented by Emanuel L. Wolf; 90 minutes; Rated PG: April release.

CAST

Sergeant Bosselet	Jean Carmet
Paul Rechampot	Jacques Dufilho
Marinette	Catherine Rouvel
Hubert Fresnoy	Jacques Spiesser
Maryvonne	Dora Doll
Caprice	Maurice Barrier
Jacques Rechampot	Claude Legros
Pere Simon	Jacques Monnet
Pere Jean De La Croix	Peter Berling
Barthelemy	Marius Beugre Boignan
Lamartine	Baye Macoumba Diop
Fidele	Aboutbakar Toure
Kraft	Dieter Schidor
Major Anglais	Marc Zuber
Haussmann	Klaus Huebl
Oscar	Mamadou Coulibaly
Assomption	Memel Atchori
Marius	Jean-Francois Eyou N'Geussan
Charlotte	Natou Koly
John	Tanoh Kouao

and the inhabitants of Niofouin (Ivory Coast)

Left: Jacques Spiesser

Peter Berling, Jacques Monnet

Catherine Rouvel

1976 ACADEMY AWARD FOR BEST FOREIGN LANGUAGE FILM

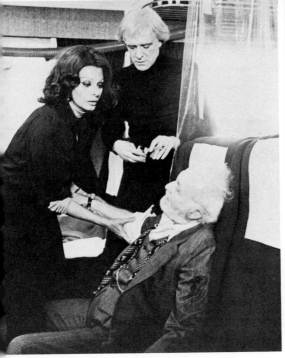

Sophia Loren, Richard Harris,
Lee Strasberg Right: Fausta Avelli, Sophia Loren

THE CASSANDRA CROSSING

(AVCO EMBASSY) Producer, Carlo Ponti; Executive Producer, Giancarlo Pettini; Director, George Cosmatos; Screenplay, Robert Katz, George Cosmatos, Tom Mankiewicz; Photography, Enio Guarnieri; Art Director, Aurelio Crugnola; Editors, Francois Bonnot, Roberto Silvi; Assistant Directors, Antonio Gabrielli, Joe Pollini; Costumes, Andriana Berselli; Sound, Carlo Palmieri; Presented by Sir Lew Grade and Carlo Ponti in Panavision and Technicolor; Rated R; 125 minutes; February release.

CAST

Jennifer	Sophia Loren
Chamberlain	Richard Harris
Nicole	Ava Gardner
Mackenzie	Burt Lancaster
Navarro	Martin Sheen
Elena	Ingrid Thulin
Kaplan	Lee Strasberg
Stack	John Phillip Law
Susan	Ann Turkel
Father Haley	O. J. Simpson
Conductor	Lionel Stander
Tom	Raymond Lovelock
Mrs. Chadwick	Alida Valli
Swede (Driver)	Lou Castell
Attendant	Stefano Patrizi
Patient	Carlo De Mejo
Katherine	Fausta Avelli

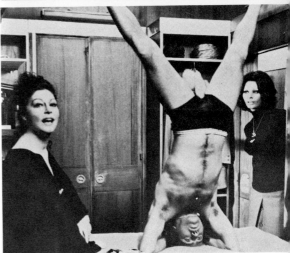

Ava Gardner, Martin Sheen, Sophia Loren
Above: Martin Sheen, Ava Gardner

FELLINI'S CASANOVA

(UNIVERSAL) Producer, Alberto Grimaldi; Director, Federico Fellini; Screenplay, Federico Fellini, Bernardino Zapponi; Photography, Giuseppe Rotunno; Designer, Danilo Donati; Editor, Ruggero Mastroianni; Music, Nino Rota; Assistant Director, Maurizio Mein; Choreography, Gino Landi; In Technicolor; 165 minutes; Rated R; February release.

CAST

Giacomo Casanova .... Donald Sutherland
Maddalena .... Margareth Clementi
Anamaria .... Clarissa Mary Roll
Giselda .... Daniela Gatti
Madame D'Urfe .... Cicely Browne
Marcolina .... Clara Algranti
DuBois .... Daniel Emilfork Berenstein
Henriette .... Tina Aumont
Giantess .... Sandra Elaine Allen
Lord Talou .... John Karlsen
Prince del Brando .... Hans Van Den Hoek
Isabella .... Olimpia Carlisi
Duke of Wurtenberg .... Dudley Sutton
Faulkircher .... Reggie Nalder
The Pope .... Luigi Zerbinati
Doll Woman .... Adele Angela Lojodice
Madame Charpillon .... Carmen Scarpitta
Silvana .... Silvana Fusacchia

Donald Sutherland
(also at top)

Top: Margareth Clementi

NASTY HABITS

(BRUT) Executive producer, George Barrie; Produced and Written by Robert J. Enders; Based on novel "The Abbess of Crewe" by Muriel Spark; Director, Michael Lindsay-Hogg; Editor, Peter Tanner; Music, John Cameron; Photography, Douglas Slocombe; In color; 91 minutes; Rated PG; March release.

CAST

Alexandra	Glenda Jackson
Gertrude	Melina Mercouri
Walburga	Geraldine Page
Winifred	Sandy Dennis
Mildred	Ann Jackson
Geraldine	Anne Meara
Felicity	Susan Penhaligon
Hildegarde	Edith Evans
Priest	Jerry Stiller
Maximilian	Rip Torn
Monsignor	Eli Wallach
Bathildis	Suzanna Stone
Baudouin	Peter Bromilow
Officer	Shane Rimmer
Ambrose	Harry Ditson
Gregory	Chris Muncke

Right: Anne Jackson, Glenda Jackson

Susan Penhaligon Above: Geraldine Page, Glenda Jackson, Sandy Dennis, Anne Jackson

Eli Wallach, Jerry Stiller
Above: Melina Mercouri

THE DOMINO PRINCIPLE

(AVCO EMBASSY) Executive Producer, Martin Starger; Producer-Director, Stanley Kramer; Screenplay, Adam Kennedy; Based on his novel; Associate Producer, Terry Morse, Jr; Assistant Director, Michael S. Glick; Designer, Bill Creber; Art Director, Ron Hobbs; Photography, Fred Koenekamp, Ernest Laszlo; Editor, John Burnett; Composer, Billy Goldenberg; Costumes, Rita Riggs; In color and Panavision; Presented by Sir Lew Grade for Associated General Films; 100 minutes; Rated R; March release.

CAST

Roy Tucker	Gene Hackman
Ellie Tucker	Candice Bergen
Tagge	Richard Widmark
Spiventa	Mickey Rooney
Ross Pine	Edward Albert
General Tom Reser	Eli Wallach
Ditcher	Ken Swofford
Gaddis	Neva Patterson
Captain Ruiz	Jay Novello
Ruby	Claire Brennan
Schnaible	Ted Gehring
Bowcamp	Joseph Perry
Mrs. Schnaible	Majel Barrett
Lenny	Jim Gavin
Henemeyer	George Fisher
Murdock	Denver Mattson
Brookshire	Bob Herron
Nebraska	Wayne King
Harley	Charles Horvath
Truck Driver	Bear Hudkins
Bank Official	Farnesio De Bernal
Travel Agency Girl	Patricia Luke
Assassination Victim	George Sawaya

Left: Gene Hackman, Candice Bergen

Gene Hackman, Richard Widmark
Above: Mickey Rooney, Gene Hackman

Richard Widmark, Candice Bergen, Gene Hackman
Above: Edward Albert, Eli Wallach

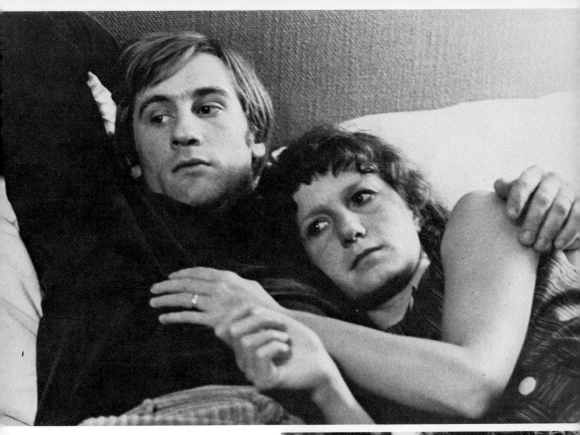

Gerard Depardieu, Dominique Labourier

THE WONDERFUL CROOK

(NEW YORKER FILMS) Executive Producers, Yves Gasser,
Yves Peyrot; Direction and Screenplay, Claude Goretta; Photog-
raphy, Renato Berta; Editor, Joele Van Effenterre; Music, Arie
Dzierlatka, Patrick Moraz; Design, Serge Etter, Nicolas Philibert;
Costumes, Charlotte Dubreuil, Monique Tourret; In color; 112
minutes; March release.

CAST

Pierre	Gerard Depardieu
Nelly	Marlene Jobert
Marthe	Dominique Labourier
Julien	Philippe Leotard
Pierre's Father	Jacques Debary
Foreman Francois	Michel Robin
Drunkard	Paul Crauchet
Couple	Pierre Walker, Marblum Jequier

Gerard Depardieu, Marlene Jobert

THE EAGLE HAS LANDED

(COLUMBIA) Producers, Jack Winer, David Niven, Jr.; Director, John Sturges; Screenplay, Tom Mankiewicz; Based on novel by Jack Higgins; Photography, Tony Richmond, Peter Allwork; Designer, Peter Murton; Art Director, Charles Bishop; Assistant Director, David Anderson; Editor, Irene Lamb; In color; 134 minutes; Rated PG; March release.

CAST

Col. Kurt Steiner	Michael Caine
Liam Devlin	Donald Sutherland
Col. Max Radl	Robert Duvall
Molly Prior	Jenny Agutter
Heinrich Himmler	Donald Pleasence
Admiral Wilhelm Canaris	Anthony Quayle
Joanna Grey	Jean Marsh
Capt. Ritter Neumann	Sven-Bertil Taube
Father Philip Verecker	John Standing
Pamela Verecker	Judy Geeson
Capt. Harry Clark	Treat Williams
Col. Clarence E. Pitts	Larry Hagman
Sgt. Brandt	Siegfried Rauch

Top: Michael Caine, Sven-Bertil Taube, Robert Duvall Right: John Standing, Caine

Leigh Dilley (C) Above: Michael Caine, Donald Sutherland Left: Sutherland, Jenny Agutter

MOTHER KUSTERS GOES TO HEAVEN

(NEW YORKER FILMS) Director, Rainer Werner Fassbinder; Screenplay, Mr. Fassbinder, Kurt Raab; Photography, Michael Ballhaus; Music, Peer Raben; Editor, Thea Eymesz; A Tango Film in color; German with English subtitles; 108 minutes; March release.

CAST

Mother Kusters	Brigitte Mira
Corinna Corinne, her daughter	Ingrid Caven
Ernst, her son	Armin Meier
Helene, her daughter-in-law	Irm Hermann
Journalist	Gottfried John
Mr. Thalmann	Karlheinz Bohm
Mrs. Thalmann	Margit Carstensen
Nightclub Manager	Peter Kern

Right: Brigitte Mira, Armin Meier

Karlheinz Bohm, Brigitte Mira, Margit Carstensen

THE HOUSE BY THE LAKE

(AMERICAN INTERNATIONAL) Formerly "Death Week-end"; Executive Producers, Andre Link, John Dunning; Producer, Ivan Reitman; Direction and Screenplay, William Fruet; Editors, Jean Lafleur, Debbie Karjala; Assistant Director, Gary Flanagan; Costumes, Erla Gliserman; In Movielab Color; 89 minutes; Rated R; March release.

CAST

Diane	Brenda Vaccaro
Lep	Don Stroud
Harry	Chuck Shamata
Runt	Richard Ayres
Frankie	Kyle Edwards
Stanley	Don Gransberry
Spragg	Ed McNamara
Ralph	Michael Kirby
Policeman	Richard Donat
Smokey	Denver Mattson
Mr. Doobie	Al Bernardo
Mrs. Doobie	Roselle Stone
Campground Girl	Elaine Yarish

Left: Chuck Shumata, Brenda Vaccaro, also below with Don Stroud

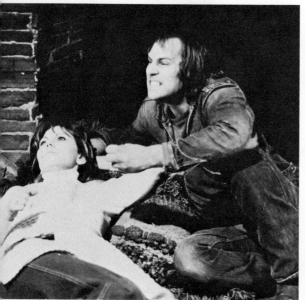

Brenda Vaccaro, Don Stroud

Brenda Vaccaro, and above with Don Stroud

THE LITTLEST HORSE THIEVES

(BUENA VISTA) Formerly "Escape from the Dark"; Producer, Ron Miller; Director, Charles Jarrott; Screenplay, Rosemary Anne Sisson; Story, Miss Sisson and Burt Kennedy; Associate Producer, Hugh Attwooll; Photography, Paul Beeson; Music, Ron Goodwin; Art Director, Robert Laing; Editor, Richard Marden; Costumes, John Furniss; Assistant Director, Allan James; In Technicolor; 104 minutes; Rated G; March release.

CAST

Lord Harrogate	Alastair Sim
Richard Sandman	Peter Barkworth
Luke Armstrong	Maurice Colbourne
Violet	Susan Tebbs
Miss Coutts	Geraldine McEwan
Bert	Joe Gladwin
Dave	Andrew Harrison
Tommy Sadler	Benjie Bolgar
Alice Sandman	Chloe Franks
Mrs. Sandman	Prunella Scales
Foreman Carter	Leslie Sands

and Jeremy Bulloch, Derek Newark, Duncan Lamont, Ian Hogg, Richard Warner, Don Henderson, Tommy Wright, John Hartley, Ken Kitson, Peter Geddis, Roy Evans, Gordon Kaye, James Marcus, Donald Bisset, Gordon Christie

Top: Flash, Chloe Franks, Benjie Bolgar, Andrew Harrison

Chloe Franks, Benjie Bolgar

159

MOHAMMAD, MESSENGER OF GOD

(ANTHONY BIRLEY-TARIK FILMS) Producer-Director, Moustapha Akkad; Screenplay, H. A. L. Craig; Photography, Jack Hildyard; Music, Maurice Jarre; A Filmco International Production in Panavision and Eastmancolor; Editor, Jack Bloom; Rated PG; 180 minutes; March release.

CAST

Hamza	Anthony Quinn
Hind	Irene Papas
Bu-Sofyan	Michael Ansara
Bilal	Johnny Sekka
Khalid	Michael Forest
Zaid	Damien Thomas
Ammar	Garrick Hagon

and Ronald Chenery, Michael Godfrey, Peter Madden, Habib Ageli, George Camiller, Neville Jason, Martin Benson, Robert Brown, Wolfe Morris, Bruno Barnabe, John Humphry, John Bennett, Donald Burton, Andre Morell, Rosalie Crutchley, Ewen Solon, Elaine Ives Cameron, Nicholas Amer, Gerard Hely, Hassan Joundi, Earl Cameron, Ronald Leigh-Hunt, Leonard Trolley, Wahshi, Mohammad Al Gaddary

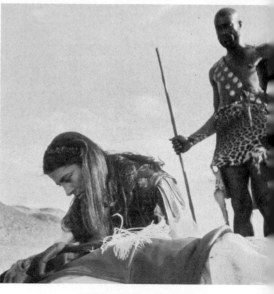

Top: Anthony Quinn Below: Johnny Sekka, Michael Ansara

Anthony Quinn, Irene Papas
Top: Irene Papas

UNCLE VANYA

(ARTHUR CANTOR) Producer, Chichester Festival of 1963; Director, Laurence Olivier; Director for film, Stuart Burge; Written by Anton Chekhov; Translation, Constance Garnett; A British Home Entertainment Production in black and white; 120 minutes; March release.

CAST

Nurse	Sybil Thorndike
Astrov	Laurence Olivier
Vanya	Michael Redgrave
Telyegin	Lewis Casson
Sonya	Joan Plowright
Ilyena	Rosemary Harris
Maman	Fay Compton
Yefim	Robert Lang
Professor	Max Adrian

Right: Michael Redgrave, Joan Plowright

Robert Lang, Rosemary Harris, Joan Plowright, Max Adrian, Michael Redgrave, Sybil Thorndike, Laurence Olivier, Lewis Casson

LES ZOZOS

(BAUER INTERNATIONAL) Producer, Albina du Boisrouvray; Director-Editor, Pascal Thomas; Screenplay, Pascal Thomas, Roland Duval; Photography, Colin Mounier; Music, Vladimir Cosma; In color; French with English sub-titles; 105 minutes; April release.

CAST

Frederic	Frederic Duru
Francois	Edmond Railard
Paringaux	Jean-Marc Chollet
Venus	Jean-Claude Antezack
Uncle Jacques	Daniel Ceccaldi
Elisabeth	Annie Cole
Martine	Virginie Thevenet
Nelly	Caroline Cartier
Jacqueline	Michele Andre
French teacher	Serge Rousseau
Vice Principal	Jacques Debary

Left: Frederic Duru, Edmond Railard, Jean-Marc Chollet

Daniel Ceccaldi Above: Annie Cole, Frederic Duru

Frederic Duru, Edmond Railard

AGUIRRE, THE WRATH OF GOD

(NEW YORKER) Produced, Directed and Written by Werner
Herzog; Photography, Thomas Mauch; Music, Popol Vuh; Editor, Beate Mainka-Jellinghaus; In color; German with English
sub-titles; 90 minutes; April release.

CAST

Don Lope de Aguirre	Klaus Kinski
Don Pedro de Ursua	Ruy Guerra
Brother Gaspar de Carvajal	Del Negro
Inez (wife of Ursua)	Helena Rojo
Flores (daughter of Aguirre)	Cecilia Rivera
Don Fernando de Guzman	Peter Berling
Perucho	Dany Ades

Top: Klaus Kinski, Helena Rojo

Klaus Kinski

MAN ON THE ROOF

(CINEMA 5) Directed, Written and Edited by Bo Widerberg;
Based on novel "The Abominable Man" by Maj Sjowall and Per
Wahloo; Music, Bjorn Jason Lindh; Produced by Svensk Filmin-
dustri and Svenska Institutet; Photography, Odd Geir Safther; In
color; Swedish with English sub-titles; 110 minutes; Rated R;
April release.

CAST

Martin Beck	Carl-Gustaf Lindstedt
Lennart Kollberg	Sven Wollter
Mrs. Kollberg	Eva Remaeus
Gunvald Larsson	Thomas Hellberg
Einar Roenn	Hakan Serner
Mrs. Nyman	Birgitta Valberg
Stefan Nyman (her son)	Harald Hamrell
Ake Eriksson	Ingvar Hirdvall
Father Eriksson	Gus Dahlstroem
Mother Eriksson	Bellan Roos
Superintendent Malm	Torgny Anderberg
Melander	Folke Hjort
Hult	Carl Axel Heiknert

Right: Sven Wollter

Thomas Hellberg, Sven Wollter   **Carl Axel Heiknert, Carl-Gustaf Lindstedt**

THE WILD DUCK

(NEW YORKER) Producer, Bernd Eichinger; Direction and
Screenplay, Hans W. Geissendorfer; Photography, Harry Nap;
Editor, Gunther Witte; Music, Nils Janette Walen; A Solaris Film
Production in cooperation with Sascha Film/Wien and the West
German Broadcasting Company; Based on play by Henrik Ibsen;
in color; German with English subtitles; 100 minutes; April re-
ease.

CAST

Gina	Jean Seberg
Hjalmar	Peter Kern
Gregers	Bruno Ganz
Hedwig	Anne Bennent
Old Ekdal	Martin Florchinger
Relling	Heinz Bennent
Consul	Heinz Moog
Mrs. Sorby	Sonja Sutter
Molvik	Robert Werner
Petersen	Guido Wieland

Top: Peter Kern, Anne Bennent

Anne Bennent

165

CHINESE ROULETTE

(NEW YORKER) Produced, Directed and Written by Rainer Werner Fassbinder; Photography, Michael Ballhaus; Editor, Ila von Hasperg; Music, Peer Raben; In color; German with English sub-titles; 96 minutes; April release.

CAST

Ariane	Margit Carstensen
Kolbe	Ulli Lommel
Irene	Anna Karina
Gerhard	Alexander Allerson
Angela	Andrea Schober
Traunitz	Macha Meril
Kast	Brigitte Mira
Gabriel	V. Spengler

Right: Margit Carstensen, Anna Karina

Anna Karina, Alexander Allerson

166

JACOB THE LIAR

(MacMILLAN FILMS) Director, Frank Beyer; Screenplay, Jurek Becker from his novel; Photography, Gunter Marczinkowsky; Music, Joachim Werzlau; Editor, Rita Hiller; Costumes, Joachim Dittrich; Assistant Directors, Harold Fischer, Gunter Hoffmann; English Translation, Melvin Kornfeld; In German with English subtitles; In color; 95 minutes; April release.

CAST

Jacob	Vlastimil Brodsky
Kowalski	Erwin Geschonneck
Lena	Manuela Simon
Misha	Henry Hubchen
Rosa	Blanche Kommerell
Herr Frankfurter	Dezso Garas
Frau Frankfurter	Suzana Gordon
Prof. Kirschbaum	Friedrich Richter

Right: Vlastimil Brodsky, Manuela Simon

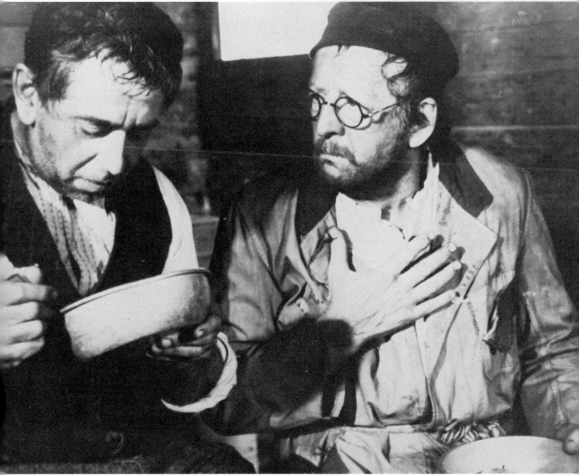

Vlastimil Brodsky (L)

ALICE IN THE CITIES

(BAUER INTERNATIONAL) Producer, Peter Genee; Director, Wim Wenders; Screenplay, Wim Wenders, Veith der Furstenberg; Photography, Robbie Muller, Martin Schafer; Editors, Peter Przygodda, Barbara von Weitershausen; Music CAN; A West German film in black and white; 110 minutes; April release.

CAST

Philip Winter .... Rudiger Vogler
Alice van Damn .... Yella Rottlander
Lisa van Damn .... Lisa Kreuzer
Edda .... Edda Kochl
Girl .... Didi Petrikat
Policeman .... Ernest Bohm
Car Salesman .... Sam Presti
Airline Girl .... Lois Moran
and Sibylle Baier, Hans Hirschmuller, Mirko

Right: Yella Rottlander

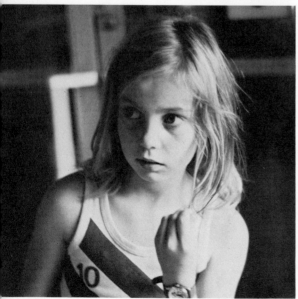

Yella Rottlander
Above: Rudiger Vogler

Rudiger Vogler, Yella Rottlander
Above: Lisa Kreuzer, Rudiger Vogler

CROSS OF IRON

(AVCO EMBASSY) Producer, Wolf C. Hartwig; Director, Sam Peckinpah; Screenplay, Julius J.Epstein, Herbert Asmodi; From book "The Cross of Iron" by Willi Heinrich; Photography, John Coquillon; Editors, Tony Lawson, Mike Ellis; Designers, Ted Haworth, Brian Ackland Snow; Music, Ernest Gold; Assistant Directors, Bert Batt, Chris Carreras; In Technicolor; 133 minutes; Rated R; May release.

CAST

Steiner	James Coburn
Stransky	Maximilian Schell
Brandt	James Mason
Kiesel	David Warner
Kruger	Klaus Lowitsch
Kern	Vadim Glowna
Triebig	Roger Fritz
Anselm	Dieter Schidor
Maag	Burkhardt Driest
Schnurrbart	Fred Stillkraut
Dietz	Michael Nowka
Marga	Veronique Vendell
Zoll	Arthur Brauss
Eva	Senta Berger
Mikael	Slavco Stimac

Top: Maximilian Schell, James Coburn
Below: James Mason

James Coburn, Senta Berger Above: Roger Fritz,
Maximilian Schell Top: David Warner   **169**

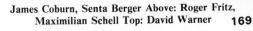

Jose Luis Lopez Vasquez, Lina Canalejas

Maria Clara Fernandez

COUSIN ANGELICA

(NEW YORKER) Producer, Elias Querejeta; Director, Carlos Saura; Screenplay, Rafael Azcona, Carlos Saura; Photography, Luis Cuadrado; Editor, Pablo Del Amo; Music, Luis De Pablo; Art Director, Roberto Parra; In Spanish with English sub-titles; In color; 106 minutes; May release.

CAST

Luis .... Jose Luis Lopez Vazquez
Angelica (as a woman) .... Lina Canalejas
Angelica (as a child) .... Maria Clara Fernandez
Anselmo .... Fernando Delgado
Aunt Pilar (aged) .... Josefina Diaz
Aunt Pilar (middle aged) .... Lola Cardona
Nun .... Julieta Serrano
Luis' mother .... Encarna Paso
Luis' father .... Pedro Sempson

REBELLION IN PATAGONIA

(TRICONTINENTAL FILM CENTER) Producer, Fernando
Ayala; Director, Hector Olivera; Associate Producer, Luis Osvaldo Repetto; Screenplay, Osvaldo Bayer, Fernando Ayala, Hec-
or Olivera; Based on "The Avengers of Tragic Patagonia" by
Osvaldo Bayer; Photography, Victor Hugo Caula; Music, Oscar
Cardozo Ocamp; Costumes, Maria Julia Bertotto; Editor, Oscar
Montauti; Assistant Director, Horacio Guisado; In Eastmancolor; In Spanish with English subtitles; 109 minutes; May re-
ease.

CAST

Antonio Soto	Luis Brandoni
Jose Font (Facon Grande)	Federico Luppi
Schultz	Pepe Soriano
Outerello	Osvaldo Terranova
Commander Zavala	Hector Alterio
Felix Novas	Pedro Aleandro
Mendez Garzon	Jose Maria Gutierrez
Minister Gomez	Alfredo Iglesias
Don Bernardo	Carlos Munoz
Carballeira	Eduardo Munoz
Captain Arzeno	Hector Pelegrini
Mathews	Jorge Rivera Lopez
Gaucho Cuello	Jorge Villalba
Danielewski	Max Berliner
Judge Velar	Juan Pablo Boyadgian
Farina, the Chilean	Franklin Caicedo
Grana, the Spaniard	Fernando Iglesias
Don Federico	Maurice Jouvet
Seriff Micheri	Claudio Lucero
The Tuscan	Mario Luciani
Sergeant	Antonio Monaco
The "68"	Luis Orbegozo

JABBERWOCKY

(**CINEMA 5**) Producer, Sandy Lieberson; Director, Terry Gilliam; Executive Producer, John Goldstone; Screenplay, Charles Alverson, Terry Gilliam; Associate Producer, Julian Doyle; Photography, Terry Bedford; Editor, Michael Bradsell; Designer, Roy Smith; Art Director, Millie Burns; Costumes, Hazel Pethig, Charles Knode; Music, De Wolfe; An Umbrella Entertainment Production; A Michael White Presentation in color; 100 minutes; Rated PG; May release.

CAST

Dennis Cooper	Michael Palin
King Bruno the Questionable	Max Wall
Princess	Deborah Fallender
Chamberlain	John Le Mesurier
Griselda Fishfinger	Annette Badland
Mr. Fishfinger	Warren Mitchell
Mrs. Fishfinger	Brenda Cowling
Squires	Harry H. Corbett, Rodney Bewes
Landlord	Bernard Bresslaw
Betsy	Alexandra Dane
Bishop	Derek Francis
Merchants	Peter Cellier, Frank Williams, Anthony Carrick
Herald	John Bird
Herald and Drummer	Neil Innes
Mr. Cooper, Sr	Paul Curran
Fanatics' Leader	Graham Crowden
King's Taster	Gordon Rollings
Gate Guards	Glenn Williams, Bryan Pringle
Poacher	Terry Jones
Armourer	Brian Glover
Prince	Simon Williams
Sister Jessica	Gordon Kaye
Wat Dabney	Jerrold Wells
Red Herring Knight/Black Knight	Dave Prowse
Peasants	John Gorman, Julian Hough, Harold Goodwin, Tony Sympson

**Right: Deborah Fallender, Michael Palin
Top: Michael Palin**

Michael Palin, Annette Badland

Deborah Fallender

172

WE ALL LOVED EACH OTHER SO MUCH

(CINEMA 5) Producers, Pio Angeletti, Adriano De Micheli; Director, Ettore Scola; Screenplay, Age, Scarpelli, Scola; Photography, Claudio Cirillo; Music, Armando Trovaioli; Editor, Raimondo Crociani; In color, black and white; 124 minutes; May release

CAST

Giovanni	Vittorio Gassman
Antonio	Nino Manfredi
Luciana	Stefania Sandrelli
Nicola	Stefano Satta Flores
Elide	Giovanna Ralli
Catenacci	Aldo Fabrizi
Boarding House Landlady	Isa Barzizza
Nicola's Wife	Marcella Michelangeli
Themselves	Federico Fellini, Marcello Mastroianni, Vittorio De Sica

EQUINOX FLOWER

(NEW YORKER) Director, Yasujiro Ozu; Screenplay, Yasujiro Ozu, Kogo Noda; Based on novel by Ton Satomi; Photography, Yushun Atsuta; Art Director, Tatsuo Hamada; Music, Takayori Saito; Editor, Yoshiyasu Hamamura; In color; 118 minutes; May release.

CAST

Wataru Hirayama	Shin Saburi
Kiyoko Hirayama	Kinuyo Tanaka
Setsuko Hirayama	Ineko Arima
Hisako Hirayama	Miyuki Kuwano
Masahiko Taniguchi	Keiji Sada
Hajime Sasaki	Chieko Naniwa
Yukiko Sasaki	Fujiko Yamamoto
Toshihiko Kawai	Nobuo Nakamura
Shukichi Mikami	Chishu Ryu
Fumiko Mikami	Yoshiko Kuga
Shotaro Kondo	Teiji Takahashi
Ichiro Naganuma	Fumio Watanabe

Left: Ineko Arima, Fujiko Yamamoto,
Yoshiko Kuga Top: Yoshiko Kuga,
Shin Saburi

THE LITTLE GIRL WHO LIVES DOWN THE LANE

(AMERICAN INTERNATIONAL) Producer, Zev Braun; Executive Producers, Harold Greenberg, Alfred Pariser; Director, Nicolas Gessner; Screenplay, Laird Koenig from his novel; Co-Producers, Denis Heroux, Leland Nolan, Eugene Lepicier; Photography, Rene Verzier; Score, Christian Gaubert; Editor, Yves Langlois; Costumes, Denis Sperdouklis, Valentino; In color; 94 minutes; Rated PG; May release.

CAST

Rynn	Jodie Foster
Frank Hallet	Martin Sheen
Mrs. Hallet	Alexis Smith
Miglioriti	Mort Shuman
Mario	Scott Jacoby
Town Hall Clerk	Dorothy Davis
Bank Manager	Clesson Goodhur
Bank Clerks	Hubert Noel, Jacques Famery
Tellers	Mary Morter, Judie Wildman

Martin Sheen, Jodie Foster

Eva Mattes, Harry Baer

JAIL BAIT

(NEW YORKER) Formerly titled "Wild Game"; Direction and Screenplay, Rainer Werner Fassbinder; Based on play by Franz Xaver Kroetz; Photography, Dietrich Lohmann; Editor, Thea Eymesz; Art Director, Kurt Raab; Music, Ludwig von Beethoven; Produced by Intertel in color; In German with English subtitles; 99 minutes; May release.

CAST

Hanni .... Eva Mattes
Franz .... Harry Baer
Erwin (Hanni's father) ....Jorg von Liebenfels
Hilda (Hanni's mother) .... Ruth Drexel
Franz's Friends .... El Hedi Ben Salem,
Rudolph Waldemar Brem
Doctor ....Hanna Schygulla
Boss ....Kurt Raab
Policeman ....Karl Scheydt, Klaus Lowitsch
Police Officials.........................Irm Hermann, Marquand Bohm

GODS OF THE PLAGUE

(NEW YORKER) Direction and Screenplay, Rainer Werner Fassbinder; Photography, Dietrich Lohmann; Editor, Franz Walsch; Music, Peer Raben; Produced by Antiteater; In black and white; 90 minutes; June release.

CAST

Franz Walsch .... Harry Baer
Guenther ("Gorilla") .... Guenther Kaufmann
Johanna ....Hanna Schygulla
Margarethe ....Margarethe von Trotta
Carla .... Carla Aulaulu
Magdalena Fuller ....Ingrid Caven
Policeman .... Jan George
Marian Walsch .... Marian Seidowski
Pornography Customer.....................Rainer Werner Fassbinder

Harry Baer, Ingrid Caven

KATZELMACHER

(NEW YORKER) Direction and Screenplay, Rainer Werner Fassbinder; Photography, Dietrich Lohmann; Editor, Franz Walsch; Music, Peer Raben after Franz Schubert; Produced by Antiteater; In black and white; 88 minutes; June release.

CAST

Marie	Hanna Schygulla
Erich	Hans Hirschmueller
Helga	Lilith Ungerer
Paul	Rudolf Waldemar Brem
Rosy	Elga Sorbas
Franz	Harry Baer
Elisabeth	Irm Hermann
Peter	Peter Moland
Gunda	Doris Mattes
Jorgos	Rainer Werner Fassbinder

Hanna Schygulla, Hans Hirschmuller, Rudolph Waldemar Brem, Lilith Ungerer Top: Lilith Ungerer, Rudolf Waldemar Brem

Marc Chagall

HOMAGE TO CHAGALL

"The Colours of Love"; Produced, Directed and Written by Harry Rasky; Narrated by James Mason and Joseph Wiseman; Photography, Kenneth W. Grigg; Editor, Aria Saare; Music, Louis Applebaum; In color, 90 minutes; Not rated; June release. A documentary on the life and art of Marc Chagall.

LA GRANDE BOURGEOISE

(ATLANTIC/BUCKLEY BROS.) Formerly "The Murri Affair"; Produced by Lira Films-Filmarpa/Rome; Director, Mauro Bolognini; Photography, Ennio Guarnieri; Music, Ennio Morricone; In color; 115 minutes; Not rated; July release.

CAST

Linda Murri	Catherine Deneuve
Tullio Murri	Giancarlo Giannini
Augusto Murri	Fernando Rey
Rosa Bonetti	Tina Aumont
Francesco Bonmartini	Paolo Bonicelli
Pio Naldi	Corrada Pani
Carlo Secchi	Eltore Mani
Augusto Stanzani	Marcel Bozzuffi

Top; Giancarlo Giannini, Catherine Deneuve
Below: Giancarlo Giannini

Catherine Deneuve, Giancarlo Giannini
Above: Fernando Rey, Deneuve

TOUCHED IN THE HEAD

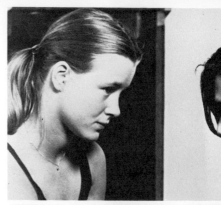

(BAUER INTERNATIONAL) Producer-Director, Jacques Doillon; Screenplay, Jacques Doillon, Philippe Defrance; Photography, Yves Lafaye; Editor, Noelle Boisson; Art Director, Manuel Durouchoux; In black and white; 104 minutes; July release.

CAST
Liv	Ann Zacharias
Chris	Christophe Soto
Leon	Olivier Bousquet
Rosette	Roselyne Villaume
Boss	Martin Thevieres
Union Official	Pierre Fabien
Replacement	Gabriel Bernard
Commune girl	Marilyn Even
Girl on grass	Joelle Marin
Ping Pong player	Alain Vibe

Right: Ann Zacharias, Christophe Soto, Olivier Bousquet Top: Ann Zacharias, Christophe Soto

Ann Zacharias, Christophe Soto, Olivier Bousquet, Roselyne Villaume

STROSZEK

(NEW YORKER) Produced, Directed and Written by Werner Herzog; Photography, Thomas Mauch; Assistant Director, Ed Lachman; Editor, Beate Mainka-Jellinghaus; Music, Chet Atkins, Sonny Terry; German with English subtitles; 108 minutes; In color; Not rated; July release.

CAST

Stroszek .... Bruno S.
Eva.. Eva Mattes
Scheitz .... Clemens Scheitz
Pimps........................Wilhelm von Homburg, Burkhard Driest
Scheitz's Nephew .... Clayton Szlapinski
Indian ....Ely Rodriguez
Prison Governor .... Alfred Edel
Bank Employee .... Scott McKain
Auctioneer .... Ralph Wade

Top Right: Bruno S. (R)

Eva Mattes, Bruno S.

THE SPY WHO LOVED ME

(UNITED ARTISTS) Producer, Albert R. Broccoli; Director, Lewis Gilbert; Screenplay, Christopher Wood, Richard Maibaum; Designer, Ken Adam; Music, Marvin Hamlisch; Theme Song, Marvin Hamlisch, Carole Bayer Sager; Performed by Carly Simon; Photography, Claude Renoir; Editor, John Glen; In color; 125 minutes; Rated PG; July release.

CAST

James Bond	Roger Moore
Major Anya Amasova	Barbara Bach
Stromberg	Curt Jurgens
Jaws	Richard Kiel
Naomi	Caroline Munro
General Gogol	Walter Gotell
Minister of Defense	Geoffrey Keen
"M"	Bernard Lee
Captain Benson	George Baker
Captain Carter	Shana Rimmer
Commander Talbot	Bryan Marshall
Sergei	Michael Billington
Felicca	Olga Bisera
"Q"	Desmond Llewelyn
Sheik Hosein	Edward De Souza
Max Kalba	Vernon Dobtcheff
Hotel Receptionist	Valerie Leon
Miss Moneypenny	Lois Maxwell
Liparus Captain	Sydney Tafler
Fekkesh	Nadim Sawalha
Log Cabin Girl	Sue Vanner
Arab Beauties	Felicity York, Dawn Rodrigues, Anika Pavel, Jill Goodall

Left: Roger Moore, Barbara Bach

Barbara Bach, Curt Jurgens, Roger Moore

Roger Moore, Barbara Bach Top: (L) Dawn Rodrigues, Jill Goodall, Roger Moore,
Anika Pavel, Felicity York (R) Moore, Richard Kiel Below: Moore, Milton Reid

183

OUTRAGEOUS!

(CINEMA 5) Producers, William Marshall, Hendrick J. Van Der
Kolk; Direction and Screenplay, Richard Benner; Based on story
from "Butterfly Ward" by Margaret Gibson; Music, Paul Hoffert;
Associate Producer, Peter O'Brien; Photography, James B. Kelly;
Editor, George Appleby; Original Lyrics, Brenda Hoffert; Assis-
tant Director, Barbara Laffey; Art Director, Karen Bromley;
Gowns, Michael Daniels; A Herbert R. Steinmann-Billy Baxter
presentation; In Eastmancolor; 100 minutes; August release.

CAST

Robin Turner	Craig Russell
Liza Connors	Hollis McLaren
Perry	Richard Easley
Martin	Allan Moyle
Bob	David McIlwraith
Jason	Gerry Salzberg
Anne	Andree Pelletier
Jo	Helen Shaver
Nurse Carr	Martha Gibson
Mrs. Connors	Helen Hughes
Dr. Beddoes	Jonah Royston
Stewart	Richard Moffatt
Hustler	David Woito
Jimmy	Rusty Ryan
Miss Montego Bay	Trevor Bryan
Jackie Loren	Jackie Loren
Performer in gold	Michael Daniels
Drunk	Mike Ironside
Manatee D. J.	Rene Fortier
Peggy O'Brien	Maxine Miller
Performer in pink	Michel

**Craig Russell, and top
with Hollis McLaren**

184

JOSEPH ANDREWS

(PARAMOUNT) Producer, Neil Hartley; Director, Tony Richardson; Screenplay, Allan Scott, Chris Bryant; Story, Tony Richardson from novel by Henry Fielding; Photography, David Watkin; Editor, Thom Noble; Music, John Addison; Songs, Bob Stewart, Jim Dale; Design, Michael Annals; Art Director, Bill Brosie; Assistant Director, Andrew Grieve; In Movielab Color; 103 minutes; Rated R; September release.

CAST

Lady Booby .... Ann-Margret
Joseph Andrews .... Peter Firth
Parson Adamis .... Michael Hordern
Mrs. Slipslop .... Beryl Reid
Peddler .... Jim Dale
Fanny Goodwill .... Natalie Ogle
Sir Thomas Booby .... Peter Bull
Wicked Squire .... Kenneth Cranham
Pamela .... Karen Dotrice
Mr. Booby .... James Villiers

Right: Ann-Margret, Beryl Reid Below:
Peter Bull, Ann-Margret, Peter Firth

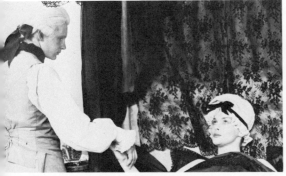

Peter Firth, Ann-Margret
(also above)

Peter Firth, Ann-Margret

185

THE AMERICAN FRIEND

(NEW YORKER) Direction and Screenplay, Wim Wenders; Based on novel "Ripley's Game" by Patricia Highsmith; Photography, Robby Muller; Editor, Peter Przygodda; Music, Jurgen Knieper; Assistant Directors, Fritz Muller-Scherz, Emmanuel Clot, Serge Brodskis; Art Director, Sickerts; German with English subtitles; In color; 127 minutes; Not rated; September release.

CAST

Jonathan Zimmermann	Bruno Ganz
Tom Ripley	Dennis Hopper
Marianne Zimmermann	Lisa Kreuzer
Raoul Minot	Gerard Blain
Derwatt	Nicholas Ray
The American	Samuel Fuller
Marcangelo	Peter Lilienthal
Ingraham	Daniel Schmid
Friendly Man	Jean Eustache
Gantner	Rudolf Schundler
Doctor in Paris	Sandy Whitelaw
Rodolphe	Lou Castel

Left: Dennis Hopper

Bruno Ganz

Bruno Ganz, Dennis Hopper
Above: Lisa Kreuzer, Bruno Ganz

THE MAN WHO LOVED WOMEN

(CINEMA 5) Director, Francois Truffaut; Screenplay, Francois Truffaut, Michel Fermaud, Suzanne Schiffman; Music, Maurice Jaubert; Photography, Nestor Almendros; Editor, Martine Barraque-Curie; In color; French with English subtitles; 119 minutes; Not rated; September release.

CAST

Vera	Leslie Caron
Bertrand Morane	Charles Denner
Genevieve Bigey	Brigitte Fossey
Delphine Grezel	Nelly Borgeaud
Helene	Genevieve Fontanel
Martine Desdoits	Nathalie Baye
Doctor	Jean Daste
Bernadette	Sabine Glaser
Fabienne	Valerie Bonnier

Top: Brigitte Fossey, Charles Denner
Top Right: Leslie Caron

Charles Denner
Above: Nelly Borgeaud

A SPECIAL DAY

(CINEMA 5) Producer, Carlo Ponti; Director, Ettore Scola; Story and Screenplay, Ruggero Maccari, Ettore Scola, Maurizio Costanzo; Music, Armando Trovaioli; Photography, Pasqualino De Santis; Editor, Raimondo Crociani; Assistant Directors, Silvio Ferri, Claude Fournier; Costumes, Enrico Sabbatini; A Canadian-Italian Co-Production in color; 110 minutes; Not rated; October release.

CAST

Antonietta	Sophia Loren
Gabriele	Marcello Mastroianni
Emanuele	John Vernon
Caretaker	Francoise Berd
Figlia Del Cavaliere	Nicole Magny
Romana	Patrizia Basso
Arnaldo	Tiziano De Persio
Fabio	Maurizio Di Paolantonio
Littorio	Antonio Garibaldi
Umberto	Vittorio Guerrieri
Maria Luisa	Allessandra Mussolini

Sophia Loren, and top
with Marcello Mastroianni

188

Sophia Loren, Marcello Mastroianni
(also top)

THE LACEMAKER

(NEW YORKER) Executive Producers, Yves Peyrot, Yves Gasser; Associate Producers, Klaus Hellwig, Lise Fayolle; Director, Claude Goretta, Pascal Laine; From novel by Pascal Laine; Photography, Jean Boffety; Editor, Joele Van Effenterre; Music, Pierre Jansen; In color; French with English subtitles; 108 minutes; Not rated; October release.

CAST

Pomme	Isabelle Huppert
Francois	Yves Beneyton
Marylene	Florence Giorgetti
Pomme's Mother	Anne Marie Duringer
Francois' Friend	Renata Schroeter
The Painter	Michel De Re
Francois' Mother	Monique Chaumette
Francois' Father	Jean Obe

Right: Isabelle Huppert

Yves Beneyton, Isabelle Huppert

VALENTINO

(UNITED ARTISTS) Producers, Irwin Winkler, Robert Chartoff; Director, Ken Russell; Screenplay, Ken Russell, Mardik Martin; Associate Producer, Harry Benn; Music, Ferde Grofe, Stanley Black; Photography, Peter Suschitzky; Art Director, Philip Harrison; Costumes, Shirley Russell; Editor, Stuart Baird; Choreography, Gillian Gregory; Assistant Director, Jonathan Benson; In color; 132 minutes; October release.

CAST

Rudolph Valentino	Rudolf Nureyev
Nazimova	Leslie Caron
Natasha Rambova	Michelle Phillips
"Fatty's" Girl	Carol Kane
June Mathis	Felicity Kendal
George Ullman	Seymour Cassel
Rory O'Neil	Peter Vaughan
Jesse Lasky	Huntz Hall
Joseph Schenck	David De Keyser
Richard Rowland	Alfred Marks
Baron Long	Anton Diffring
Agnes Ayres	Jennie Linden
"Fatty"	William Hootkins
Jail Cop	Bill McKinney
George Melford	Don Fellows
Sidney Olcott	John Justin
Billie Streeter	Linda Thorson
Bianca De Saulles	June Bolton
Lorna Sinclair	Penny Milford
Willie	Dudley Sutton
Jack De Saulles	Robin Brent Clarke
Vaslav Nijinsky	Anthony Dowell

**Top: Michelle Phillips, Rudolf Nureyev
Below: Carol Kane Top Right: Nureyev,
Seymour Cassel**

**Rudolf Nureyev Above: Michelle
Phillips, Leslie Caron**

THAT OBSCURE OBJECT OF DESIRE

(FIRST ARTISTS) Executive Producer, Serge Silberman; Director, Luis Bunuel; Screenplay, Luis Bunuel, Jean-Claude Carriere; From novel "La Femme et Le Pantin" by Pierre Louys; Photography, Edmond Richard; Editor, Helene Plemiannikov; Art Director, Pierre Guffroy; In color; 100 minutes; Rated R; November release.

CAST

Mathieu	Fernando Rey
Conchita	Carole Bouquet, Angela Molina
Judge	Julien Bertheau
Traveler	Milena Vukotic
Psychologist	Pieral

Left: Carole Bouquet, Fernando Rey

Fernando Rey, Angela Molina

Carole Bouquet, Fernando Rey
(also top)

Susannah MacMillan

THE CONFESSIONS OF AMANS

(BAUER INTERNATIONAL) Direction and Photography, Gregory Nava; Assistant Director, Anna Thomas; Screenplay, Gergory Nava, Anna Thomas; Costumes, Cornejo; In color; 90 minutes; November release.

CAST

Amans .... William Bryan
Absalom .... Michael St. John
Anne .... Susannah MacMillan
Petrus..Richard Gardener
Arnolfo .... Leon Liberman
Nicholas............................Feliciano Ituero Bravo
Landlord .... Stephen Bateman
Steward .... Robert Case
Maidservant................................... Maria Rodriquez
Nurse ....Jeanne Graham
Cook ....Delfina Bayon
Child .... Mari Carmen Moza

Michael St. John, William Bryan

DERSU UZALA

(NEW WORLD) Director, Akira Kurosawa; Screenplay, Akira Kurosawa, Yuri Nagibin; Based on story by Vladimir Arseniev; Photography, Asakadru Nakai, Yuri Gantman, Fyodor Dobronavov; A Soviet-Japanese co-production in Russian with English subtitles; 137 minutes; November release. 1975 Academy Award for Best Foreign Language Film.

CAST

Dersu Uzala .... Maxim Munzzuk

Right: Masim Munzuk

Yuri Solomin, Maxim Munzuk

1900

(PARAMOUNT) Director, Bernardo Bertolucci; Screenplay, Mr. Bertolucci, Franco Arcalli, Giuseppe Bertolucci; Executive Producer, Alberto Grimaldi; Photography, Vittorio Storaro; Editor, Franco Arcalli; Music, Ennio Morricone; In color; 245 minutes; November release.

CAST

Alfredo .... Burt Lancaster
Giovanni .... Romolo Valli
Eleonora .... Anna-Maria Gherardi
Regina .... Laura Betti
Alfredo (grandson) .... Robert De Niro
Alfredo as a child .... Paolo Pavesi
Ada .... Dominique Sanda
Leo Dalco .... Sterling Hayden
Olmo Dalco ....Gerard Depardieu
Olmo as a child.................................Roberto Maccanti
Anita Foschi .... Stefania Sandrelli
Attila .... Donald Sutherland
Octavio .... Werner Bruhns
Signora Pioppi.. Alida Valli
Sister Desolata .... Francesca Bertini

**Left: Burt Lancaster
Below: Robert DeNiro**

Robert DeNiro, Gerard Depardieu

Robert DeNiro, Dominique Sanda
Above: Donald Sutherland

Juliet Berto, Alain Delon

MR. KLEIN

(QUARTET) Producers, Raymond Danon, Alain Delon, Jean-Pierre Labrande, Robert Kupferberg; Director, Joseph Losey; Screenplay, Franco Solinas; Photography, Gerry Fisher; Editor, Henri Lanoe; Art Director, Alexander Trauner; Music, Egisto Macchi, Pierre Porte; In Eastmancolor; A Basil Film Presentaion; 122 minutes; Rated PG; November release.

CAST

Mr. Klein	Alain Delon
Florence	Jeanne Moreau
Pierre	Michel Lonsdale
Janine	Juliet Berto
Concierge	Suzanne Flon
Nicole	Francine Berge
Man	Jean Bouise
Mr. Charles	Massimo Girotti

Jeanne Moreau

ANOTHER MAN, ANOTHER CHANCE

(UNITED ARTISTS) Producers, Alexandre Mnouchkine, Georges Dancigers; Direction and Screenplay, Claude Lelouch; Photography, Jacques Lefrancois, Stanley Cortez; Editors, Georges Klotz, Fabien Tordjmann; Designer, Robert Clatworthy; Music, Francis Lai; In DeLuxe Color; 129 minutes; Rated PG; November release.

CAST

David Williams	James Caan
Jeanne Leroy	Genevieve Bujold
Francis Leroy	Francis Huster
Mary	Jennifer Warren
Debbie/Alice	Susan Tyrrell
Simon	Rossie Harris
Sarah	Linda Lee Lyons
Mary's Mother	Diana Douglas
Mary's Father	Fred Stuthman
Springfield	Bernard Behrens
Evans	Oliver Clark
Telegrapher	William Bartman
Sheriff Murphy	Burton Gilliam
Stagecoach Driver	Richard Farnsworth
Foster	Walter Barnes
Bill	Walter Scott

Top: Genevieve Bujold, Francis Huster
Below: James Caan, Bujold

Genevieve Bujold, Linda Lee Lyons, James Caan,
Rossie Harris Top: Susan Tyrrell, Caan

IPHIGENIA

(CINEMA 5) Direction and Screenplay, Michael Cacoyannis; Based on "Iphigenia in Aulis" by Euripides; Executive Producer, Yanoula Wakefield; Photography, Georges Arvantis; Music, Mikis Theodorakis; Editors, Michael Cacoyannis, Takis Yannopoulos; A Greek Film Center Production; In Greek with English subtitles; In color; 130 minutes; Not rated; November release

CAST

Clytemnestra .... Irene Papas
Agamemnon .... Costa Kazakos
Menelaus .... Costa Carras
Iphigenia .... Tatiana Papamoskou
Ulysses...Christos Tsangas
Achilles .... Panos Michalopoulos
Servant... Angelos Yannoulis
Calchas .... Dimitri Aronis
Orestes... Georges Vourvahakis
Nurse .... Irene Koumarianou
Messenger .... Georges Economou

Christos Tsangas
Above: Costa Kazakos

Irene Papas, Tatiana Papamoskou

199

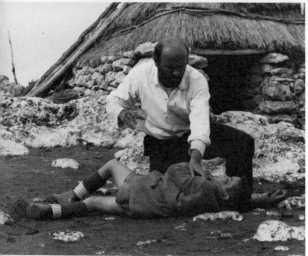

PADRE PADRONE

(CINEMA 5) Producer, Giuliani G. De Negri; Direction and Screenplay, Paolo Taviani, Vittorio Taviani; From novel by Gavino Ledda; Photography, Mario Masini; Music, Egisto Macchi; Costumes, Lina Nerli Taviani; Editor, Roberto Perpignani; Assistant Director, Marco De Poli; Italian with English subtitles; In Technicolor; 114 minutes; Not rated; December release.

CAST

Gavino's Father .... Omero Antonutti
Gavino .... Saverio Marconi
Gavino's Mother .... Marcella Michelangeli
Gavino as a child .... Fabrizio Forte
Servant/Shepherd .... Marino Cenna
Sebastino .... Stanko Molnar
Cesare .... Nanni Moretti

Left: Omero Antonutti, Fabrizio Forte

Omero Antonutti, Saverio Marconi
Above: Saverio Marconi

Saverio Marconi

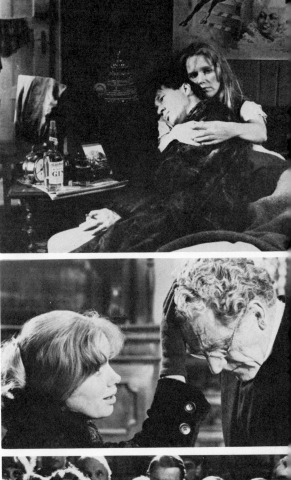

THE SERPENT'S EGG

(PARAMOUNT) Producer, Dino DeLaurentiis; Director, Ingmar Bergman; Executive Producer, Horst Wendlandt; Screenplay, Ingmar Bergman; Photography, Sven Nykvist; Designer, Rolf Zehetbauer; Costumes, Charlotte Flemming; Assistant Director, Wieland Liebske; Music, Rolf Wilhelm; Choreography, Heino Hallhuber; Editor, Petra Von Oelffen; Art Directors, Werner Achmann, Friedrich Thaler; In color; 120 minutes; Rated R; December release.

CAST

Manuela Rosenberg	Liv Ullmann
Abel Rosenberg	David Carradine
Inspector Bauer	Gert Froebe
Hans Vergerus	Heinz Bennent
Mr. Rosenberg	Toni Berger
Student	Christian Berkel
Mrs. Hemse	Paula Braend
Mrs. Rosenberg	Edna Bruenell
Cabaret Comedian	Paul Buerks
Woman with baby	Gaby Dohm
Cupid	Emil Feist
Priest	James Whitmore

and Kai Fischer, Georg Hartmann, Edith Heerdegen, Klaus Hoffmann, Grischa Huber, Volkert Kraeft, Gunther Malzacher, Lisi Mangold, Guenter Meisner, Kyra Mladeck, Heide Picha, Hans Quest, Charles Regnier, Walter Schmidinger, Irene Steinbeisser, Fritz Strassner, Glynn Turman, Ellen Umlauf, Wolfgang Wieser, Ralf Wolter

Top: Liv Ullmann, and Right
with David Carradine

Liv Ullmann, David Carradine
Above: Ullmann, James Whitmore

Hugh Griffith, Donald Pleasence
in "The Passover Plot"

"People of the Wind"

THE PASSOVER PLOT (Atlas) Producer, Wolf Schmidt; Executive Producer, Menahem Golan; Director, Michael Campus; Screenplay, Millard Cohan, Patricia Knop; From book by Hugh J. Schonfield; Photography, Adam Greenberg; Editor, Dov Hoenig; Music, Alex North; Art Director, Kuli Sander; Costumes, Mary Wills; In DeLuxe Color; 108 minutes; Rated PG; January release. CAST: Harry Andrews (Yohanan the Baptist), Hugh Griffith (Caiaphas), Zalman King (Yeshua), Donald Pleasence (Pontius Pilate), Scott Wilson (Judah), Dan Ades (Andros), Michael Baseleon (Mattai), Lewis van Bergen (Yoram), William Burns (Shimon), Daniel Hedaya (Yaacov), Helena Kallianiotes (Visionary), Kevin O'Connor (Irijah), Robert Walker (Bar Talmi), William Watson (Roman Captain)

CAGLIOSTRO (Rampart) Producer, Rodolfo Puttignani; Director, Daniele Pettinari; Screenplay, Pier Carpi, Enrico Bonacorti, Daniele Pettinari; Photography, Giuseppe Pinori; Editor, Adriano Tagliavia; Music, Manuel De Sica; In color; 103 minutes; January release. CAST: Bekim (Cagliostro), Curt Jurgens (Cardinal), Rossana Schiaffino (Lorenza), Evelyn Stewart (Serafina), Massimo Girotti (Casanova), Robert Alda (Pope)

DUNKERKLUMPEN (Select) Director, Per Ahlin; Story, Song Lyrics, Bebbe Wolgers; Executive Producer, Gunnar Karlsson; Music, Toots Thielemans; In color; 96 minutes; Rated G; January release. An animated feature.

PRIVATE PROJECTION (Albina) Director, Francois Leterrier; Screenplay, Francois Leterrier, Madeleine Chapsal, Bernard Revon; Photography, Jean Badal; Editor, Marie-Joseph Yoyotte; Music, Serge Gainsbourg, Jean-Claude Vannier; In color; 93 minutes; January release. CAST: Francois Fabian (Marthe), Jean-Luc Bideau (Denis), Jane Birkin (Kate), Bulle Ogier (Camille), Jacques Weber (Philippe), Barbara Laage (Madeleine)

THE RIGHT TO LOVE (Cougar) Director, Eric Le Hung; Screenplay, Jean-Claude Carriere, Francoise Xenakis, Jean Bolvary, Eric Le Hung; From book by Miss Xenakis; Photography, Henri Decae; Music, Philippe Sarde; In Eastmancolor; 92 minutes; January release. CAST: Omar Sharif (Pierre), Florinda Bolkan (Helena), Pierre Michael (Commander), Georges Douking (Old Man), Gilles Segal (Prisoner), Didier Haudepin (Young Man)

SEBASTIAN (Discopat) Producers, Howard Malin, James Whaley; Direction and Screenplay, Paul Humfress, Derek Jarman; Photography, Peter Middleton; Editor, Paul Humfress; Music, Biran Eno, Andrew Wilson; In Eastmancolor; 85 minutes; Rated X; January release. CAST: Leonardo Treviglio (Sebastian), Barney James (Severus), Neil Kennedy (Maximus), Richard Warwick (Justin), Donald Dunham (Claudius), Ken Hicks (Adrian)

THE SCARLET LETTER (A. J. Bauer) Producers, Peter Genee, Primitivo Alvaro; Director, William Wenders; Screenplay Mr. Wenders, Bernardo Fernandez; From novel by Nathaniel Hawthorne; Photography, Robby Muller; Editor, Peter Przygodda; Music, Jurgen Knieper; In color; 94 minutes; January release. CAST: Senta Berger (Hester), Hans Christian Blech (Chillingworth), Lou Castel (Dimmesdale), Yelena Samarina (Hibbins), Yella Rottlander (Pearl)

PEOPLE OF THE WIND (Tricontinental) Producers, Anthony Howarth, David Koff; Director, David Koff; Written by David Koff; Photography, Mike Dodds; Editor, Carolyn Hicks; Music, G. T. Moore, Shusha; In DeLuxe Color; 108 minutes; Not rated; January release. A Chronicle of Jafar Qoli, the chief of the Babadi tribe of western Iran, featuring the voice of James Mason.

FLAVIA (World Wide) Director, Gianfranco Mingozzi; In Technicolor; Rated R; No other credits available; January release. CAST: Florinda Bolkan, Maria Casares, Claudio Cassinelli, Anthony Corlan

THE TATTOOED HIT MAN (New Line) Written by Jack Sholder; In Eastmancolor; Rated R; No other credits available; January release. Starring Bud Sugawara.

GET CHARLIE TULLY (TBS) Producer, E. M. Smedley Aston; Director, Cliff Owen; Screenplay, John Warren, John Singer; Photography, Ernest Steward; 97 minutes; Rated PG; January release. CAST: Dick Emery (Charlie), Derren Nesbit (Sid), Ronald Fraser (Reggie), Pat Coombs (Libby), William Franklyn (Arnold), Cheryl Kennedy (Jo)

LES GALETTES DE PONT AVEN (PRO) Direction and Screenplay, Joel Seria; Editor, Marcel Combes; Music, Philippe Sarde; 100 minutes; Not rated; January release. CAST: Jean-Pierre Marielle (Henri), Jeanne Goupil (Marie), Dolores MacDonough (Angela), Romain Bouteille (Le Cure)

WELCOME TO MY NIGHTMARE (Producers Releasing Organization) Produced, Directed, Choreographed by David Winters; Co-Producer, Joe Gannon; Executive Producer, William B. Silberkleft; Photography, Larry Pizer; Editor, Stuart Baird; Music and Songs, Alice Cooper, Dick Wagner, Bob Ezrin; Assistant Director, Emma Gowing; In Eastmancolor; 85 minutes; Not rated; January release. A documentary

DIRTY MONEY (Allied Artists) Directed and Written by Jean-Pierre Melville; Photography, Walter Wottitz; Editor, Patricia Renaut; Music, Michel Comobier; Art Director, Theo Meurisse; In Eastmancolor; 100 minutes; Rated PG; January release. CAST: Alain Delon (Coleman), Catherine Deneuve (Cathy), Richard Crenna (Simon), Riccardo Cucciolla (Paul), Michael Conrad (Costa), Andre Pousse (Albouis), Paul Crauchet (Morand), Simone Valere (Wife), Jean Desailly (Man)

ROD STEWART & FACES & KEITH RICHARD (Apache) Executive Producer, Roger Grod; 71 minutes; Not rated; No other credits available; January release. A documentary featuring Rod Stewart, Faces, and Keith Richard.

THE MINISTER AND ME (Rioma) Producer, Jacques Gelman; Director, Miguel Delgado; Screenplay, Tito Davison; Story, Mario Mareno, Tito Davison; Photography, Jorge Stahl, Jr.; Editor, Gloria Schoemann; Music, Gustave C. Carreon; In Panavision and Eastmancolor; 100 minutes; Not rated; January release. CAST: Mario Moreno (Cantinflas), Lucia Mendez, Celia Castro, Angel Garasa, Hector Suarez

THE DAY THAT SHOOK THE WORLD (American International) Director, Veljko Bulajic; Screenplay, Paul Jarrico; Photography, Jan Curik; Editor, Roger Dwyre; Music, Juan Carlos Calderon, Libus Fiser; An Oliver A. Unger presentation of a Mundo Film; In Movielab Color; Rated PG; 111 minutes; January release. CAST: Christopher Plummer (Archduke Ferdinand), Florinda Bolkan (Duchess Sophie), Maximilian Schell (Djuro Sarac), Irfan Mensur (Gavrilo Princip)

Eva Ziegler, Arthur Brauss in
"The Goalie's Anxiety. . . ."

Ingrid Thulin, Helmut Berger
in "Madam Kitty"

KINGS OF THE ROAD (A. J. Bauer) Direction and Screenplay, Wim Wenders; Photography, Robby Muller; January release. CAST: Rudiger Vogler (Bruno), Hanns Zischler (Robert), Lisa Kreuzer, Rudolf Schundler, Marquand Bohm, Patrick Kreuzer

THE SICILIAN CONNECTION (Joseph Green) Director, Ferdinando Baldi; In Technicolor; No other credits available; January release. CAST: Ben Gazzara, Silvia Monti, Fausto Tozzi, Jess Hahn

THE GOOD, THE BAD AND THE LOSER (Stirling Gold) Producer, Y. C. Lai; Direction and Screenplay, Kar S. Mak; In color; Rated R; January release. CAST: Lau Ka-Wing, Carter Wong, Roy Chiao

JOURNEY (EPOH) Direction and Screenplay, Paul Almond; Photography, Jean Boffety; In color; 87 Minutes; Rated PG; January release. CAST: Genevieve Bujold (Saguenay), John Vernon (Boulder), George Sperdakos (Vid), Elton Hayes (Piers), Luke Gibson (Luke)

DOGPOUND SHUFFLE (Paramount) Produced, Directed and Written by Jeffrey Bloom; In color; Rated PG; January release. CAST: Ron Moody, David Soul, Pamela McMyler, Ray Stricklyn

VIXENS OF KUNG FU (Chang) Director, Chiang; In color; Rated X; No other credits available; January release. CAST: Bree Anthony, Peonies Jong, C. J. Laing, Anthony Wong, Tony Blue, Jamie Gillis, Bobby Astyr

THE AMAZING MR. BLUNDEN (Goldstone) Director, Lionel Jeffries; In color; Rated G; No other credits available; January release. CAST: Laurence Naismith, Lynne Frederick, Garry Miller

THE VOYAGE (United Artists) Director, Vittorio de Sica; Screenplay, Diego Fabbri, Massimo Franciosa, Luisa Montagnana; Based on novel by Luigi Pirandello; Music, Manuel de Sica; Photography, Ennio Guarnieri; In color; 101 minutes; Rated PG; January release. CAST: Sophia Loren (Adriana), Richard Burton (Cesar), Ian Bannen (Antonio), Renato Pinciroli (Doctor), Daniele Pitani (Notary), Barbara Leonard (Mother), Sergio Bruno (Armando), Ettore Ger (Rinaldo), Olga Bomanelli (Clementina)

ULTIMATUM (Inter Planetary) Director, Stelvio Massi; Rated PG; In color; No other credits available; January release. CAST: Lee J. Cobb, Franco Gasparri, Nino Benvenuti

ORIENTAL TREATMENT (Carbon Canyon) Director, Harold Lee; A Beagle Brothers Presentation in color; Rated X; January release. CAST: Kyoto Gee, Bob Rose

BEWARE OF A HOLY WHORE (New Yorker) Direction and Screenplay, Rainer Werner Fassbinder; 103 minutes; No other credits available; January release. CAST: Lou Castel, Werner Schroefer, Eddie Constantine, Hanna Schygulia, Margarethe von Trotta

THE GOALIE'S ANXIETY AT THE PENALTY BLOCK (Bauer International) Producer, Peter Genee; Director, Wim Wenders; Screenplay, Wim Wenders, Peter Handke; Photography, Robbie Muller; Editor, Peter Przygodda; Music, Jurgen Knieper; Sound, Rainer Lorenz, Martin Muller; Art Direction, R. Schnieder Manns, Burghard Schlicht; In color; 101 minutes; January release. CAST: Arthur Brauss (Josef Bloch), Kai Fischer (Hertha), Erika Pluhar (Gloria), Libgart Schwarz (Anna), Marie Bardischewski (Maria), Michael Toost (Salesman), Edda Kochl (Girl), Rudiger Vogler (Idiot)

MADAME KITTY (Trans-American Films) Executive Producer Carla Cipriani; Producers, Giulio Sbarigia, Ermanno Donati; Director, Tinto Brass; Screenplay, Ennio De Concini, Maria Pia Fusco, Tinto Brass; Photography, Silvano Ippoliti; Designer, Ken Adam; Editor, Tinto Brass; Costumes, Ugo Pericoli, Jost Jacob; Music, Fiorenzo Carpi; Choreography, Tito Ledu; Music, Bruno Nicolai; Lyrics, Derry Hall; Sung by Annie Ross; Rated X; 111 minutes; January release. CAST: Helmut Berger (Wallenberg), Ingrid Thulin (Kitty), Theresa Ann Savoy (Margherita), Bekim Fehmiu (Hans), John Steiner (Biondo), Stefan Satta Flores (Dino), Dan Van Husen (Rauss), John Ireland (Clift), Alexandra Bofojevich (Gloria), Rosemarie Lindt (Susan), Paola Senatore (Marika), Sara Sperati (Helga), Tina Aumont (Herta), Maria Michi (Hilde), Gianfranco Bullo (Wolff), Tito Leduc (Frank), Gigi Ballista (Generale), Giancarlo Badessi (Geraca), Claus Rhule (Margherita's Father), Margherita Horowitz (Margherita's Mother)

WARHEAD (Worldwide) Director, John O'Connor; In color; Rated R; No other credits available; February release. CAST: David Janssen, Karin Dor, Chris Stone, Art Metrano

DON'T JUST LIE THERE, SAY SOMETHING (K-Tel) Producer, Andrew Mitchell; Director, Bob Kellet; Screenplay, Michael Pertwee; In color; Rated PG; February release. CAST: Leslie Phillips, Joan Sims, Brian Rix, Katy Manning, Joanna Lumley

FUNERAL FOR AN ASSASSIN (Epoh) Director, Ivan Hall; Screenplay, Walter Brough; In color; Rated PG; No other credits available; February release. CAST: Vic Morrow, Peter Von Dissel, Gaby Getz, Gillian Garlick, Siegfried Mayhardt, Stewart Parker

NAUGHTY WIVES (Cannon) Producer, David Grant; Director, Wolf Rilla; Screenplay, Roy Nicholas; In color; Rated R; February release. CAST: Brendan Price, Jean Harrington, Elizabeth Romilly, Jacqueline Logan

HOUSE OF 1,000 PLEASURES (Group I) Director, Anthony M. Dawson; Screenplay, Dino Verde, Antonio Margheriti; In color; Rated R; February release. CAST: Barbara Bouchet, Femi Benussi, Barbara Marzano, Esmeralda Barros, Pupo De Luca, Gigi Battista, Amparo Pilar, Ray O'Connor

THE LOVE FACTOR (Film Ventures International) Presented by Edward L. Montoro; In color; Rated R; February release. Starring Anna Gael

HORROR OF THE ZOMBIES (Independent International) Director, Amando de Ossorio; Music, A. Garcia Abril; Photography, Raul Artigot; In color; Rated R; 85 minutes; February release. CAST: Maria Perschy, Jack Taylor, Carlos Lemos, Manuel de Blas, Barbara Rey, Blanca Estrada

BLACK SAMURAI (B.J.L.J. International) Producer, Barbara Holden; Director, Al Adamson; Executive Producer, Laurence Joachim; Screenplay, B. Readick; Based on novel by Marc Olden; In color; Rated PG; February release. Starring Jim Kelly

FRENCH PUSSYCAT (Cineworld) Producer, Elio Romano; Direction and Screenplay, Henry Billion; In color; Rated R; February release. CAST: Sybil Danning, Katie Buchele, Marlene Appel

THE DEVIL HAS SEVEN FACES (Libert) Producer-Director, Osvaldo Civirani; In color; February release. CAST: Carroll Baker, Stephen Boyd, George Hilton

Tisa Farrow, Stuart Whitman
in "Strange Shadows in an Empty Room"

Ana Torrent, Geraldine Chaplin
in "Cria!"

STRANGE SHADOWS IN AN EMPTY ROOM (American International) Producer, Admondo Amati; Director, Martin Herbert; Screenplay, Vincent Mann, Frank Clark; Photography, Anthony Ford; Editor, Vincent P. Thomas; Art Director, Michel Proulux; Costumes, Louise Jobin; Music, Armando Trovajoli; In Panavision, Cinemascope and color; Rated R; 99 minutes; February release. CAST: Stuart Whitman (Tomy), John Saxon (Sgt. Matthews), Martin Landau (Doctor), Tisa Farrow (Julie), Carole Laure (Louise), Jean Leclerc (Mystery Woman), Gayle Hunnicutt (Margie Cohn)

MY HUSBAND, HIS MISTRESS AND I (Joseph Green) Director, Sergio Gobbi; Screenplay, Paul Gegauff, Sergio Gobbi; Photography, Daniel Vogel; Music, Vladimir Cosma; In color; 95 minutes; Rated R; February release. CAST: Bibi Andersson (Blanche), Jean Piat (Edgar), Genevieve Fontanel (Clair), Maurice Biraud

ONDINE (GP) Director, Rolf Thiele; Photography, Wolf Wirth; In color; Rated R; February release. CAST: Angela von Radloff, Ingo Thouret

MAFIA JUNCTION (Rumson) Producer, Ross MacKenzie; Director, Massimo Dallamano; In color; Rated R; February release. CAST: Ivan Rassimov, Stephanie Beachm, Patricia Hayes

LITTLE GIRL, BIG TEASE (Cannon) Producer-Director, Roberto Mitrotti; In color; Rated R; February release. CAST: Jody Ray, Rebecca Brooke

MONDO MAGIC (Peppercorn-Wormser) Producers, Alfred Castiglioni, Angelo Castiglioni, Guido Gerasio; Narrated by Mac Mauro Smith; In Eastmancolor; 100 minutes; Rated X; February release. A documentary on bizarre tribal customs in remote areas of the world.

THE SEX MACHINE (Seymour Borde) Producer, Silvio Clementelli; Direction and Screenplay, Pasquale Festa Campanile; Music, Fred Bongusto; Photography, Franco DiGiacomo; Editor, Sergio Montanari; In Technicolor; Rated R; February release. CAST: Agostina Belli (Francesca), Luigi Proietti (Professor), Eleonora Giorgi (Piera), Christian De Sica (Daniel), Mario Scaccia (Monsignior), Adriana Asti (Irene)

LES BORDELLO GIRLS (Independent) In Eastmancolor; Rated X; No other credits available; February release. Starring Darby Lloyd Rains

KING, QUEEN, KNAVE (AVCO Embassy) Producer, David Wolper; Director, Jerzy Skolimowsky; Screenplay, Davie Seltzer, David Shaw; From novel by Vladimir Nabokov; Photography, Charly Steinberger; Editor, Mel Shapiro; Art Director, Rolf Zeherbauer; Music, Stanley Myers; In Eastmancolor; 92 minutes; Rated R; February release. CAST: David Niven (Charles), Gina Lollobrigida (Martha), John Moulder Brown (Frank), Mario Adorf (Ritter), Carl Fox-Duering (Entricht)

ONE-ARMED BOXER VS. THE FLYING GUILLOTINE (In-Frame Films) Producer, Wong Cheuk Hon; Direction and Screenplay, Jimmy Wang Yu; Photography, Chiu Yau Wu; Choreography, Lau Brothers; Music, Chan Fung Ki; In color; 83 minutes; Rated R; February release. CAST: Jimmy Wang Yu (One-Armed Boxer), Kam Kong (Fung Sheng), Lung Kun Yee (Wu Shao), Cheng Cheng Po (Thai Boxer)

GODZILLA VS. COSMIC MONSTER (Downtown) Formerly "Godzilla VS. The Bionic Monster"; Director, Jun Fukuda; In Tohoscope and color; 80 minutes; Rated G; Presented by Cinema Shares International; March release. CAST: Akihiko Hirata, Hiroshi Koizumi, Barbara Lynn

UNCLE TOM'S CABIN (Independent International) Director, Geza Radvanyi; Screenplay, Fred Denger, Geza Radvanyi; Based on novel by Harriet Beecher Stowe; U. S. Sequences, Al Adamson; Music, Peter Thomas; A Kroger Babb presentation in Eastmancolor; Rated R; March release. CAST: John Kitzmiller (Uncle Tom), Herbert Lom (Legree), Olive Moorefield (Cassy), Prentiss Moulden (Napoleon), Mary Ann Jenson (Melissa), O. W. Fisher (St. Clair), Gertraud Mitter-Mayr (Eva), Juliette Greco (Dinah), Charley Fawcett, Elonora Rossi-Drago, Mylene Demongeot, Aziz Saad, Catana Cayetano, Erika Von Thellman

THE LOVE PILL (Cannon) Producers, Laurence Barnett, John Lindsay; Director, Kenneth Turner; In color; Rated R; March release. CAST: Toni Sinclair, Henry Woolf, Melinda Churcher, David Pugh

MYSTERIES OF THE GODS (Hemisphere) Producer, Ellis P. Eisenstein; Director, Chuck Romine; Based on "Miracles of the Gods" by Erich von Daniken; Narrated by William Shatner; In color; 93 minutes; Rated G; March release. A documentary.

THE KEYHOLE (Centrum) Executive Producer, R. Burton; Direction and Screenplay, Paul Gerber; In Eastmancolor; Rated X; March release. CAST: Marie Ekorre, Bent Warburg, Max Horn, Torben Larsen

THE FELINES (Memory) Producer, Rene Levy-Balensi; Director, Daniel Daert; Photography, Stanley Mills, Patrick Godaert; Music, Vladimir Cosma; In color; 70 minutes; Rated X; March release. CAST: Janine Reynaud, Nathalie Zeiger, Pauline Larrieu, Jacques Insermini, Georges Guerret

CHAMPION OF DEATH (United Artists) Director, Kazuhiko Yamagushi; A Toei Company production in color; Rated R; March release. Starring Sonny Chiba.

THE CONFESSIONAL (Atlas) Producer-Director, Pete Walker; Screenplay, David McGillivray; Story, Pete Walker; Music, Stanley Myers; Photography, Peter Jessop; In color; 104 minutes; Rated R; March release. CAST: Anthony Sharp (Meldrum), Susan Penhaligan (Jenny), Stephanie Beacham (Vanessa), Norman Eshley (Bernard), Sheila Keith (Miss Brabazon), Hilda Barry (Mrs. Meldrum), Stewart Beven (Terry), Julia McCarthy (Mrs. Davey), Jon Yule (Robert), Mervyn Johns (Father Duggan), Victor Winding (Dr. Gaudio), Kim Butcher (Valerie), Bill Kerr (Davey), Ivor Salter (Gravedigger), Jack Allen, Jane Hayward, Andrew Sachs, Austin King, Melinda Clancy

LET THE BALLOON GO (Inter Planetary) Producer, Richard Mason; Director, Oliver Howes; Screenplay, Richard Mason, Oliver Howes, Ivan Southall; From novel by Ivan Southall; Photography, Dean Semler; Music, George Dreyfus; Art Director, David Copping; Assistant Director, Elisabeth Knight; In color; Rated G; 92 minutes; February release. CAST: Robert Bettles (John), Jan Kingsbury (Mrs. Sumner), Ben Gabriel (Mr. Sumner), Sally Whiteman (Mamie), Matthew Wilson (Cecil), Terry McQuillan (Harry), Bruce Spence, John Ewart, Kenneth Goodlet, Ray Barrett, Nigel Lovell, Babette Stephens, Brian Anderson, Charles Metcalfe, Phillip Ross, Scott Griffiths, Goff Vockler, Bob Lee

SWEET TASTE OF HONEY (Act IV) Director, Max Pecas; In Eastmancolor; Rated X; No other credits available; March release. CAST: Karine, Pierre Danny, Richard Darbois

HOUSE OF THE LIVING DEAD (Worldwide) Producer, Matt Druker; Director, Ray Austin; Screenplay, Marc Marais; Executive Producer, Philip N. Krasne; In color; Rated PG; March release. CAST: Mark Burns, Shirley Anne Field

BEYOND FEAR (Cine III) Direction and Screenplay, Yannik Andrei; Photography, Pierre Petit; Music, Alain Goraguer; In Eastmancolor; 95 minutes; Not rated; March release. CAST: Michel Bouquet (Claude), Michel Constantin (Guilloux), Marilu Tolo (Nicole), Paul Crauchet (Inspector), Michel Creton (Legoff)

ONCE UPON A TIME (G.G. Communications) Producer-Director, Rolf Kauka; Art Director, Louis Gaviolo; Music, Peter Thomas; In Movielab Color; 83 minutes; March release. An animated film.

ALICE OR THE LAST ESCAPADE (Filmel) Direction and Screenplay, Claude Chabrol; Photography, Jean Rabier; Editor, Monique Fardoulis; Music, Pierre Jansen; In Eastmancolor; 93 minutes; March release. CAST: Sylvia Kristel (Alice), Charles Vanel (Vergennes), Jean Carmet (Colas), Andre Dussollier (Man), Fernand Ledoux (Doctor), Thomas Chabrol (Boy), Bernard Rousselet (Husband)

CHRISTIAN THE LION (Scotia American) Produced and Directed by Bill Travers, James Hill; Photography, Simon Trevor; Editor, Andrew Borthwick; Narrated by Bill Travers, Virginia McKenna; Music, Pentangle; In color; 89 minutes; Rated G; March release. CAST: Bill Travers, Virginia McKenna, George Adamson, Terence Adamson, Anthony Bourke, John Rendall

ANKUR ("The Seedling") (Bonanza Films) Direction and Screenplay, Shyam Benegal; No other credits available; April release. Starring Shabana Azmi (Laxmi).

THE BEAST (Jayson Allen) Producer, Anatole Dauman; Direction and Screenplay, Walerian Borowczyk; Photography, Bernard Daillencourt, Marcel Grigon; French with English subtitles; In color; 100 minutes; Rated X; April release. CAST: Sirpa Lane (Romilda), Lisbeth Hummerl (Lucy), Elisabeth Kaza (Virginia), Pierre Benedietti (Mathurin), Guy Treian (Marquis)

TORO-SAN, THE INTELLECTUAL (Shochiku) Producer, Kiyoshi Shimazu; Direction, Story and Screenplay, Yoji Yamada; Editor, Iwao Ishil; Photography, Tetsuo Takaba; 97 minutes; Not rated; April release. CAST: Kiyoshi Atsumi (Kuruma), Chieko Baisho (Sakura), Fumie Kashiyama, Junko Sakurada, Masami Shimojo, Chieko Misaki, Gin Maeda, Hayato Nakamura, Keiju Kobayashi, Masakane Yonekura, Hideii Otaki, Gajiro Sato

ESKIMO NELL (Cinema Shares International) Director, Martin Campbell; In color; Rated R; April release. CAST: Roy Kinnear, Anna Quayle, Katy Manning, Michael Armstrong, Sheila Bernette, Richard Galdicot, Terrence Edmond, Jeremy Hawke, Rosaline Knight, Diane Langton, George Moon, Beth Porter, Christopher Timothy

SUPERBUG, THE WILD ONE (Central Park) Director, David Mark; Screenplay, Alexander Callier; In color; Rated G; April release. CAST: Richard Lynn, Constance Siech, Jim Browne, Bob Mackay

THE VALLEY (Circle Associates) Director, Barbet Schroeder; Screenplay, Barbet Schroeder, Paul Gegauff; Photography, Nestor Almendros; Music, Pink Floyd; In Eastmancolor; 100 minutes; April release. CAST: Bulle Ogier (Viviane), Jean-Pierre Kalfon (Gaetan), Michael Gothard (Olivier), Valerie Lagrange (Hermine), Jerome Beauvarlet (Yann), Monique Giraudy (Monique)

THE BODY (United Pictures) Director, Luigi Scattini; In color; Rated R; April release. CAST: Zeudi Araya, Carroll Baker, Leonard Mann, Enrico Maria Salerno

FRUSTRATED WIVES (Cineworld) Producer, Leslie Berens; Director, Arnold Miller; In color; April release. CAST: Hilary Labow, Kim Alexander, Amber Kammer, Tristan Rogers

LE SAMOURAI (Films Inc.) Director, Jean-Pierre Melville; In Eastmancolor; April release; No other credits available. CAST: Alain Delon, Nathalie Delon, Francois Perier

FAMILY JEWELS (Alpha) Director, Jean-Claude Laureux; Screenplay, Michel Parmentier, Jean-Claude Laureux; In Eastmancolor; 90 minutes; April release. CAST: Francoise Brion, Corinne O'Brian, Jacqueline Staup, Alexandre Rignault

VANESSA (Intercontinental) Director, Hubert Frank; Screenplay, Joos De Ridder; Photography, Franz X. Lederle; Executive Producer, Erich Tomek; 91 minutes; In color; Rated X; April release. CAST: Olivia Pascal, Anton Diffring, Gunther Clemens, Uschi Zech, Eva Eden, Henry Heller, Eva Louise, Astrid Bohner, Giesela Krauss, Peter M. Kruger, Tom Garven

CRY OF A PROSTITUTE (Joseph Brenner) Producer, Mauro Righi; Director, Andrew Bianchi; In Technicolor; Rated R; April release. CAST: Henry Silva, Barbara Bouchet, Mario Landi

IMPOSSIBLE LOVE (Athena) Director, Jose Antonio Nieves Conde; In color; Rated PG; 90 minutes; April release. CAST: Stephen Boyd, Sara Lezana

THAT MOST IMPORTANT THING: LOVE (Seaberg) Director, Andrej Zulawski; Screenplay, Andrej Zulawski, Christopher Frank; From book by Mr. Frank; Photography, Ricardo Aronovitch; Editor, Christiane Lack; Music, Georges Delerue; In Eastmancolor; 110 minutes; Rated R; April release. CAST: Romy Schneider (Nadine), Fabio Testi (Servais), Jacques Dutronc (Jacques), Klaus Kinski (Karl), Claude Dauphin (Mazelli), Roger Blin (Father), Michel Robin (Lapade)

ZORRO (Allied Artists) Director, Duccio Tessari; Screenplay, Giorgio Arlorio; Photography, Giulio Albonico; Editor, Mario Morra; In Eastmancolor; 120 minutes; Rated G; April release. CAST: Alain Delon (Zorro), Stanley Baker (Huerta), Ottavia Piccolo (Girl), Moustache (Sergeant), Adriana Asti (Countess)

THE SAVAGE (Atlas) Title changed to "Lovers Like Us"; Director, Jean-Paul Rappeneau; Screenplay, Jean-Paul Rappeneau, Elisabeth Rappeneau, Jean-Loup Dabadie; Photography, Pierre Lhomme; Editor, Marie-Josephe Yoyotte; Music, Michel Legrand; In Eastmancolor; 110 minutes; Rated PG; April release. CAST: Catherine Deneuve (Nelly), Yves Montand (Martin), Luigi Vanucchi (Vittorio), Tony Roberts (Alex), Dana Wynter (Wife)

CRIA! (Jason Allyn) Producer, Elias Quereieta; Direction and Screenplay, Carlos Saura; Editor, Pablo G. Del Amo; Photography, Teodoro Escamilla; 115 minutes; Rated PG; May release. CAST: Geraldine Chaplin (Ana), Ana Torrent (Ana as a child), Conchita Perez (Irene), Maite Sanchez Alexandros (Maite), Monica Randall (Paulina)

THE SAGA OF ANATAHAN (Twyman) Producer, Takimura; Direction, Screenplay and Photography, Josef von Sternberg; Adapted from book by Maruyama; 95 minutes; Rated PG; May release. CAST: Akemi Negishi (Queen Bee), Suganume (Husband), Narrator, Josef von Sternberg

TOKKAN (ATG) Directed and Written by Kihachi Okamoto; Photography, Daisuke Kimura; 95 minutes; Not rated; May release. CAST: Toshitaaka Ito (Senta), Yusuke Okada (Manjiro), Etsushi Takahashi (Judayu), Hiroko Isayama (Oito), Emiko Senba (Teru)

TANGE-SAZEN (Shochiku) Directed and Adapted by Seiichiro Uchikawa from the novel by Fubo Hayashi; Photography, Yoshikawa Ototu; In color; 95 minutes; Not rated; No other credits; May release. CAST: Tetsuro Tamba (Tange-Sazen), Keisuke Sonoi, Haruko Wanibuchi, Michiko Saga

TENDERNESS OF THE WOLVES (Monument) Producer, Rainer Werner Fassbinder; Director, Ulli Lommel; Screenplay, Kurt Raab; Photography, Jurgen Jorges; Music, Peer Ragen; Editors, Thea Evans, Franz Walsch; A Tango Films production in color; German with English subtitles; 95 minutes; May release. CAST: Kurt Raab (Haarmann), Jeff Roden (Granz), Margit Carstensen (Frau Linder), Brigitte Mira (Cafe owner), Ingrid Caven (Dora), Hannelore Riefenbrunner (Frau Bucher), Tanara Schanzara (Frau Schluss), Wolfgang Schenk, Rainer Hauer (Commissars), Rainer Werner Fassbinder (Wittkowski), Heinrich Giskes (Einarmiger)

THE LEGEND OF FRANK WOODS (Variety International) Producer, Deno Paoli; Director, Hagen Smith; In color; Rated R; May release. CAST: Troy Donahue, Kitty Vallacher, Brad Stewart

SEVEN TO ONE (Independent) Producer-Director, Ho Chang; In Eastmancolor; Rated R; May release. CAST: Shang Kuan, Ling Fung

RIP OFF (Unlimited International) Producer, Michael Benet; Direction and Screenplay, Manolis Tsafos; Music, Jaime Mendoza, Antonios Roussos, Peter Bravos; In Eastmancolor; Rated R; May release. CAST: Michael Benet, James Masters, Barbara Bourbon, Vasilis Koudounis, Michele Simone, Johnny Dark, Stelios Manios, Al Ward

THE GROOVE ROOM (Constellation) Producer-Director, Vernon P. Becker; Screenplay, Barry E. Downes, Vernon P. Becker; Photography, Tony Forsberg; In 3-D and Eastmancolor; 83 minutes; Rated R; May release. CAST: Sue Longhurst (Alice), Ollie Soltoft (Jack), Malou Cartwright (Penny), Diana Dors (Madam), Charlie Elvegard (Sampson), Martin Ljung (The Ripper)

A GIRL CALLED TIGRESS (Chang) Director Wang Hun Chang; Screenplay, Chu Hsiang Ken; In color; Rated R; May release. CAST: Shang Kuan, Ling Fu, Kam Kang, Yasuki Kurata

LE TETE DE NORMANDE ST. ONGE (Cinepix) Director, Gilles Carle; Screenplay, Gilles Carle, Ben Barzman; In Eastmancolor; 105 minutes; May release. CAST: Carole Laure, Reynald Bouchard, Raymond Cloutier, Renee Girard, Carmen Giroux, J. Leo Gagnon, Gaetan Guidmond, Anne-Marie Ducharme

SUDDEN DEATH (Topar) Producers, Caruth C. Byrd, James Wilson; Director, Eddie Romero; Screenplay, Oscar Williams; Presented by Tom, Maurice and Rick Parker; In color; Rated R; May release. CAST: Robert Conrad, Don Stroud, Felton Perry, John Ashley, Nancy Conrad, Jenny Green, Eddie Garcia

BIBI (Cineworld) Producer, Chris Nebe; Director, Joe Sarno; In Eastmancolor; May release. CAST: Maria Forsa, Annie Sebring, Nadia Phillips

CURSE OF THE DEVIL (Goldstone) In Technicolor; rated R; No other credits available; May release. CAST: Paul Naschy, Vidal Molina, Maritza Olivares

ONE MAN AGAINST THE ORGANIZATION (Rampart) Producer, P. Joseph; In color; Rated R; No other credits available; May release. Starring Stephen Boyd

BEL AMI (Mature) Producer, Inge Ivarson; Director, Bert Torn; Based on novel by Guy de Maupassant; Music, Olivier Toussain; Photography, Henri Alexandre; In color; 90 minutes; Rated X; May release. CAST: Harry Reems, Christa Linder, Maria Lynn, Bie Warburg, Jacqueline Laurent, Bent Warburg, Lucienne Camille, Preben Mahrt, Lisa Olssen

THE SELL OUT (Distrib Venture) Producer, Josef Shaftel; Director, Peter Collinson; Screenplay, Murray Smith, Judson Kinberg; Based on story by Mr. Smith; Photography, Arthur Ibbetson; Music, Mick Green, Colin Frichter; In color; 88 minutes; Rated PG; May release. CAST: Richard Widmark (Sam), Oliver Reed (Gabriel), Gayle Hunnicutt (Deborah), Sam Wanamaker (Sickles), Vladek Sheybal (Dutchman), Ori Levy (Major), Assaf Dayan (Lt. Elan), Shmuel Rodensky (Zafron), Peter Frye (Kasyan)

NIGHTS AND DAYS (Polski) Direction and Screenplay, Jerzy Antczak; Based on novel by Maria Dabrowska; Photography, Stanislaw Loth; Music, Waidemar Kazanecki; In color; 275 minutes; May release. CAST: Jadwiga Baranska (Barbara), Jerzy Binczycki (Her Husband), Barbara Ludwizanka (Her Mother)

THE ORDERS (Films 13) Director, Michel Brault; Screenplay, Michel Brault, Guy Dufresne; Photography, Michel Brault; Music, Philippe Gagnon; In color, black and white; 107 minutes; May release. CAST: Jean Lapointe (Taxi Driver), Helene Loiselle (Wife), Claude Gauthier (Lavoie), Louise Forestier (Social Worker), Guy Provost (Doctor)

SWALLOWS AND AMAZONS (LDS) Producer, Richard Pilbrow; Director, Claude Whatham; Screenplay, David Wood; From book by Arthur Ransome; Photography, Denis Lewiston; Editor, Michael Bradsell; Music, Wilfred Josephs; Art Director, Simon Holland; In Technicolor; 92 minutes; May release. CAST: Virginia McKenna (Mrs. Walker), Ronald Fraser (Uncle Jim), Brenda Bruce (Mrs. Dixon), Jack Woolgar (Old Billy), John Franklyn-Robbins (Young Billy), Simon West (John), Zanna Hamilton (Susan), Sophie Neville (Titty), Stephen Grendon (Roger), Kit Seymour (Nancy), Lesley Bennett (Peggy)

TI-CUL TOUGAS (Nu-Image) Direction and Screenplay, Jean-Guy Noel; Photography, Francois Beachemin; Editor, Marthe de la Chevrotiere; Music, Georges Langford; Art Director, Fernand Durand; Costumes, Mickie Hamilton; Assistant Director, Francois Labonte; In color; 83 minutes; May release. CAST: Claude Maher (Ti-Cul), Micheline Lanctot (Odette), Gilbert Sicotte (Martin), Suzanne Garceau (Gilberte)

HIGH STREET Executive Producers, Pierre Drouot, Alain Guilleaume; Director, Andre Ernotte; Screenplay, Andre Ernotte, Elliot Tiber; Music, Mort Schuman; Photography, Walter van den Ende; In French with English subtitles; 90 minutes; Not rated; June release. CAST: Annie Cordy (Mimi), Mort Schuman (David), Bert Struys (The Man), Ester Christiniat (Young Mimi), Olivier Krickler (Boy), Claude Batelle (David)

THE LAST SAMURAI (Shochiku Films of America) Director, Kenil Misumi; Screenplay, Takeo Kunihiro; Story, Shotaro Ikenami; Photography, Masao Kosugi; In color; 160 minutes; Not rated; June release. CAST: Hideki Takahashi (Toranosuke), Ken Ogata (Hanjiro), Takahiro Shimura (Ikemoto), Masaomi Kondo (Iba), Teruhiko Saigo (Okita), Keiko Matsuzaka (Reiko), Kiwako Taiji (Nun)

MATATABI (ATG) Director, Kon Ichikawa; Screenplay, Kon Ichikawa, Shuntaro Tanigawa; Photography, Setsu Kobayashi; Editor, Saburohyoe Hirano; 100 minutes; Not rated; June release. CAST: Kenichi Ogihara (Mokutaro), Ichiro Ogura (Genta), Isao Bito (Shinta), Reiko Inoue (Okyo), Tadao Ninomiya (The Boss)

THE OTHER FRANCISCO (Tricontinental) Direction and Screenplay, Sergio Giral; Based on novel "Francisco" by Anselmo Romero; Photography, Livio Delgado; Editor, Nelson Rodriguez; Music, Leo Brouwer; Produced by Cuban Film Institute; In Spanish with English subtitles; In black and white; 100 minutes; Not rated; June release. CAST: Miguel Benavides (Francisco), Alina Sanchez (Dorotea), Ramon Veloz (Ricardo), Margarita Balboa (Ricardo's mother), Adolfo Llaurado (Overseer)

OSSESSIONE (ICI) Producer, Liberto Solaroli; Director, Luchino Visconti; Screenplay, Mario Alicata, Antonio Pietrangeli, Gianni Puccini, Giuseppe de Santis, Luchino Visconti; Photography, Aldo Tonti, Domenico Scala; Editor, Mario Serandrei; 135 minutes; Not rated; June release. CAST: Clara Calamal (Giovanna), Massimo Girotti (Gino), Juan de Landa (Husband), Elia Marcuzzo (Spaniard), Dhia Cristani (Anita), Vittorio Duse (Lorry driver)

PHARAOH (Horizon) Director, Jerzy Kawalerowicz; Screenplay, Jerzy Kawalerowicz, Tadeusz Konwicki; Based on novel by Boleslav Prus; Photography, Jerzy Woicik; Editor, Wieslawa Otocka; Music, Adam Walacinski; English dialogue, Robert Cushman, John Henderson Produced by KADR Film Unit Film Polski; 140 minutes; Not rated; June release. CAST: George Zeinik (Rameses XIII), Christine Mikolayevska (Sarah), Barbara Bryl (Kama), Piotr Paulovski (Herhor), Leszek Herdegen (Penther), Jerzy Buczacki (Tutmosis), Stanislav Milski (Mephres), Eva Kryzyevska (Hebron)

THE TEASERS (Group I) Producer, Victor Sims; Director, George Lancer; In color; Rated R; June release. CAST: Gloria Guida, Alice Ames, Sherry Wilson

AUTOPSY (Joseph Brenner) Director, Armando Crispino; Music, Ennio Morricone; In color; Rated R; June release. CAST: Mimsy Farmer, Barry Primus, Ray Lovelock, Gaby Wagner, Angela Godwin

LEGEND OF THE WOLF WOMAN (Dimension) Producer, Diego Alchimede; Direction and Screenplay, Rino Di Silvestro; In color; 84 minutes; Rated R; June release. CAST: Annik Borel, Frederick Stafford, Dagmar Lassander, Howard Ross

DEMONIACS (Clark) Direction and Screenplay, Jean Rollin; In color; Rated R; June release. CAST: Lieva Lone, Patricia Hermenier, Joelle Coeur

VALENTINA ... THE VIRGIN WIFE (Silverstein) Director, Franco Martinelli; In color; Rated R; June release. CAST: Edwige Fenech, Carroll Baker, Renzo Montagnani, Ray Lovelock, Michele Cammino, Florence Baines

FRENCH TEENS (Gail) Director, J. Angel Bardines; In Eastmancolor; Rated X; June release. CAST: Jaculiene Bardot, Pepe, Sharon Mitchell, Bobby Astyr

FAUSTINE AND THE BEAUTIFUL SUMMER (Cinema International) Direction and Screenplay, Nina Companeez; Photography, Ghislain Cloquet; Presented by Mag Bodard; In Eastmancolor; 96 minutes; June release. CAST: Muriel Catala, Mariane Egerika, Isabelle Adjani, Georges Marchal, Francis Huster, Claire Vernet, Jacques Spiesser, Maurice Garrel, Jacques Weber, Isabelle Huppert

THE PORN BROKERS (Artemis) An Elmside Films Production; In color; Rated X; June release. CAST: Ilsa Stupp, John Collin, Elvira Clark, Jamie Gillis, Helen Madigan, Lasse Braun

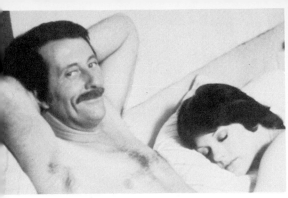

**Jean Rochefort, Anny Duperey
in "Pardon Mon Affaire"**

**Sergio Corrieri
in "The Man from Maisinicu"**

LAND OF THE MINOTAUR (Crown International) Formerly "The Devil's Men"; Producer, Frixos Constantine; Director, Costa Carayiannis; Screenplay, Arthur Rowe; A Getty Picture in color; Rated PG; June release. CAST: Donald Pleasence, Peter Cushing, Luan Peters, Nikos Verlekis, Vanna Revilli, Costas Skouras, Fernando Bislani, Bob Behling, Anna Mantzourani

INFRA-MAN (Joseph Brenner) Producer, Runne Shaw; Director, Hua Shan; In color; A Shaw Brothers production in color; Rated PG; 92 minutes; June release. CAST: Li Hsiu-hsien, Wang Hsieh, Terry Liu, Lin Wen-wei

ALOISE (Framo Diffusion) Director, Liliane De Kermadec; Screenplay, Liliane De Kermadec, Andre Techine; Photography, Jean Penzer; In Eastmancolor; 115 minutes; June release. CAST: Delphine Seyrig (Aloise), Isabelle Huppert (Aloise younger), Michel Lonsdale (Doctor), Roger Blin (Teacher), Marc Eyraud (Father)

THE TRUE NATURE OF BERNADETTE (Campagnie France) Direction and Screenplay, Gilles Carle; Photography, Rene Verzier; Art Director, Jocelyn Joly; Music, Pierre F. Brault; In Panavision and Eastmancolor; 97 minutes; June release. CAST: Micheline Lanctot (Bernadette), Donald Pilon (Thomas), Reynald Bouchard (Rock), Maurice Beaupre (Octave), Ernest Guimond (Moise), Julien Lippe (Auguste), Robert Rivard (Felecien), Willie Lamothe (Antoine)

THE WOMAN WITH RED BOOTS (Gamma III) Direction and Screenplay, Juan Bunuel; Photography, L. Vilasenor; In Eastmancolor; 92 minutes; June release. CAST: Catherine Deneuve (Francoise), Fernando Rey (Perrot), Adalberto Maria Merli (Man), Jacques Weber (Painter), Laura Betti (Leonore), Jose Sacristan (Valet)

PARDON MON AFFAIRE (First Artists) Producers, Alain Poire, Yves Robert; Director, Yves Robert; Screenplay, Jean-Loup Dabadie, Yves Robert; Music, Vladimir Cosma; 105 minutes; Rated PG; June release. CAST: Jean Rochefort (Etienne), Claude Brasseur (Daniel), Guy Bedos (Simon), Victor Lanoux (Bouly), Daniele Delorme (Marthe), Anny Duperey (Charlotte), Martine Sarcey (Mme. Esperanza)

RABID (New World) Executive Producers, Ivan Reitman, Andre Link; Producer, John Dunning; Direction and Screenplay, David Croenenberg; Editor, Jean LaFleur; Art Director, Claude Marchand; Photography, Rene Verzier; Associate Producer, Dan Goldberg; A Cinema Entertainment Enterprises Production in Panavision and Eastmancolor; 91 minutes; Rated R; July release. CAST: Marilyn Chambers (Rose), Frank Moore (Hart), Joe Silver (Murray), Howard Ryshpan (Dr. Dan Keloid), Patricia Gage (Dr. Roxanne Keloid), Susan Roman (Mindy), J. Roger Periard (Lloyd), Lynne Deragon (Nurse), Terry Schonoium (Judy), Victor Desy (Claude), Julie Anna (Rita), Gary McKeehan (Smooth Eddy), Terrance G. Ross (Farmer), Miguel Fernandes (Man in cinema), Robert O'Ree (Sergeant), Greg Van Riel (Young man in plaza)

STRONGMAN FERDINAND (Bauer International) Produced, Directed and Written by Alexander Kluge; Photography, Thomas Mauch; Editor, Heidi Genee; Music, Emil Waldteutel; Sound, Heiko Hinderks; In color; 98 minutes; Not rated; July release. CAST: Heinz Schubert (Ferdinand), Verena Rudolph (Gertie), Joachim Hackethal (Kniebling), Heinz Schimmelpfennig (Ganter), Gert Gunther Hoffmann (Wilutzki), Enrich Kleiber (Rosotschke), Daphne Wagner (Dr. Haferkamp), Siegfried Wischnewski (Kobras), Hans Fabe (Minister)

IN THE REALM OF THE SENSES (Arges) Producer, Anatole Dauman; Direction and Screenplay, Nagisa Oshima; Photography, Kenichi Okamoto, Hideo Ito; Editor, Kelichi Uraoka; Music, Minoru Miki; Japanese with English subtitles; 115 minutes; Not rated; July release. Cast not listed.

THE MAN FROM MAISINICU (Tricontinental) Directed and Written by Manuel Perez; Photography, Jorge Herrera; Editor, Gloria Arguelles; Produced by the Cuban Film Institute; In black and white; 124 minutes; Not rated; July release. CAST: Sergio Corrieri (Alberto), Reinaldo Miravalles, Raul Pomares, Adolfo Llaurado

FRENCH POSTCARD GIRL (Gail) In Eastmancolor; Rated X; No other credits available; July release. CAST: Jaquliene Bardot, Rina Russell, Marcelle Letig

NURSES FOR SALE (Independent International) Director, Rolf Olsen; In color; Rated R; 84 minutes; July release. CAST: Curt Jurgens, Joan Kozian

JAWS OF THE DRAGON (Worldwide Entertainment) Producer, Robert Jeffery; Director, James Nam; Presented by Jack H. Harris; In color; Rated R; July release. CAST: James Nam, Johnny Taylor, Jenny Kam

SCHOOL DAYS (Cinema Shares International) A Dania Film in Eastmancolor; Rated R; July release. CAST: Lilli Carr, Nikky Kennedy, Mike Gable

BRUCE LEE: THE MAN/THE MYTH Directed by Ng See Yuen; 90 minutes; Rated PG; No other credits available; August release. Starring Bruce Li

DAUGHTER OF DECEIT (Bauer International) Producer, Oscar Dancigers; Director, Luis Bunuel; Screenplay, Raquel Rojas, Luis Alcoriza; Photography, Jose Ortiz Ramos; Music, Manuel Espereon; 80 minutes; Not rated; Spanish with English subtitles; August release. CAST: Fernando Soler (Don Quintin), Alicia Caro (Marta), Ruben Rojo (Paco), Nacho Contra (Jonron), Fernando Soto (Angel), Lily Aclemar (Jovita)

**Frank Moore, Marilyn Chambers
in "Rabid"**

Jessica Harper, Alida Valli, Joan Bennett
in "Suspiria"

Volker Spengler, Margit Carstensen
in "Satan's Brew"

DEATH IN THE GARDEN (Bauer International) Producers, David Mage, Oscar Dancigers; Director, Luis Bunuel; Screenplay, Luis Bunuel, Luis Alcoriza, Raymond Queneau; Story, Jose-Andre Lacour; Photography, Jorge Stahl, Jr.; Music, Paul Misraki; Editor, Marguerite Renoir; French with English subtitles; 97 minutes; Not rated; August release. CAST: Simone Signoret (Djin), Georges Marchal (Chark), Michel Picolli (Father Lisardl), Michele Girardon (Maria), Charles Vanel (Castin), Tito Junco (Chenko), Luis Aceves Castaneda (Alberto), Jorge Martines de Hoyos (Capt. Ferrero), Raul Ramirez (Alvaro), Alberto Pedret (Lt.)

THE GREAT MADCAP (Bauer International) Producer, Oscar Dancigers, Ultramar Films; Director, Luis Bunuel; Screenplay, Raquel Rojas, Luis Alcoriza; From comedy by Adolfo Torrado; Photography, Ezequiel Carrascu; Music, Manuel Esperon; Editor, Carlos Savage; Spanish with English subtitles; 90 minutes; Not rated; August release. CAST: Fernando Soler, Andres Soler, Luis Alcoriza, Rosario Granados, Maruja Grifell, Antonio Bravo, Ruben Rojo, Gustavo Rojo, Francisco Jambrina.

THE ILLUSION TRAVELS BY STREETCAR (Bauer International) Director, Luis Bunuel; Screenplay, Maurice de la Serna, Jose Revueltas, Juan de la Cabada; Photography, Raul Martinez Solares; Music, Luis Hernandez Breton; In Spanish with English subtitles; 84 minutes; Not rated; August release. CAST: Lilia Prado, Carlos Navarro, Domingo Soler, Agustin Isunza; Fernando Soto

SANDAKAN 8 (Peppercorn-Wormser) Director, Kei Kumai; Screenplay, Kei Kumai, Sakae Hirozawa; Photography, Mitsuhi Kaneo; Story, Tomoko Yamazaki; Japanese with English subtitles; 120 minutes; Not rated; August release. CAST: Kinuyo Tanaka (Old Woman), Yoko Takashi (Young Woman), Komaki Kurihara (Young Writer)

DUTCH TREAT (Asom) Produced, Directed and Written by Navred Reef; In color; Rated X; August release. CAST: Lucy Dubois, Carrah Major-Minor, Cristy Kluiver, Roger Caine, Zebedy Colt

SATAN'S BREW (New Yorker) Direction and Screenplay, Rainer Werner Fassbinder; Photography, Michael Ballhaus; Editors, Thea Eymez, Gabi Eichel; Music, Peer Raben; German with English subtitles; In color; 110 minutes; Not Rated; August release. CAST: Kurt Raab (Walter), Margit Carstensen (Andree), Helen Vita (Luise), Ingrid Caven (Lisa), Marquard Bohm (Rolf), Ulli Lommel (Lauf), Volker Spengler (Ernst)

THE SENSUAL MAN (Peppercorn-Wormser) Directed and Written by Marco Vicario; Based on novel by Vitaliano Brancati; Editor, Bompiani; Music, Armando Trovaloli; In Italian with English subtitles; 108 minutes; In color; Rated R; August release. CAST: Giancarlo Giannini (Paolo), Rossana Podesta (Lilia), Lionel Stander (Il Nonno), Gastone Moschin (Edmondo), Marianne Comtell (Marietta)

SUSPIRIA (International Classics) Producer, Claudio Argento; Directed and Written by Dario Argento; Photography, Luciano Tovoli; Music, The Goblins; 92 minutes; Rated R; August release. CAST: Jessica Harper (Susy), Stefania Casini (Sara), Joan Bennett (Mme. Blank), Alida Valli (Miss Tanner), Flavio Bucci (Daniel)

MARCH OR DIE (Columbia) Producers, Dick Richards, Jerry Bruckheimer; Director, Dick Richards; Screenplay, David Zelag Goodman; Story, David Zelag Goodman, Dick Richards; Music, Maurice Jarre; Photography, John Alcott; Editors, John C. Howard, Stanford C. Allen, O. Nicholas Brown; Associate Producer, Georges-Patrick Salvy-Guide; Designer, Gil Parrondo; Assistant Directors, Jose Lopez Rodero, Andre Delacroix, Larry Franco, Mustapha Laghaz; Art Director, Jose Maria Tapiador; In Technicolor; Presented by Sir Lew Grade for Associated General Films; 100 minutes; Rated PG; August release. CAST: Gene Hackman (Maj. Foster), Terence Hill (Marco), Max Von Sydow (Francois), Catherine Deneuve (Simone), Ian Holm (El Krim), Rufus (Sgt. Triand), Jack O'Halloran (Ivan), Marcel Bozzuffi (Lt. Fontaine), Andre Penvern (Top Hat), Paul Sherman (Fred), Vernon Dobtcheff (Mean cpl.), Marne Maitland (Leon), Gigi Bonds (Andre), Wolf Kahler, Mathias Hell (Germans), Jean Champion (Minister), Walter Gotell (Col. Lamont), Paul Antrim (Mollard), Catherine Willmer (Petite Lady), Arnold Diamond (Her Husband), Maurice Arden (Pierre), Albert Woods (Henri), Liliane Rovere (Lola), Elisabeth Mortensen (French street girl), Leila Shenna (Arab street girl), Francois Valorbe (Detective), Villena (Gendarme), Guy Deghy (Ship's captain), Jean Rougerie, Guy Mairesse (Legionnaires), Eve Brenner (Singing girl), Guy Marly (Singing legionnaire), Margaret Modlin (Lady in black)

HEART OF GLASS (New Yorker) Producer-Director, Werner Herzog; Screenplay, Werner Herzog, Herbert Achternbusch; Photography, Jorg Schmidt-Reitwein; Editor, Beate Mainka-Jellinghaus; Music, Popol Vuh; Art Directors, Henning Von Gierke, Cornelius Siegel; Costumes, Gisela Storch, Ann Poppel; German with English subtitles; In color; 93 minutes; August release. CAST: Josef Bierbichler (Hias), Stefan Guttler (Factory Owner), Clemens Scheitz (Adalbert), Sonja Skiba (Ludmilla), Brunhilde Klockner (Paulin), Wilhelm Friedrich (Father of factory owner)

DEATH PROMISE (Howard Mahler) Producer, Serafim Karalexis; Director, Robert Warmflash; Screenplay, Norbert Albertson, Jr.; Associate Producers, Howard Mahler, Hank Stern; In color; Rated R; August release. CAST: Miou-Miou, Bernard Menez, Jean Lefebvre, Annie Duperey, Pamela Moore, Henri Guibet, Renee Saint-Cyr

Gene Hackman, Catherine Deneuve
in "March or Die"

Jean Rochefort, Jean-Pierre Marielle
in "Femmes Fatales"

Mariangela Melato, Yves Beneyton
in "By the Blood of Others"

KID VENGEANCE (Irwin Yablans) Producer, Menahem Golan; Director, Joe Manduke; Screenplay, Budd Robbins, Jay Telfer; Based on story by Kenneth Globus; Executive Producer, Yoram Globus; Co-Producer, Alex Hacohen; In color; Rated PG; August release. CAST: Jim Brown, Lee Van Cleef, John Marley, Glynnis O'Connor, Matt Clark, Timothy Scott, Leif Garrett

CHAC (Libra) Produced, Directed and Written by Rolando Klein; Photography, Alex Phillips, Jr., William Kaplan, Jr.; Music, Victor Forzado, Elisabeth Waldo; Editor, Harry Keramidas; Art Director, Jesus Dura; Assistant Director, Mario Cisneros; In DeLuxe Color; 95 minutes; August release. CAST: Villagers of Tenejapa, State of Chiapas, Mexico

GODZILLA ON MONSTER ISLAND (Downtown) A Toho Production in association with Toho Eizo Co.; Presented by Cinema Shares; In color and widescreen; Rated G; August release; No other credits.

ALLEGRO NON TROPPO (Specialty) Director, Bruno Bozzetto; Screenplay, Bruno Bozzetto, Guido Manuli, Maurizio Nichetti; Animators, Bruno Bozzetto, Giuseppe Lagana, Walter Cavazzuti, Giovanni Ferrari, Giancarlo Cereda, Giorgio Valentini, Guido Manuli, Paolo Albicocco, Giorgio Forlani; Editor, Giancarlo Rossi; Music, Debussy, Dvorak, Ravel, Sibelius, Vivaldi, Stravinsky; In color; 75 minutes; Rated PG; September release. An animated feature with Maurisio Nichetti, Nestor Garay, Maurizio Micheli, Maria Luisa Giovannini

THE CRIMINAL LIFE OF ARCHIBALDO DE LA CRUZ also released as "Rehearsal for a Crime"; Producer, Alfonso Patino Gomez; Director, Luis Bunuel; Screenplay, Luis Bunuel, Eduardo Ugarte Pages; Story, Rodolfo Usigli; Photography, Agustin Jimenez; Music, Jorge Perez Herrera; Editor, Jorge Bustos; 91 minutes; Not rated; Spanish with English subtitles; September release. CAST: Ernesto Alonso (Archibaldo), Miroslava Stern (Lavinia), Rita Macedo (Patricia), Ariadna Weler (Carlota), Rodolfo Landa (Alejandro), Andres Palma (Cervantes), Carlos Riquelme (Chief of Police), Jose Maria Linares Rivas (Willy), Leonor Llansas (Governess), Eva Calvo (Mother)

FEMMES FATALES (New Line Cinema) Formerly "Calmos"; Producer, Bernard Artigues; Director, Bertrand Blier; Screenplay, Bertrand Blier, Philippe Dumarcay; Photography, Claude Renoir; Editor, Claudine Merlin; Music, Georges Delerue; In French with English subtitles; 81 minutes; Not rated; September release. CAST: Jean-Pierre Marielle (Paul), Jean Rochefort (Albert), Bernard Blier (Le Cure), Brigitte Fossey (Suzanne), Claude Pieplue (L'Ancien Combattant), Michel Peyrelon (Le P. D. G.), Micheline Kahn (Genevieve), Pierre Bertin (Le Chanoine), Claudine Becarrie (Cliente Cossue)

LET JOY REIGN SUPREME (Specialty Films) Producer, Michelle de Broca; Director, Bertrand Tavernier; Screenplay, Jean Aurenche, Bertrand Tavernier; Photography, Pierre William Glenn; Editor, Armand Psenny; Music, Philippe d'Orleans; In color; 120 minutes; Not rated; September release. CAST: Philippe Noiret (Philippe), Jean Rochefort (Abbe), Jean Pierre Marielle (Marquis), Marina Vlady (Mme. de Bourbon), Alfred Adam (Villeroi), Gerard Desarthe (Duc de Bourbon), Christine Pascal (Emilie), Gilles Guillot (Caussimon)

BY THE BLOOD OF OTHERS (Joseph Green) Director, Marc Simenon; Producers, Kangourou Films, Mylene Demongeot, Marc Simenon; Screenplay, Jean Max; Photography, Rene Verzier; Music, Francis Lai; Editor, Etienette Muse; Art Director, Jean Andre; In Eastmancolor; 95 minutes; September release. CAST: Mariangela Melato (Maryse), Yves Beneyton (The Man), Denise Filiatrault (Genevieve), Nathalie Guerine (Caroline), Bernard Blier (Mayor), Charles Vanel (Priest), Georges Geret (Police Chief), Mylene Demongeot (Juliette), Claude Pieplu (Prefect), Francis Blanche (Dr. Senequier), Robert Castel (Francesco), Riccardo Cucciolla (Scarpelli), Monita Derrieux (Amelie), Jacques Godin (Francis), Daniel Pilon (Georges)

LEONOR (New Line) Director, Juan Bunuel; Screenplay, Juan Bunuel, Philippe Nuridzany, Pierre Maintigneux, Jean-Claude Carriere, Clement Biddle Wood; Story, Ludwig Tieck; Photography, Luciano Tovoli; Editor, Pablo Del Amo; Music, Ennio Morricone; In Eastmancolor; 100 minutes; Rated R; September release. CAST: Liv Ullmann (Leonor), Michel Piccolo (Richard), Ornella Mutti (Catherine), Antonio Ferrandis (Thomas), Jose Maria Caffarel (Doctor), Angel Del Pozo (Chapelain)

ONE SINGS, THE OTHER DOESN'T (Cinema 5) Direction and Screenplay, Agnes Varda; Photography, Charlie Van Damme; Editor, Joelle Van Effenterre; Music, Francois Wertheimer; In Eastmancolor; 120 minutes; September release. CAST: Valerie Mairesse (Pauline), Therese Liotard (Suzanne), Robert Dadies (Jerome), Ali Affi (Darius), Jean-Pierre Pellegrin (Pierre), Francois Wertheimer (Francois II)

20th CENTURY OZ (Inter Planetary) Producers, Chris Lofven, Lyne Helms; Associate Producer, Jane Scott; Direction and Screenplay, Chris Lofven; Music, Ross Wilson; Photography, Dan Burstall; Editor, Les Luxford; In Eastmancolor; Rated R; September release. CAST: Joy Dunstan (Dorothy), Graham Matters (The Wizard), Bruce Spence (Surfie), Michael Carmen (Mechanic), Gary Waddell (Bikie), Robin Ramsay (Good Fairy), Paula Maxwell (Jane), Ned Kelly (Truckie)

Liv Ullmann
in "Leonor"

209

Alicia Alonzo, Azari Plisetski
in "Alicia"

Richard Alfieri
in "Children of Rage"

A WOMAN'S DECISION (Tinc) Produced by Film Polski; Directed and Written by Krzysztof Zanussi; Photography, Slawomir Idziak; Music, Wojciech Kilar; Polish with English subtitles; In color; 99 minutes; Not rated; September release. CAST: Maya Komorowska (Marta), Piotr Franczewski (Marta's husband), Marek Piwowski (Jacek)

THE RIVER AND DEATH (Bauer International) Director, Luis Bunuel; Screenplay, Luis Bunuel, Luis Alcoriza; From novel "Muro Blanco Sobre Roca Negra" by Miguel Alvarez Acosta; Photography, Raul Martinez Solaris; Music, Raul Lavista; Editor, Jorge Bustos; Produced by Clasa Films Mundiales; 90 minutes; Not rated; September release. CAST: Columba Dominguez (Mercedes), Miguel Torruco (Felipe), Joaquin Cordero (Gerardo), Jaime Fernandez (Romulo), Victor Alcocer (Polo), Silvia Derbez (Elsa), Humberto Almazan (Crescencio), Alfredo Varela, Jr. (Chinelas)

THE SWISS CONSPIRACY (S. J. International) Producer, Maurice Silverstein; Director, Jack Arnold; Screenplay, Norman Klenman, Philip Saltzman, Michael Stanley; Executive Producer, Raymond P. Homer; 89 minutes; Rated PG; In color; September release. CAST: David Janssen (David), Senta Berger (Denise), John Ireland (McGowan), Elke Sommer (Rita), John Saxon (Hayes), Ray Milland (Hurtil), Anton Diffring (Franz), Arthur Brauss (Korsak), Curt Lowens (Andre), David Hess (Tony), Inigo Gallo (Hans), Sheila Ruskin (Corinne), Irmgard Forst (Florelle)

LOVE CAMP #27 (Group I) Formerly "Nazi Love Camp"; Director, William Hawkins; Music, Francesco De Masi; In color; Rated R; September release. CAST: Sirpa Lane, Carl Sisti, Robert Post, Christy Borg, Mike Morris

PIPPI ON THE RUN (G. G. Communications) Director, Olle Hellbom; Presented by N. W. Russo; In Movielab Color; Rated G; September release. CAST: Inger Nilsson, Par Sundberg, Maria Persson

GASP....! (Dan Tana) Director, Vlatko Gilic; In color; 91 minutes; September release. CAST: Dragan Nikolic, Stanislava Janjic, Predrag Lakovic, Pavlo Stevanovic, Nikola Gvozdenovic

THE SCHOOL THAT COULDN'T SCREAM (Newport) Formerly "What Have They Done to Solange?"; Producer, Leo Pescarolo; Director, Massimo Dallamano; Story and Screenplay, Bruno Di Geronimo, Massimo Dallamano; Music, Ennio Morricone; In Eastmancolor; Rated R; September release. CAST: Fabio Testi, Karin Baal, Joachim Fuchsberger, Christine Galbo, Camille Keaton, Gunther W. Stoll, Claudia Butenuth, Maria Monte, Pilar Castel

SWEDISH MINX (Cambist) Producer, Inge Ivarson; Director, Mac Ahlberg; Screenplay, Edward Mannering; In color; 99 minutes; Rated X; September release. CAST: Maria Lynn, Bie Warburg, Harry Reems, Brigette Maier, Erik Limstrom, Bent Warburg, Fritz Franchy

CHILDREN OF RAGE (Coliseum) Producer, George R. Nice; Direction and Screenplay, Arthur Allan Seidelman; No other credits available; October release. CAST: Helmut Greim, Richard Alfieri, Olga Georges-Picot, Simon Ward, Cyril Cusack, Robart Salvio, Simon Andreu

ALICIA (Tricontinental Film Center) Producer, Instituto Cubano del Arte e Industria Cinematograficos; Director, Manuel Duchesne Cuzan; In Cinemascope and color; 75 minutes; October release. A documentary celebrating Cuba's prima-ballerina Alicia Alonzo

VOLCANO (Cinema 5) Produced by the National Film Board of Canada; Executive Producer, James De B. Domville; Directed and Written by Donald Brittain with John Kramer; Narrator, Donald Brittain; Photography, Douglas Kiefer; Design, Denis Boucher; Editor, John Karmer; Music, Alain Clavier; In color; 100 minutes; October release. A documentary on the life and death of Malcolm Lowry with his words spoken by Richard Burton

THE DEMISE OF FATHER MOURET (Images Film Library) Producer, Vera Belmont; Director, Georges Franju; Screenplay, Georges Franju, Jean Ferry; Based on novel by Emile Zola; Photography, Marcel Fradatai; Music, Jean Wiener; French with English subtitles; 90 minutes; Not rated; October release. CAST: Francis Huster (Serge Mouret), Gillian Hills (Albine), Andre Lancombe (Archangias), Margo Lion (La Teuse), Lucien Barjon (Bambaousse), Hugo Fausto Tozzi (Jeanbernat), Tino Carroro (Dr. Pascal)

THE LONELY WOMAN (Independent International) Director, Robert Belen (Rovira Beleta); Photography, Michel Kelber; Music, Piero Piccioni; In color; Rated R; October release. CAST: Gina Lollobrigida, Danielle Darrieux, Susan Hampshire, Renaud Verley, Conchita Velasco, Mariebel Martin, Javier Loyola, Giacomo Rossi Stewart, Eduardo Fajardo

THE LAST FOUR DAYS (Group I) Director, Carlo Lizzani; Screenplay, Carlo Lizzani, Fabio Pittorru; In Eastmancolor; Rated PG; October release. CAST: Rod Steiger (Mussolini), Lisa Gastoni (Clara), Henry Fonda (Cardinal), Franco Nero (Valerio), Lino Capolicchio (Pedro)

MASTER OF THE FLYING GUILLOTINE (Seymour Borde) Director, Ho Meng-hua; Screenplay, I. Kuang; In Shawcolor; Rated R; October release. CAST: Ma Teng, Hsing Kang, Hsu Shuang-kun, Li Yu-ping, Wan-chu, Hsieh Tien-fu, Lo Peng, Yung Cheng

2069, A SEX ODYSSEY (Burbank International) Producer, Gunther Koph; Director, George Keil; Screenplay, Willie Pribil; In color; Rated X; October release. CAST: Alena Penz, Nina Fredric, Gerti Sneider, Raul Retzer, Cathrene Conti, Heidy Hammer, Michael Mein, Herb Heesel

THE GOOD AND THE BAD (Paramount) Directed, Written and Photographed by Claude Lelouch; Music, Francis Lai; Editor, Georges Klotz; 125 minutes; Rated R; October release. CAST: Jacques Dutronc (Jacques), Marlene Jobert (Lola), Bruno Cremer (Blanchot), Jacques Villeret (Simon), Brigitte Fossey (Wife), Jean-Pierre Kalfon (Lafont), Serge Reggiani (Resistance Chief)

Olga Georges-Picot, Helmut Greim
in "Children of Rage"

"Voyage to Grand Tartary"

MISTER SCARFACE (PRO International) Director, Fernando Di Leo; In color; Rated R; September release, CAST: Jack Palance, Edmund Purdom, Al Cliver, Harry Baer, Gisela Hahn, Enzo Pulcrano, Roberto Reale, Vittorio Caprioli

CRAZY HOUSE (Constellation) Produced and Written by Clive Exton, Terry Nation; Director, Peter Sykes; Music, Harry Robinson; An Anglo EMI Film in Technicolor; Rated PG; September release. CAST: Frankie Howerd, Ray Milland

A SLIGHTLY PREGNANT MAN (S. J. International) Direction and Screenplay, Jacques Demy; Photography, Andreas Windin; Music, Michel Legrand; In Eastmancolor; Rated PG; 92 minutes; October release. CAST: Catherine Deneuve, Marcello Mastroianni, Micheline Presle, Raymond Gerome, Claude Melki, Marisa Pavan

BILITIS (Topar) Producers, Sylvio Tabet, Jacques Nahum; Director, David Hamilton; Screenplay, Robert Bouissinot, Jacques Nahum, Catherine Breillat from book by Pierre Louys; Photography, Bernard Daillencourt; Editor, Henri Colpi; Music, Francis Lai; In Eastmancolor; 95 minutes; Rated R; October release. CAST: Patti D'Arbanville (Bilitis), Mona Kristensen (Melissa), Bernard Giraudeau (Lucas), Gilles Kohler (Pierre), Mathieu Carriere (Nikias)

OTHER SIDE OF PARADISE (New World) Formerly "Foxtrot"; Producer, Gerald Green; Executive Producers, Maximiliano Vega Tato, Anuar Badin; Director, Arturo Ripstein; Screenplay, Arturo Ripstein, Jose Emilio Pacheco, H. A. L. Craig; Photography, Alex Phillips, Jr.; Editor, Peter Zinner; Music, Pete Rugolo; Title Song, Jay Livingston, Ray Evans, Pete Rugolo; Art Director, Lucero Isaac; Assistant Directors, Luis Gaytan, Valerio Olivio; In Technicolor; 91 minutes; Rated R; October release. CAST: Peter O'Toole (Liviu), Charlotte Rampling (Julia), Max Von Sydow (Larsen), Jorge Luke (Eusebio), Helena Rojo (Alexandra), Claudio Brook (Paul), Max Kerlow (Captain), Christa Walter (Gertrude), Mario Castillon (Sailor), Anne Porterfield (Marianna)

STAR PILOT (Monarch) Director, Peter Francisci; Screenplay, Michael Elder; Presented by Allan Shackleton; In color; Rated PG; October release. CAST: Kirk Morris, Gordon Mitchell, Leonora Ruff

SALO, 120 DAYS OF SODOM (Zebra) Executive Producer, Alberto Grimaldi; Director, Pier Paolo Pasolini; Screenplay, Mr. Pasolini with Sergio Citti; Based on novel "120 Days of Sodom" by Marquis de Sade; Photography, Tonino Delli Colli; Editor, Nino Baragli; Music, Ennio Morricone; In color; 117 minutes; Rated X; Italian with English subtitles; October release. CAST: Paolo Bonacelli (Duke), Giorgio Cataldi (Bishop), Umberto P. Quinavalle (Magistrate), Aldo Valletti (President), Caterino Boratto (Signora Castelli), Elsa De Giorgi (Signora Maggi), Helene Surgere (Signora Vaccari), Sonia Savlange (Virtuosa)

VOYAGE TO GRAND TARTARIE (New Line) Direction and Screenplay, Jean-Charles Tacchella; Photography, M. Andre du Breuil; Music, Gerard Anfosso; An MK2 Production; 100 minutes; Not rated; November release. CAST: Jean-Luc Bideau (Alexis), Micheline Lanctot (Daphne), Lou Castel (Sports Champion), Catherine Verlor (Orlane), Catherine Laborde (Pamela), Fulbert Janin (Pamela's husband), Sybil Maas (Nelly)

WHY DOES HERR R. RUN AMOK? (New Yorker) Direction and Screenplay, Rainer Werner Fassbinder, Michael Fengler; Photography, Dietrich Lohmann; Editors, Franz Walsch, Michael Fengler; Music, Christian Anders; German with English subtitles; In color; 88 minutes; Not rated; November release. CAST: Kurt Raab (Herr R), Lilith Ungerer (His wife), Amadeus Fengler (Son), Harry Baer, Peter Holand, Lilo Pempeit (Colleagues of Herr R), Hanna Schygulla (Schoolfriend)

THE ASCENT (Amicus) Director, Larissa Shepitko; Screenplay, Yuri Klepikov, Larissa Shepitko; Photography, V. Chuhnov; Music, A. Shnitke; In black and white; 105 minutes; Not rated; November release. CAST: Boris Plotnikov, Vladimir Gostjuhin, Sergei Jakovlev, Anatoli Solonitzin, Ludmila Poliakova

"Why Does Herr R. Run Amok?"

"The Ascent"

**Bernardo Bertolucci
in "The Cinema according to Bertolucci"**

**Malcolm McDowell, Christopher Plummer,
Peter Firth in "Aces High"**

SUMMER HEAT (World Wide) In Eastmancolor; Rated X; No other credits available; November release. CAST: Alice Arno, Karine Jeantet, Gerry Huart, Nicole Avril, Patrice Pascal, Bob Garry

CREAM'S FAREWELL CONCERT (Film Shows) Presented by Sandy Oliveri; In color; Rated G; November release. CAST: Eric Clapton, Ginger Baker, Jack Bruce

LIZ (Group I) Producer, Goran Sjostedt; Director, Paul Gerber; In DeLuxe Color; Rated X; November release. CAST: Elona Glenn, Ulf Brunnberg, Per-Axel Arosenius, Marie Ekorre, Richard Roman, Joanne Phillips

READY, WILLING AND ABLE (Martin) Producer, Henry Willeg; Director, Jerry Macc; Executive Producer, Martin Friedmann; Music, Raymond Rosenberger; In color; Rated R; November release. CAST: Ingrid Steeger, Christine Schubert, Monica Rohde

MASTERMIND (Goldstone) Producer, Malcolm Stuart; Director, Alex March; A Master Associates presentation in Eastmancolor; Rated G; November release. CAST: Zero Mostel, Bradford Dillman, Gawn Grainger, Keiko Kishi, Frankie Sakai

EMANUELLE IN BANGKOK (Monarch) Director, Joe D'Amato; Screenplay, Maria Pia Fusco; Music, Nico Fidenco; Presented by Allan Shackleton; In color; 94 minutes; Rated X; November release. CAST: Laura Gemser, Debra Berger, Chris Avram, Ivan Rassimov, Gabriele Tinti, Giacomo Rossi Stuart, Venantino Venantino

VOYAGE TO THE END OF THE WORLD (Pacific International) Conceived and Directed by Jacques-Yves, Philippe Cousteau; Photography, D. Meyrand, Philippe Cousteau; Editor, Edwige Bienvenu; In Eastmancolor; Rated G; 92 minutes; November release. A documentary

THE CINEMA ACCORDING TO BERTOLUCCI or "The Making of 1900" (Bauer International) Producer, Ovidio Assonitis; Direction and Screenplay, Giuseppe Bertolucci; Photography, Tonino Nardi; Editor, Giuseppe Bertolucci; In color; Italian with English subtitles; 70 minutes; Not rated; December release. CAST: the cast and crew of "1900" including Bernardo Bertolucci, Vittorio Storaro, Giuseppe Bertolucci, Robert De Niro, Gerard Depardieu, Dominique Sanda, Burt Lancaster, Donald Sutherland, Sterling Hayden, Stefania Sandrelli, Laura Betti, Alida Valli

THE PHANTOM BARON (Raymond Rohauer) Director, Serge de Poligny; Dialogue, Jean Cocteau; Screenplay, Jean Cocteau, Serge de Poligny; Editor, Jean Feyte; Photography, Roger Hubert; 100 minutes; Not rated; December release. CAST: Jean Cocteau (Baron), Alain Cuny (Herve), Odette Joyeaux (Eify), Jany Holt (Anne), Claude Samval (Alberic)

NIGHT OF THE HOWLING BEAST (Constellation) Director, M. I. Bonns; In Gevacolor; Rated R; December release. CAST: Paul Naschy, Grace Mills, Gil Vidal, Silvia Solar, Louis Induni

BUTTERFLY (Leisure Time) Direction and Screenplay, Joseph W. Sarno; Music, Gunter Moll; In Eastmancolor and Widescreen; 92 minutes; Rated X; December release. CAST: Maria Forsa, Harry Reems, Eric Edwards, Natascha Verell, Nadia Henkowa, Zoe Uva, Irene Wendlin, Marius Alcher

PLAYGIRLS OF MUNICH (Asom) Produced, Directed and Written by Navred Reef; In color; Rated X; December release. CAST: Gretchen Kolber, Karen Hapsburg, Sylvia Reynard, Roger Caine, Zebedy Colt

THE KUNG FU BROTHERS (Goldstone) In Technicolor; Rated R; No other credits available; December release. CAST: Kao Yung, Jeanette Su, Chan Sing

ACES HIGH (Cinema Shares) Producer, S. Benjamin Fisz; Director, Jack Gold; Screenplay, Howard Baker; Inspired by R. C. Sheriff's play "Journey's End"; Photography, Gerry Fisher; Editor, Anne Coates; Music, Richard Hartley; Associate Producer, Basil Keys; Assistant Director, Derek Cracknell; In Technicolor; Rated PG; December release. CAST: Malcolm McDowell (Gresham), Christopher Plummer (Sinclair), Simon Ward (Crawford), Peter Firth (Croft), John Gielgud (Headmaster), Trevor Howard (Lt. Col. Silkin), Richard Johnson (Col. Lyle), Ray Milland (Brig. Whale), David Wood (Thompson), David Daker (Bennett), Elliott Cooper (Wade), Pascale Christophe (Croft's girl friend), Jeanne Patou (Chanteuse)

MAX HAVELAAR (Netherlands) Producers, Fons Rademakers, Hiswara Darmaputera; Director, Fons Rademakers; Screenplay, Gerard Soeteman; Based on book by Multatuli; Photography, Jan de Bont; Costumes, Elly Claus; Editor, Pieter Bergema; In Eastmancolor; 170 minutes; December release. CAST: Peter Faber, Sacha Bulthuis, Herry Iantho, Menny Zulaini, Rina Melati, Elang Mohamad Adenan Soesilaningrat, Maruli Sitompul, Rutger Hauer

THE CHILDREN OF THEATRE STREET (Peppercorn-Wormser) Producer and Co-Director, Earle Mack; Director, Robert Dornhelm; Written by Beth Gutcheon; Narrated by Princess Grace of Monaco; Photography, Karl Kofler; In color; 90 minutes; Not rated; December release. A documentary on the Kirov School of Ballet in Russia.

"The Children of Theatre Street"

242

246

251